LOST FILMS
OF THE LOST WORLD
& THE MOVIES THAT TIME FORGOT

JOHN LEMAY
with contributions by
**Mike Bogue, Neil Riebe,
Matthew B. Lamont, Blake Matthews
& Lee Powers**

Bicep
Books

BICEP BOOKS
Roswell, New Mexico, U.S.A.

For Mike Bogue, aka Kount Kaiju, one of my greatest encouragers

TABLE OF CONTENTS

ACKNOWLEDGMENTS

For their help with this tome, I would like to sincerely thank Allen Debus, Matthew B. Lamont, Neil Riebe, Mike Bogue, Blake Matthews and Lee Powers for their contributions to the book (as well as help with research).

THE CROWNING TRIUMPH OF THE MOTION PICTURE

WORLD PICTURES

THE
GHOST OF
SLUMBER
MOUNTAIN

Produced By HERBERT M·DAWLEY
Presented By CINEMA DISTRIBUTING CORP.
Distributed By WORLD PICTURES

THESE GIANT MONSTERS OF THE PAST ARE SEEN TO BREATHE.
TO LIVE AGAIN, TO MOVE AND BATTLE AS THEY DID AT DAWN OF LIFE.

PREFACE

A ll kids love dinosaurs, and I was no exception. The first films I ever saw were the animated *The Land Before Time* (1988) and the live-action *The Land That Time Forgot* (1974). Unlike many kids, I never grew out of that love. I also notice that most dinosaur fans that retain their love of saurians into adulthood tend to fall into one of two camps. There are the fans of real dinosaurs who lean heavily into paleontology, and then there are those of us who simply love dinosaur movies. I am definitely more so one of the latter.

One of my favorite books of all time is Mark F. Berry's *The Dinosaur Filmography*. It's one of the most comprehensive tomes on the subject, and in the back is a little appendix on unmade dinosaur movies. It's been a long time now, but I have a feeling that little appendix is probably what inspired me to do a whole book on unmade Godzilla and Gamera movies from Japan in 2016. The resultant *The Big Book of Japanese Giant Monster Movies: The Lost Films* was the most successful book I had ever written up to that point. Plus, I had a blast writing it, so next came *Kong Unmade*, and after the big ape, *Jaws Unmade*. And now here we are with *Lost Films of the Lost World & The Movies That Time Forgot*.

On the cover, in true Samuel Z. Arkoff tradition, I proclaimed that this book was "ALL NEW! NEVER BEFORE SEEN!" Well, that was a lie. Typically, dinosaur films with that slogan tended to be proliferated with the infamous stock footage from 1940's *One Million B.C.* In that tradition, I suppose you could say this book has "stock footage" too. If you're a reader of my other books and *The Lost Films Fanzine*, this tome will have a lot of stuff you've seen before interspersed between the new entries. For instance, *Creation*, the unmade 1930 dinosaur dream of Harry Hoyt is reprised here from *Kong Unmade* with few alterations. However, strictly Kong-focused films, dinosaur-laden though they may be, are relegated to the Appendix. The same is true for Godzilla movies besides two exceptions: *The Lost World*-inspired *Bride of Godzilla* (unproduced by Toho in 1956) and the unmade Americanization of *Godzilla Raids Again*, to be called *The Volcano Monsters*, which would have turned Godzilla and Anguirus into a

9

duo of a nondescript Tyrannosaurus and Ankylosaurus. There are also a few paleontological purists who might argue that Godzilla doesn't belong in this book to begin with. And in that vein, neither does Reptilicus or Gorgo.

As a kid, my favorite VHS was Goodtimes' cassette of *Fantastic Dinosaurs of the Movies*. It was a feature-length compilation of monster movie trailers with a short dinosaur documentary of sorts tacked onto the beginning. If you've seen *Fantastic Dinosaurs of the Movies*, you know it's really a hodgepodge of content that includes previews for non-dinosaur flicks like *Jason and the Argonauts*, *The Giant Gila Monster*, and many Godzilla movies. Heck, they even threw in a promotional making-of feature for *The Golden Voyage of Sinbad*. I didn't nitpick, though. You've heard of *Chicken Soup for the Teenage Soul*? Well, *Fantastic Dinosaurs of the Movies* was like heroin for my dinosaur-addicted child brain. There wasn't much in the vein of the dreaded "people parts," just a non-stop smorgasbord of celluloid saurian action. Basically, being comprised of trailers, it was just the money shots. Before you could get bored with anything, it moved onto something else.

It's my hope that this book can do the same for you as an adult. It's not as scholarly as *Kong Unmade*, or even as cohesive. Like *Fantastic Dinosaurs of the Movies*, some of the entries in this book are questionable as far as dinosaurs go. (Looking at you especially *Goliath and the Dragon*.) They're also a bit shorter, hitting the high points and moving on. For instance, a whole book could be—and I hope will be—written on the history of 1925's *The Lost World's* various cuts, restorations, and missing footage. Here, I just hit the high-points, but I also tell you where you can find the more in-depth stuff at least.

Nor did very many of the projects in this book truly go unmade. *Gwangi*, for instance, eventually got produced as *Valley of Gwangi*. Heck, even *Creation* evolved into *King Kong* and another unmade project called *The Lost Atlantis*, which may have itself ended up in 1951's *The Lost Continent*. I also detail the many changes that existing films went through. For instance, the Beast from 20,000 Fathoms started out as an ancient alien as opposed to a dinosaur. Then there's the fact that D.W. Griffith almost directed *One Million B.C.* instead of Hal Roach, among other interesting tidbits.

Lastly, some of these movies aren't lost at all. As movies that were mostly forgotten over the years or barely seen at all, like Mexico's *One Million B.C.*-inspired *The Beautiful Dreamer*, I wanted to review them. They are included under the monicker of "Films That Time Forgot."

Basically, as I struggled to have my cake and eat it, too, when formatting this book, I decided upon the following criteria. Most importantly are what I classified as UNCOMPLETED PROJECTS, like *Gwangi*, which Willis O'Brien's version of was never completed. Next up were entries included on the basis of LOST FOOTAGE, like *Jungle Manhunt's* deleted dinosaur scene, which was shot but left on the cutting room floor. Next up is what I call PROJECT DEVELOPMENT, showing how existing movies like

Gorgo started out as something a bit different, in this case the South Pacific-set *Kuru Island*. Lastly are this book's true guilty pleasures, the short reviews of FILMS THAT TIME FORGOT, which although not lost or completely forgotten, certainly are obscure to the general public.

Anyhow, it's my hope that this eclectic title can give adult dinosaur junkies a quick fix in the same vein that *Fantastic Dinosaurs of the Movies* did for myself and many other dino-kids of the VHS era. Afterall, *G-Fan* editor J.D. Lees once called me the "premiere cinematic paleontologist" who dug up lost films like scattered dinosaur bones. So, on that note, I hope you find these old fossils of interest...

SILENT SAURIANS
1905-1929

BEFORE ONE MILLION B.C:
THE FIRST ONSCREEN DINOSAURS

ADAPTED FROM MATERIAL ORIGINALLY PUBLISHED IN *THE LOST FILMS FANZINE PRESENTS MOVIE MILESTONES* #1

Like 1940's *One Million B.C.*, the very first dinosaur film ever shot focused on cavemen living side by side with prehistoric saurians. It was released in 1905 and called *Prehistoric Peeps* because it was based upon a comic strip. Said comic strip was written and drawn by Edward Tennyson Reed starting in the 1890s and appearing in *Punch* magazine. The simple short began in the present with a scientist falling asleep and dreaming of dinosaurs. When the scientist suddenly finds himself in a prehistoric cave, a giant saurian chases him out. As it does so, he fires at it with his revolver to no avail. As the scientist flees the cave, he comes across a gaggle of prehistoric cave women. How exactly the dream concludes is unknown, but sources say that the scientist is awakened from his dream when his wife splashes some water on him from a siphon. Perhaps he was cheating on her with one of the cave women?

Still from *Brute Force.*

Supposedly the dinosaurs in the film adaptation of *Prehistoric Peeps* were brought to life by men in costumes. I say supposedly because *Prehistoric Peeps* is a lost film, hence it's inclusion in this book. Remarkably not lost is the D.W. Griffith produced *Man's Genesis*, another caveman tale (sans dinosaurs) from 1912. It begins in the modern day with a grandfather regaling his grandchildren with tales of the prehistoric age as they climb up a hill. It seemed to set the template for several similar films to follow, as it focused on a weak caveman trying to woo a cavewoman away from a strong alpha male. The story ends with the hero, Weakhands, developing the first club, to beat the villain, Bruteforce.

In 1914, Griffith was at it again with *Brute Force,* a live-action comedy short that begins in the modern-day. A man named Harry is upset that his girlfriend, Priscilla, has left a party with another man. "Oh, for the good old days of brute force and marriage by capture!" Harry's title card reads. Harry then has a flashback to the "good ol' days" of prehistoric times. In the scene, a caveman and his mate survive various perils, including something resembling a winged dragon more so than a dinosaur. Also popping up is a Ceratosaurus, animated via stop-motion. As such, this was the first stop-motion dinosaur ever created.

Charlie Chaplin in *His Prehistoric Past.*

Charlie Chaplin produced a similar prehistoric comedy that year, too, in *His Prehistoric Past* shown above. Apparently 1914 was a big year for caveman movies, for it also saw the release of the short *The Primitive Man!* Next came *The Dinosaur and the Missing Link: A Prehistoric Tragedy*, a short film animated by Willis O'Brien in 1915. O'Brien, of course, is a cinema legend and arguably the true father of the onscreen dinosaur as we know it. Obie, as he's affectionately known, had shown some dinosaur test footage he had made to Herman Wobber, an exhibitor. Wobber then provided Obie with $5,000 to make his stopmotion short.

The movie was released in 1917 by Thomas Edison's film company Conquest Pictures. The comical story followed the efforts of a caveman trying to impress a cavewoman, with his attempts being thwarted by an ape, the missing link. That same year saw the release of two more O'Brien spoofs. *R.F.D. 10,000 B.C.* focused yet again on rivalry between cavemen competing for a woman. In this case, one was a prehistoric mailman who rode a dinosaur on his route! *Prehistoric Poultry* showcased a prehistoric chicken monster of a sort. At least one of O'Brien's shorts, 1917's *Curious Pets of Our Ancestors*, is lost completely.

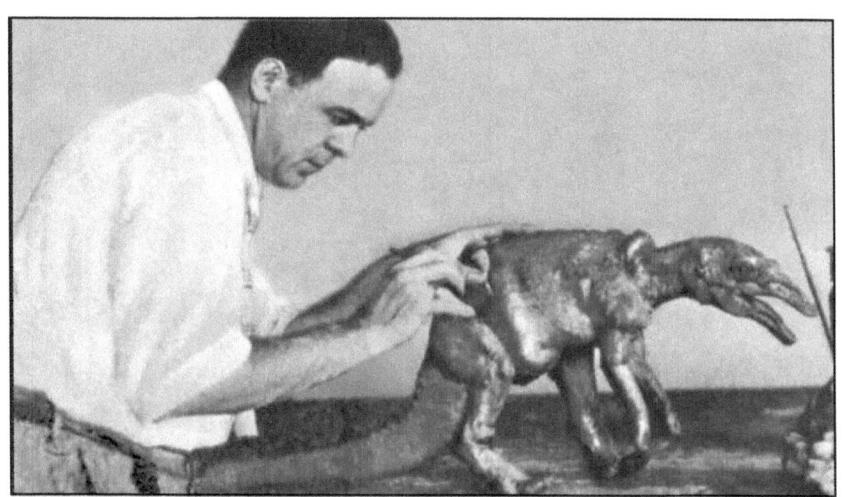

Herbert M. Dawley and the duckbill model from *Along the Moonbeam Trail.*

In 1918, Obie connected with sculptor Herbert M. Dawley, who had similar dreams of dinosaur movies. The two collaborated to create that same year's *The Ghost of Slumber Mountain*. Written by O'Brien, what was initially a forty-minute film even starred Dawley and O'Brien in onscreen roles. The picture opened with Dawley's character, called Holmes, regaling some child relatives with a story about the time he found a strange cabin inhabited by the ghost of an old hermit called Mad Dick (O'Brien's character). The ghost instructs Holmes to use his telescope to spy the crest of nearby Slumber Mountain. Holmes then witnesses fantastic scenes of stopmotion saurians battling it out in the prehistoric past. However, Holmes ends his story by telling his little relatives that he was in fact only dreaming, which causes the tikes to tackle him. Unfortunately, this is all we know about the film today.

Though the first three-reel version ran forty minutes, it was cut in half to only run nineteen minutes.[1] The first cut of the film apparently never even made it to theaters as it was requested by the distributor that it be truncated to only one reel for release. As such, the three-reel version of *The Ghost of Slumber Mountain* is essentially a lost film.[2] However, the production was at least a box office success, grossing $100,000 on a $3,000 budget, which ensured more stopmotion dinosaur movies to come—just not with Dawley and O'Brien working together again.

The World Called Him Crazy!

But he accomplished the impossible. He made his dreams come true. He fought a great battle and won! And today the world hails him as a genius.

Herbert M. Dawley went back to the Dawn of Time to bring before our very eyes the animals that lived when history began. How did he do it? How did he return? The answer is "The Ghost of Slumber Mountain."

THE GREATEST TRIUMPH OF THE MOTION PICTURE

O'Brien and Dawley parted ways after a dispute over the effects work on *Slumber Mountain*, with Dawley working on another dinosaur short called *Along the Moonbeam Trail*. The short film has a father and his two children taking a magic airplane all the way to the moon where they discover dinosaurs battling amidst the lunar landscape. The ten-minute short was thought lost for many years until it was rediscovered by Stephen Czerkas when he came across a reel of it in the Dawley archive in New Jersey. Sadly, it was only one of two reels. But the reel did seem to settle a long standing debate about *Along the Moonbeam Trail*. For many years, it had been claimed that the film's dinosaurs were simply made up of outtakes from *Ghost of Slumber Mountain* done by Willis O'Brien. As it turned out, the footage in the reel rediscovered by Czerkas was footage unique to *Moonbeam Trail* from Dawley. Next came the discovery of photos of Dawley animating the dinosaurs himself. By default, it's also now unclear just how much of *Slumber Mountain* was animated by O'Brien and how much was done by Dawley. Unlike *Ghost of Slumber Mountain*, available as a special feature on *The Lost World* Blu-Ray from Flicker Alley, *Along the Moonbeam Trail* remains out of grasp for the general public, with the Academy of Motion Pictures arranging screenings of the short sporadically.

NOTES

---

¹ There also was created an even shorter 12-minute version.
² Just what the lost footage included is a mystery, but one of the scenes that was removed was intended as some kind of strange, humorous interlude. According to the book *Tome of Terror: Horror Films of the Silent Era Workman*. "It has been suggested that the missing footage was deemed too homosexual in subtext, an idea borne out by a scene that did get restored....(in which) Jack tries to persuade Joe to remove his clothes and pose as a faun, but Joe refuses... because there are too many mosquitoes around." (Christopher; Howarth, Troy [2016]. *Tome of Terror: Horror Films of the Silent Era*. Midnight Marquee Press. p. 199]

CANNIBAL HOLOCAUST
THE LOST WORLD'S LOST FOOTAGE

RELEASE DATE February 2, 1925

DIRECTOR Harry O. Hoyt **SPECIAL EFFECTS** Willis O'Brien **SCREENPLAY** Marion Fairfax **CAST** Wallace Beery (Professor Challenger) Lloyd Hughes (Edward Malone) Bessie Love (Paula White) Lewis Stone (Sir John Roxton) Arthur Hoyt (Professor Summerlee) Zambo (Francis Finch-Smiles/Jules Cowles) The "Missing Link" (Bull Montana)

Academy Ratio, B&W, 110 Minutes (surviving version)

PLOT Professor Challenger leads a daring expedition to explore a prehistoric plateau still inhabited by dinosaurs. For a time, the explorers get stranded there. However, they find a way off with a brontosaurus in tow, which they bring with them back to London...

COMMENTARY It's not an understatement to say that 1925's *The Lost World* is one of the most important creature features of all time. No, it isn't the first dinosaur movie, nor is it as well remembered as the dino-flicks that it spawned, like *King Kong* (1933) and *Godzilla* (1954). It's the special effects that make the film of great significance more than anything. In addition to kickstarting what would be a whole "lost world" genre where explorers stumble across lost islands, valleys, and plateaus of prehistoric beasts, it also birthed the giant monster on the loose genre. This is because the film adaptation exaggerated the novel's ending. In the book, Challenger brings a baby pterodactyl back to London and it gets loose and flies home. In the film, a gigantic brontosaurus terrorizes London and causes all sorts of havoc before plunging off Tower Bridge and into the Thames to swim home. This wasn't the only change made to the novel by screenwriter Marion Fairfax, though. She also added in a significant female lead in the form of Paula White, who's missing father might be located somewhere in the Lost World. And, though the movie features a lone ape man, the book had a whole tribe of them. There are, of course, plenty of other big differences between the book and the movie, but those are the more significant ones.

21

See Gigantic Prehistoric Mons

"The LOST

The Allosaurus
attacks the
Trachodon

Only the brave

LLOYD HUGHES and
ALMA BENNETT
as Sweethearts in London.

s Battle Modern Lovers in

"WORLD"

he greatest drama of adventure and romance your eyes ever have beheld.

Imagine a Lost World--millions of years old-- and now found by a daring exploring party. Imagine this world still existing as in the beginning of time--with gigantic antediluvian monsters roaming it--ape men--prehistoric men living on it--fighting at every turn for existence--fighting the monsters who would devour them. And it all happens in this tremendous love and adventure drama--and people from your own world were brave enough to encounter hardships and dangers to bring back this story to you. Without doubt the biggest motion picture achievement.

SIR ARTHUR CONAN DOYLE'S
stupendous story, with

**BESSIE LOVE
LEWIS STONE
WALLACE BEERY
LLOYD HUGHES**

By arrangement with WATTERSON R. ROTHACKER
Research and Technical Director WILLIS H. O'BRIEN

The giant Brontosaurus— millions of years old

isk adventures such as will befall us

fight between the Brontosaurus and the Agathaumas

They saw the fight between monsters ten times their own size.

A First National Picture

23

Bessie Love reacts to one of O'Brien's stopmotion dinosaurs in *The Lost World.*

The Lost World was a huge hit when released in February of 1925, in large part due to Willis O'Brien's dinosaurs, which some theatergoers believed to be real animals. Ironically enough, a contingency plan was put in place on part of the producers should O'Brien's dinosaur footage prove unusable. One might notice upon viewing the film that the heroes don't do much in *The Lost World* apart from simply observe the dinosaurs in many instances. This is because several of the dinosaur scenes were invented by O'Brien himself, notably the prehistoric stampede that occurs in the wake of a volcanic eruption. Basically, Fairfax wrote the screenplay in such a way as to be easily adaptable if O'Brien's footage proved problematic. To that effect, she created a sequence where the heroes must face off against cannibals. In fact, this cannibal interlude would have been the main set-piece of the film had O'Brien's footage been considered subpar or unusable.

What you're about to read is a summarization of *The Lost World's* cannibal subplot, which may or may not have been in some cuts of the movie.[1] Whether they were ever edited into the film or not, they were for certain shot as stills exist of the sequence. Keep in mind that this isn't a continuous sequence, just the entire subplot as it would have been interspersed throughout the picture's first half.

As the expedition travels down the Amazon River via canoe, they enact the usual jungle explorer trope of spying what was probably just stock footage animals along the shore. Whether stock footage or not, the group is menaced by a large constrictor hanging from

24

a branch. If it comes into contact with them is uncertain, but Paula reacts in terror (likely in another close-up) and Jocko the monkey does the same. As this happens, an ominous looking native leers at them through the foliage. He is, unbeknownst to them, part of a tribe of vicious cannibals.

Later that night, as they make camp, the expedition is haunted by the ominous beating of native drums in the distance. Only Challenger and Summerlee seem unconcerned (though in the latter's case, only because he is currently enthralled in observing his collection of beetles). As Jocko retreats to the arms of Paula in fear, Malone joins her to comfort the animal. As Malone pets little Jocko, his hand brushes Paula, and a sudden flareup up of sexual tension is dissolved when Paula withdraws her hand.

SUMMERLEE (to Malone)
Those cursed war drums again! They have followed us for a week now!

CHALLENGER
They are merely signal drums of the Cucuma Indians. Degraded savages - with scarcely more intelligence than the average college professor!

SUMMERLEE (standing)
The average college professor at least has more brains than the average charlatan—

To this, Challenger only chuckles. Elsewhere, one of the expedition's native guides is filling the canteens at a watering hole where some howler monkeys have gathered. The guide's dog begins to growl. The guide peers into the foliage and puts down the canteen and raises his gun. Soon, the man is struck in the shoulder by an arrow from the deadly Nhambiquara cannibal tribe. He runs back to camp, while the dog charges into the foliage to attack. The man stumbles back into camp as Challenger and Summerlee are engaged in a debate. Roxton and Malone cock their rifles in alarm until they see it is one of their native bearers returned. The man falls near the fire, and Zambo cuts off the arrow shaft with a knife.

ROXTON
One of the poison arrows of the Nhambiquara cannibals - the poor chap will be dead in a few minutes.

25

Several still of the deleted footage including, from left to right, discussion at camp; cannibals in the jungle; and Challenger, Roxton, and Malone spying on the enemy camp.

ZAMBO
Say, Boss, dis you say - cannibules?

ROXTON
I said cannibals, Zambo - but, I'm told, they always prefer - white meat.

ZAMBO
I sho' am glad to hear you speak dem words, Boss!

As Roxton and Zambo nurse the poor victim, Gomez, the nefarious leader of the bearers (who was mostly cut from the final print, by the way) converses with the other bearers. Elsewhere, in a jungle clearing lit by the moonlight, the cannibal who shot the arrow returns to his tribe and excitedly explains what has happened. They all leap to their feet to begin playing the drums again. The drums are noticed at camp, with Gomez and the natives in particular growing uneasy.

CHALLENGER
More drum talk! These sneaking devils are telegraphing the 'good news' that they have killed one of our men!

26

Still of the cannibal encampment.

SUMMERLEE
You now admit that I am right - that they are war drums!

Challenger snorts his disgust as he turns away, angry that his opponent was right for once. The drums prompt another romantic moment between Paula and Malone.

PAULA (touching Malone's arm)
If we are ever in real danger of capture, will you promise to shoot me, Ed?

Unsure of how to respond, Malone simply kisses her hand and walks away. A jealous Roxton notices this and calls to Malone.

ROXTON
We'd better scout about a bit, young fellah-my-lad!

Afraid for both of the men she cares about, Paula asks Challenger to accompany them, and he agrees, following them into the night. With the three leaders of the expedition gone, Gomez conspires with the native bearers, mutiny on their minds. Meanwhile, Challenger, Roxton, and Malone skulk through the dark jungle forest, rifles in hand and ready to fire. In the darkness they spy a terrifying sight as the tribe of about twenty cannibals performs a war dance stomping their feet and brandishing their poison arrows. Suddenly, a jaguar bursts from the jungle and Malone readies to fire upon it. Roxton stops him, pointing at the cannibals, the implication being that it's better to risk the jaguar which has not yet spotted them than alerting the cannibals to their presence. Thankfully the jaguar skulks through the jungle without noticing them and the tension passes.

ROXTON (whispering to Malone)
We'd better go back to the canoes - these chaps'll keep this up until daylight.

MALONE (nodding)
-and we'll be miles upriver by that time!

The three men return to camp, but unbeknownst to them, Gomez and their native bearers (except Zambo) have snuck away on the canoes, leaving them all stranded. Challenger becomes enraged when he realizes what has happened. Not only have they taken the canoes but much of their supplies as well. Zambo has been injured in the departing skirmish, and his right arm has been badly cut by a machete. As for Austin and Summerlee, they are bound and gagged to a nearby tree. But where is Paula?

MALONE (shouting)
PAULA!

Summerlee points to the foliage upon being freed, and Challenger, Roxton, and Malone bound into the jungle to find her. Paula is found bound and gagged, lying facedown on the ground as Jocko clings to her. Malone cradles her in his arms while Challenger tends to the monkey. They return to camp, and Malone places Paula in a hammock. After given a sip of brandy, she begins to recount the horrific ordeal.

PAULA
Poor Zambo tried to prevent them from stealing the canoes—

Malone goes to the river's edge just to be sure all canoes are gone, while the rest of the men treat Zambo's wound. After some time, the expedition resumes their trek, crossing the river single file and carrying their provisions over their heads. At dawn the next day, the cannibals come upon the scene of the deserted camp. In a rage, the cannibals can see that not only did they pick up and leave, but they took their canoes back home and are out of reach. Ironically, the deserters have saved the lives of the expedition's remaining heroes. The scene was to end with the cannibals gathering around the dead body of the native bearer they shot with their poison arrow, clearly planning to make a meal of his dead body.

Though all lost film aficionados obviously want to see this footage today, it's clear why it was removed from the initial prints. In comparison to the dinosaurs, the scene's true nature as uninspired filler is a little too evident. But still, if the footage ever does turn up, it will be a welcome addition to the ongoing quest to construct a truly complete print of *The Lost World*.

NOTES

[1] What we know of the footage comes primarily from Roy Kinnard's *'The Lost World' of Willis O'Brien: The Original Shooting Script of the 1925 Landmark Special Effects Dinosaur Film with Photographs.*

FILMSÄSONGENS STORA SENSATION !

EN FÖRSVUNNEN VÄRLD

EFTER CONAN DOYLES VÄRLDSBERÖMDA ROMAN

med

BESSIE LOVE · LEWIS STONE
WALLACE BEERY · LLOYD HUGHES

A.-B. First National Pictures
STOCKHOLM

RESTORATION OF *THE LOST WORLD*

The history of *The Lost World's* many differing versions is a long one. When First National Pictures was acquired by Warner Brothers in 1929, they withdrew the full-length version from distribution, cutting it down from an hour and a half to only one hour. This shortened version was subsequently sub-licensed to Kodascope Libraries, a subsidiary of the Kodak Company which specialized both in short films and also in the art of cutting down feature length pictures to less than an hour in length for what was the very primitive first stages of home entertainment. Gone was the introductory scenes of Gladys and Malone plus Professor Challenger joining the expedition in South America. Even the exciting final sequence in London was subject to a few cuts.

The Lost World's next evolution came about in 1948, when Encyclopedia Britannica purchased it to create a five minute short retitled "A Lost World, As Told By A. Conan Doyle" for classroom settings. It apparently has new footage of an actor playing Conan Doyle who introduces the old footage from the film. Of course, that was just a short film. It was the Kodascope version of *The Lost World* that was still widely seen. Perhaps thanks to the looming production of *Jurassic Park, The Lost World* began to be restored little by little in the early 1990s. The first step was when Petrified Films, a stock footage company, purchased a collection of old prints from Warner Brothers. One of these reels just happened to include eight minutes worth of previously lost footage from *The Lost World.* Even better, in 1992 what appeared to be a complete print of the hour and a half version was found in the Filmovy Archiv of the Czech Republic. Yet more footage was unearthed via the Library of Congress and private collections.

George Eastman began collecting the hodgepodge of elements and footage began a restoration process. Restoring the film under the guidance of Ed Stratmann and with the financial equivalent of what we would today call Go-Fune Me, Eastman used the original script as a reference to reconstruct the picture. The problem was that the final cut of the film initially released in 1925 didn't follow the screenplay to a tee itself. As such, Eastman only used about twenty seconds of footage from the eight minute's worth of outtakes from Warner Bros. Nor did Eastman want to release the film on DVD. (Eastman did at least relent to allow 20th Century Fox to include his version of the film as a special feature on their DVD release of their inferior 1960 *Lost World* remake, and Eastman's recut was the real reason many people bought the disc.) As such, David Shepard created his own restoration of the film which was released to DVD in 2001 by Image Entertainment.

Today, significant amounts of *The Lost World* remain missing. The original footage of Sir Arthur Conan Doyle, as portrayed by an actor, sitting down at his desk to begin writing the book have vanished. As such, interview footage of the real Conan Doyle has been inserted in its place. For a full rundown of the differing versions and the most recent reconstruction, listen to Nicolas Ciccone's audio commentary on the Flicker Alley Blu-Ray release.

ATLANTIS
THE LOST WORLD'S LOST SEQUEL

PROPOSED RELEASE DATE: 1929

SPECIAL EFFECTS Willis O'Brien & Ralph Hammeras **SCREENPLAY** Earl Hudson

COMMENTARY Not to be confused with Harry O. Hoyt's *The Lost Atlantis*, which would come about a decade later, is this earlier version, simply titled *Atlantis*. This one was also pitched as a spiritual sequel to *The Lost World*. If there were any continuity ties between the two is unknown. In any case, it was announced immediately after it was apparent *The Lost World* was a hit, with Richard A. Rowland, First National Pictures' GM, announcing that February that a "sequel" would begin shooting in the company's new studio in New York.

Though *Lost World* director Harry O. Hoyt would be heavily involved in the 1938 *The Lost Atlantis*, no mention has ever been made of Hoyt in conjunction with this *Atlantis* that I can find. Instead, it was to be written and produced by Earl Hudson, and would bring back Willis O'Brien and Ralph Hammeras from *The Lost World*.

Most of what we know about *Atlantis* can be traced back to this article from *Moving Picture World* from February 21, 1925:

Rowland Announces Another Big Million Dollar Special

Another million dollar thriller, a sequel to Conan Doyle s "The Lost World" which is now amazing New York and Boston, will be made by First National, it was disclosed recently by General Manager Richard A. Rowland, prior to his departure for Hollywood.

The picture will be made under the supervision of Karl Hudson, for the most part with the same technical and research organization which made "The Lost World." Rowland declared that the test premieres of "The Lost World" in the two important cities during the past week prove conclusively the public's approval of this new and startling type of picture.

"The new picture is already under way; in fact, it has been in preparation for the past two months," said Rowland. "It will be even more fantastic and stirring than the Conan Doyle novel, difficult as that is to conceive. It will have, moreover, the same foundation of scientific procedure in the working out of the plot.

"The new story will be built around the mythical submerged continent of Atlantis, which some scientists declare to have existed in fact and to have been buried not by the wrath of pagan gods as suggested by Plato, but in the great flood of Scripture."

While on the Coast, Rowland will arrange the transportation to New York of the technical apparatus and technical experts involved in the production of "The Lost World." The new picture will be made, according to the plans of Rowland, in New York and the Azores.

"Work on the new picture was started in Hollywood before the completion of the current picture and prior to the removal of the First National unit in New York," said Rowland.

"Willis O'Brien and Ralph Hammeras, technical experts, were doing research work during the last two months of the year in which they were superintending the technical processes of "The Lost World." They are now in New York at work on the new picture. Milton Menasco, who was art director of "The Lost World," and Roy Carpenter, of the camera crew, are also here. Virtually all the experts engaged in the dinosaur drama have been retained.

"The Lost World" has unearthed a new field of drama for the motion picture which is impossible to any other field of drama. The secret developed by Willis O'Brien, after seven years of experiment, has made possible the visualization of the most extreme flights of imagination of our great authors.

"The story of Atlantis is the story of another 'lost world'— a world which mothered fierce supermen who ravaged and conquered the nations about them.

"To relieve the world of their menace, the gods, say the myths, sent an earthquake, and Atlantis settled beneath the sea. Science, however, knows that the fabled spot is shallow, and some men of erudition are inclined to believe it is the ground over which Noah floated his ark.

"Another theory of science we will bring into use is the belief that in the depths of the sea are monsters and marine life the eye of man has never seen. With the experience gained through our labors with 'The Lost World' there is every reason to believe the Atlantis story, will be even better."

From that brief description, it's apparent that it would not have been a straight dinosaur picture as *The Lost World* had been, but it's implied it would have featured dinosaurian sea serpents if nothing else. Jeff Rovin's book, *From the Land Beyond Beyond,* backed this up, as it related that the project would indeed feature "sea serpents which prowled the murky depths" in addition to scenes where "white-furred mastodons" were slaughtered in the "frozen northern reaches of Atlantis."[1]

Don O. Shay seemed to know the most about *Atlantis,* as he wrote about it in his famous article "Willis O'Brien – Creator of the Impossible" published in *Cinefex* #7. The following description of *Atlantis* reprinted below comes from a proto-version of the article that was sent to Merian C. Cooper, and obtained through the Merian C. Cooper Papers at Brigham Young University:

[*Atlantis*] concerned a vast underwater empire, the major portion of which was constructed in subterranean caverns which extended for miles and were thousands of feet high. The caverns were lit by torchlight, and pressure valves held back the sea. Huge stone statues were carved into the walls of the main cavern which were also honeycombed with small caves used as living quarters by the inhabitants of Atlantis. Huge tunnels ran from the cave auditorium to the sea and through these the inhabitants of Atlantis passed to kill horrible sea monsters and gather vegetation from the ocean floor. Small oxygen capsules enabled them to breathe underwater, thus eliminating the need for cumbersome equipment.

The Atlantians were ruled by a monarch who lived in luxury with his court. This monarch controlled an army of supermen that invaded neighboring nations, captured prisoners, and made them slaves. Large celebrations and feasts were given, to which friendly monarchs and their people were invited. Such were the inhabitants of the caves in the frozen North. These inhabitants controlled large fields of ice on which roamed herds of white, fur-bearing, prehistoric mammals. In the North, also, were huge food lockers where the meat of these massive mammals could be preserved to feed a nation.

Though no production drawings have surfaced that I know of, supposedly Obie and Hudson did many sketches for the film and had quite a few story discussions. About three month's work of very intensive work was done.

The last update on the project before it was cancelled came from *Moving Picture World* of July 11, 1925, on page 187:

Preparing for "Atlantis"

Earl Hudson has been working for months on the story of "Atlantis" and is nearing the completion of the story. Willis O'Brien, technical director of "The Lost World," has been doing research work since February for the picture. Hudson plans to make it even a greater picture than "The Lost World."

Like so many unfilmed masterpieces, *Atlantis* eventually collapsed both under the weight of its proposed budget, production delays, and the purchase of First National by Warner Bros. Though *Atlantis* had been touted as a future release as late as November of 1926, by the time Warner Bros purchased First National in 1928, *Atlantis* was discarded by the new owners.

NOTES

---

[1] Rovin, *From the Land Beyond Beyond,* p.21.

THE TRAMP IN THE LOST WORLD
BY MATTHEW B. LAMONT

DEVELOPED 1925-1930

CONCEPT/SPECIAL EFFECTS Willis O'Brien **PROPOSED CAST/CHARACTERS** The Tramp (Charlie Chaplin) **PROPOSED CREATURES** Brontosaurus, Tyrannosaurs, giant bird, ape-men

COMMENTARY The idea of a *Lost World* parody starring Charlie Chaplin was a possibility pondered by Willis O'Brien from around 1925 to 1930. As we all know, 1925's *The Lost World* was a huge hit that was also popular enough to produce merchandising ranging from toys to puzzles. Well, when something is popular, it's never safe from the jaws of parody, hence O'Brien's idea of a comical retelling starring Chaplin.

Naturally, I found the concept of Chaplin visiting the Lost World puzzling enough for me to put on my investigator hat. I discovered that before *The Lost World* was even released, Obie was already cooking up an idea of utilizing a prehistoric environment with dinosaurs and ape-men as a parody. However, it was not easy to find evidence of this project. As I was watching Steven L. Austin's awesome documentary, *Creation: The Lost World of Willis O'Brien*, the Lost World parody project was brought up briefly. Later, I saw a sample from a book entitled *Register to the Merian C. Cooper Papers* by James V. D'Arc and John N. Gillespie. There was a two-page spread with concept art of the project with a Brontosaurus (also shown in the documentary) plus a big ape-man, a T-Rex, and a giant bird. The giant gorilla, shown at a circus, was notably a precursor to *King Kong*. (This was coincidentally around the same time that Merian C. Cooper was thinking about doing a movie with his own super-sized simian.) It might even be possible that the Brontosaurus and the colossal anthropoid might fight, making for another a forerunner to *Kong*'s dinosaur battles in addition to being a callback to Obie's early claymation efforts like *The Dinosaur and The Missing Link* (1915).

One of O'Brien's storyboards for the project.

In the *Register to the Merian C. Cooper Papers* that I mentioned earlier, eleven illustrations gave a good description of the story that Obie wanted to put to film. Judging by the production drawings, it was about the lovable tramp—either being a stowaway on a ship or wandering into an expedition—winding up in an unexplored land forgotten by time. There he gets himself into all sorts of trouble: being chased by a Tyrannosaurus and a run-in with an ape-man among his adventures. At one point as he's running through the lost world, he runs into what he thinks is a huge tree trunk only to discover that it's the leg of a giant prehistoric bird which takes him to its nest to be food for its hatchlings.[1]

The meat of the story concerned the Tramp befriending a brontosaurus, which he does while he's fishing. Somehow the Tramp brings the rare but lovely plant eater to civilization, where it becomes a circus attraction. As expected, hilarity and chaos ensues and the dinosaur eventually runs amuck in the city. This idea, like two others from O'Brien (*Atlantis* and *Frankenstein*), unfortunately got rejected. That said, Obie would evolve the Chaplin story in later years for Lum and Abner in *Matilda or The Isle of Women*, which also never got made.

While we unfortunately never got Obie's *Lost World* spoof starring Chaplin, which surely would have been a classic, here are a few *Lost World* parodies that we did get:

Alleged still of *The Savage* (1926).

First, Luis Seel made *Finding A Lost World* (1926) which combined live-action and animation. However, this film is lost, so nothing is known about it. *The Lost Whirl* (1926) by John Bray, who did his version of *Gertie the Dinosaur* a decade earlier, rips off *The Lost World* in a comedic fashion. This film had animated models by Joseph L. Roop, the same man who helped Willis O'Brien with the animation in *The Lost World* (1925). Also, there was *The Savage* (1926), another silent comedy based on the short story by Ernest Pascal, which was an attempt to cash in on the 1925 hit.

NOTES

[1] "Wait a minute," you might say, "Didn't Charlie Chaplin run into a giant bird in *His Prehistoric Past* (1915)?" True, but the setting was in caveman times, like Buster Keaton and the Brontosaurus in *The Three Ages* (1923) or Laurel and Hardy with the Triceratops in *Flying Elephants* (1928). As I said, this project was planned in the mid-1920s after the success of *The Lost World.*

THE MYSTERIOUS ISLAND

METRO-GOLDWYN-MAYER'S

TECHNICOLOR
TALKING, SOUND
Dramatic Spectacle
Based on Jules Verne's
Immortal Novel

When "White Shadows in the South Seas" came to picture audiences it was hailed as a welcome novelty, a thoroughly different entertainment. You know what marvelous business "White Shadows" did wherever it played. Now comes another typical M-G-M stroke of brilliant ingenuity and daring, "The Mysterious Island." It is unique among any film attractions you may play. All the thrills, the vivid imaginative sequences, the charming love story of Jules Verne's classic companion-novel to "Twenty Thousand Leagues Under the Sea" are strikingly conceived in Technicolor in "The Mysterious Island." It has been made as both a Sound and Silent picture.

Also a
SILENT
Production

with LIONEL BARRYMORE
LLOYD HUGHES—JANE DALY
Screen Play and Direction by
LUCIEN HUBBARD

THE MOSTLY-SILENT MYSTERIOUS ISLAND

RELEASE DATE October 5, 1929

DIRECTOR Lucien Hubbard **SCREENPLAY** Lucien Hubbard **CAST** Lionel Barrymore (Count Dakkar) Jacqueline Gadsden (Sonia Dakkar) Lloyd Hughes (Nikolai Roget) Montagu Love (Falon) Harry Gribbon (Mikhail) Snitz Edwards (Anton) Gibson Gowland (Dmitry) Dolores Brinkman (Teresa)

Academy Ratio, B&W, 95 Minutes

PLOT Count Dakkar (AKA Captain Nemo) rules over a benevolent, volcanic island kingdom where he is constructing a powerful new submarine. The island is eventually invaded by the villainous Baron Falon, but Dakkar escapes his clutches. The two super

41

intellects battle it out on the sea floor in their super submarines to determine the winner.

COMMENTARY 1961's *Mysterious Island* is greatly beloved amongst the stopmotion community, but very few, including myself up until this point, were aware of a 1929 precursor called *The Mysterious Island* released by MGM. However, more than a straightforward adaptation of Jules Verne's novel, it's really more of a prequel to the *20,000 Leagues Under the Sea* story as it shows the birth of the *Nautilus*. (This is because in the *Mysterious Island* book, Nemo's backstory is given, and yes, his true name is revealed as Prince Dakkar.)

Screengrab of *The Mysterious Island's* lone dinosaur.

The film began production in 1926 and was so ambitious that it wasn't finished and ready for release until three years later. It was predominantly silent, as most of the dialogue is still given via text slates, but there are sound effects throughout and a few random lines of spoken dialogue. Furthermore, of the 8,569 feet of film shot, 7,234 of it was in the 1920s version of Technicolor. It was thought that only one color reel survived within the collection of the UCLA Film and Television Archive. As you can gather, like *The Lost World*, the complete version of *The Mysterious Island* was lost for some time. Fortunately, Deborah

42

Stoiber from the George Eastman House film archive traveled to Prague in 2013 to investigate reports of a color print of *The Mysterious Island*. It was found to be true, and with the Czech National Film Archive's help, the lost film was restored.

And yes, the picture does have a dinosaur... or maybe it's more of a dragon? In any case, it's of the *One Million B.C.* variety as opposed to the 1925 *Lost World* stopmotion saurians. Basically, the undersea dinosaur is another dimetrodon-like finned lizard. It even attacks an underwater city full of miniature people. And by miniature, I do mean miniature. Though no such beings appear in Jules Verne's *Mysterious Island*, for some reason, during the *Nautilus'* underwater voyage in this picture they come across a sunken city inhabited by miniature humanoids in diving suits. Eventually, the dinosaur-like creature comes calling and drives them all away.

The film should be of interest to silent-era aficionados as well as Jules Verne fans. If you're purely a dinosaur enthusiast though, there's not much to recommend.

THE DINOSAURS ROAR
1930-1952

CREATION
DINOSAUR ISLAND RISES & SINKS
·ORIGINALLY PUBLISHED IN *KONG UNMADE VOLUME I*·
DEVELOPED 1929–1931

This chapter: Various drawing and production art made for *Creation*.

DIRECTOR Harry O. Hoyt **SPECIAL EFFECTS** Willis O'Brien **SCREENPLAY** Beulah Marie Dix & Harry O. Hoyt (story) **MUSIC** Edison von Ottenfeld **PROPOSED CAST/CHARACTERS** Steve [Armitage family tutor] (Joel McCray, tentative), Thorton Armitage [American tycoon], Elaine Armitage [Thorton's daughter], Billy Armitage [Thorton's son], Ned Hallet [Elaine's fiancée] (Ralf Harolde), Louise [aunt], Benny [Jewish chef] (Benny Rubin, tentative), Chico [Elaine's pet monkey] **PROPOSED DINOSAURS** Brontosaurus, Triceratops, Arsinotherium, Wooly Mammoth, Stegosaurus, Tyrannosaurus, Pterodactyl, Trachodon, Agathaumas (concept art), Styracosaurus (concept art), Ankylosaurus (concept art)

Academy Ratio, Black & White, 20 Minutes (uncompleted)

PLOT A group of aristocrats is stranded on a newly formed island of dinosaurs...

COMMENTARY *King Kong*, the great-granddaddy of all giant monster movies ironically owes its birth to an uncompleted film called *Creation*. Had *Creation* not been cancelled, *King Kong* may have never been made. Perhaps not surprisingly, this lost film was all about dinosaurs and humans coming into contact on an island. In many ways, the film was both a retelling and remake of *The Lost World*, replacing the prehistoric plateau with a whole island full of dinosaurs with a few elements from the 1902 play *The Admirable Crichton*, which was set on a South Seas Isle. In fact, *Lost World* director Harry O. Hoyt was to return alongside Willis O'Brien.

The project, which was to have sound unlike *The Lost World*, was the brainchild of Hoyt, who developed the picture in the summer of 1929 and pitched it to RKO in early 1930. To do so, he screened a print of *The Lost World* and also gave RKO a 76 page "Detail for Cost Estimation" document. Hoyt told RKO he believed that O'Brien could create 37 dinosaurs (17 primary ones and 20 for the background only) in a period of only eight weeks and that in four weeks, enough models would be created for filming to commence. RKO's Bertram Millhauser felt that *Creation* could be shot in a time period of 15-20 weeks on a budget of $652,242.50 exactly. Millhauser would turn out to be very wrong.

The project was officially approved by RKO Vice President William LeBaron in late April of 1930 as "Production 359" with a whopping $1,201,813 budget.[1] *Creation's* final storyline was adapted from Hoyt's ideas by Beulah Marie Dix over the summer of 1930. Dix, who had written several Cecil B. DeMille epics, compressed Hoyt's initial ideas, combining characters and also adding in an exciting battle between a tyrannosaur and a stegosaur.

The final storyline centered on a group of wealthy aristocrats on a yacht owned by patriarch Thorton Armitage. The lead character was to be a more relatable figure for the audience: Steve, the tutor of the Armitage son, Billy, and the secret admirer of Elaine Armitage. Of course, to make a love triangle, Elaine's fiancé, Ned Hallet, is also on the voyage. For comic relief are friendly, overweight Aunt Louise and the Jewish cook, Benny, who likely inspired Charlie in *King Kong*.

The story was to begin with the luxury yacht *Titan* anchored 40 degrees south of the equator not far from Patagonia. Steve has just finished teaching Billy about the theory of evolution when he runs into Elaine below deck. She flirts with him, and so Steve grabs her and kisses her while Ned watches from the shadows. Steve is shocked when Elaine tells him that the kiss meant nothing to her, so he threatens to leave the crew. Above deck, the family watch as storm clouds brew in the distance. Soon a storm is upon the yacht and a submarine dispatched by the Chilean navy arrives to save the Armitage family and their crew. They board the sub, and the yacht is destroyed as a new island emerges from the sea.

The next scene is heavily inspired by Edgar Rice Burroughs' novel *The Land That Time Forgot* (1918). The submarine becomes thrown off course due to the violent storm and soon finds itself in a strange underwater passage filled with green water and frightening creatures. The sub is damaged when it runs aground against a rock and so must emerge as soon as possible as it fills with water. It emerges in a prehistoric lagoon that appears to be the cauldron of a dormant volcano.

With the submarine immobile, the party goes on land to explore. From here on, many scripted scenes are not coincidentally similar to scenes later recreated in *King Kong*, plus its sequels and remakes. First up is a brontosaurus stampede that was finally filmed for Peter Jackson's 2005 *King Kong*. Next up is a scene re-adapted for *King Kong* in which the party traverses a log strewn across a chasm. Instead of a giant ape, they are confronted by an Arsinotherium, a prehistoric rhino of sorts, which gores many of the sailors to death and knocks others into a raging river below. Specifically, the scene begins with the party needing to cross a river. Steve swings across on a vine, but it breaks, meaning the others will have to find another way across. The captain sends his men into the jungle to chop down a tree to make a bridge out of. There they first encounter the fearsome Arsinotherium, which gives chase. It kills the men in various different ways, including uprooting a tree onto one before it finally chases them to the log bridge over the ravine. Steve, being on the other side of the river, is one of the lone survivors of the expedition party. He watches in horror as pterodactyls, attracted by the blood, swoop down like vultures to feast on the dead men and carry a few away as the Arsinotherium chases them. Steve stumbles through the jungle where he is almost killed by a wooly mammoth. He finally reconnects with the others and all fear they are stranded in this land of terror forever.

The Arsinotherium created for *Creation* which almost appeared in *King Kong* (1933).

Still similar in narrative to *The Land That Time Forgot*, the party builds a camp high on a cliff overlooking the valley. Thirty days pass as they learn to survive in the new world. One day the villainous Ned shoots a brontosaurus, and the enraged beast begins destroying the camp. Elaine grabs a torch and puts it to the monster's mouth driving it away. Ned, ashamed and angry after having been scolded by the others, leaves camp and shoots a baby triceratops. The mother then gores him to death, and the villainous Ned can no longer complicate the relationship between Steve and Elaine.

Steve, having taken charge of the party of survivors, decides to do his best to repair the submarine's radio. Steve braves the strange waters to dive into the sunken sub and retrieve the radio. Now that he has the radio, he sees that he will need a replacement leyden jar.[2] As the crew spied some ancient ruins on the island, they decide that is a good place to look. While exploring the lost city (rife with gold and precious jewels), a large block collapses, causing Elaine to fall to the ruins below. She is plucked from the

50

air by a pterodactyl, which intends to eat her. Steve manages to rescue her by swinging on a vine Tarzan-style and slamming into the beast, causing it to drop Elaine and fly away. From there, the crew is chased by a stegosaurus into a temple where a tyrannosaurus and its young live. A battle breaks out between the two dinosaurs, thus saving the party from both as the tyrannosaurus kills the stegosaur.[3] The crew escapes as the tyrannosaurus feeds the dead stegosaur to its young. As luck has it, Elaine's pet monkey Chico has discovered the very jar they needed all along.

A radio tower for an S.O.S. message is erected and a distress message is sent just as the island's volcano erupts. The dinosaurs panic, causing a stampede and in the chaos a pterodactyl slams into the radio tower, destroying it.[4] Feeling that all hope is lost, Steve and Elaine confess their love for one another. Just as Billy collapses from heat exhaustion, they spy rescue planes in the sky. They land in the lagoon and collect the castaways. The planes fly off and escape just as the volcano consumes the island.

The film's humorous epilogue would be set on a rescue boat. As the rescuers doubt the group's tales of dinosaurs on the island, an exhausted pterodactyl suddenly drops onto the ship's deck. Steve and Elaine share a laugh with the rest, and the film would come to a close.

O'Brien began working on the dinosaurs with Byron Crabbe and Ernest Smythe on July 9, 1930. Most sources confirm that one adult triceratops and two babies were built along with two brontosauri, two stegosauri, two tyrannosauri, a styracosaurus, an Arsinotherium, a pterodactyl, a Diamorphodon, and a few birds for good measure. Also built was a full-sized juvenile triceratops by mechanical expert Charles Christatoro. The mechanical dinosaur had the ability to walk and to create the illusion of breathing. Also built was a full-scale triceratops head for the adult mother.

However, by October, no footage had been shot, and Millhauser's 20 week production period had been eclipsed long ago. But, considering the massive amount of pre-production work—most importantly, a working script and dinosaurs—RKO wasn't going to abandon *Creation* yet. They approved of the shooting of some test footage—namely the scene where Ned shoots a young triceratops. Three weeks were allotted to shoot the sequence. All in all four concept drawings plus 20 other sketches were completed for the scene. There was also a detailed description for the shooting process and the camera angles.

Stills from the surviving four minutes of *Creation* featuring the Triceratops.

Another still (above) and production drawing (below).

Shooting finally began on November 15th and would end up lasting 61 days! Things had changed since O'Brien had animated *The Lost World* in 1925. Back then films were projected at 16 frames per second but in the age of 'talkies' that had been upped to 24 frames per second, meaning it would take O'Brien considerably longer to animate the dinosaurs. Instead of completing 40 feet of film per day as promised by Hoyt, O'Brien could only complete 25 feet (only about 20 seconds of film) per day.

The completed scene shows a triceratops and her two young, who are playing tug of war with a vine. One of the babies wanders off into the jungle, where it spies a chimpanzee, a jaguar, and finally, Ned Hallet.[5] The scene, which takes place when Ned is angry at his fellow castaways, shows him viewing the juvenile triceratops through the scope of his rifle and shooting it in the eye. The baby falls over and a mock-up of the dead baby was built for actor Ralf Harolde to inspect before being chased by the mother. The adult triceratops is spectacular, and although it doesn't appear in *King Kong,* it does appear in *Son of Kong.* Unfortunately, the footage of the mother goring Ned to death is lost. Reportedly, Cooper considered actually using this footage in *King Kong* but felt that it just didn't mix well enough. In both the novelization and the script of *King Kong,* there is a scene for the triceratops even though it didn't make it into the finished film. However, some of the triceratops footage was later used on the computer game *Dinosaur Museum* by Perspective Visuals and also the educational video *More Dinosaurs.*

Actually, much harder to manage in the triceratops scene were the real animals: Snooky the Chimpanzee (the star of several "two-reel novelties" for Universal), a live jaguar from Olga Celeste, a stork, and a kinkajou. The jaguar naturally terrified the crew when it did not behave as hoped. The jaguar was to be released from a cage to catch a chicken, grab it, then dart into another cage to eat its prize. Instead, it grabbed the chicken and ran loose on set until Miss Celeste grabbed it by the scruff of the neck and forced it back into its cage.

Snooky, the baby chimp, was even more terrifying. Snooky was to toss a branch at the baby triceratops. The branch was intentionally loosened so that the slightest move from Snooky would cause it to drop. Instead, on the third take, Snooky fell from the loose branch and became enraged. The baby chimp, strong as a man with sharp teeth, ran amuck on the set, wrecking props and equipment. Then the chimp stuck his face in some plaster of Paris. If Snooky, something of a beloved animal star, ingested the plaster, it would poison the chimp. Snooky's trainer chased the ape down and forced it to spit out the plaster. After the debacle, Willis O'Brien declared, "No more live animals!"

THE SOUND OF *CREATION*

Not only was test footage shot, but a musical score by a young, upcoming composer, Edison von Ottenfeld, was being scored. When the film came to naught, Ottenfeld salvaged portions of his score to create the Dinosaur Suite, which he performed at the Hollywood Bowl. Speaking of sound, had it been finished, *Creation* would have been the first talking special effects film.

Portions of the shipwreck sequence were shot by Karl Brown as well. Alongside this was also filmed the destruction of a coastal village, parts of the island rising out of the sea, and a few submarine sequences. Brown recalled to Orville Goldner, an effects technician who later co-authored *The Making of King Kong*, that:

Most of this work was done entirely underwater. For the storm at sea, I poured in carbon tetrachloride, which created [turbulence]. We had to show a mountain rising from the sea, along with lava, steam and explosions. The mountain was built in sections, and the steam was canned milk. When a twister was supposed to come along...we used a canoe paddle to create a vortex in the water and poured in negrosin, a black powdered dye soluble only in alcohol, down to the funnel. We couldn't make it come forward to the camera, so we moved the camera up to it and got the same effect.[6]

Goldner recalled further difficulties with filming the island rising from the sea, which no matter how slowly they cranked the film didn't look immense enough. To remedy this, they tried thickening the water with clear gelatin.[7]

Though these scenes are mostly lost, the shipwreck scene is said to have been salvaged to be the shipwreck in *The Most Dangerous Game*, a companion piece of sorts to *King Kong* filmed at the same time. In total, about twenty minutes worth of footage for *Creation* was shot. Today, sans the possible scene from *The Most Dangerous Game*, only four minutes survive, those being the triceratops scene minus Ned's death.

Concept art from the sequence where the brontosaurus attacks camp.

By January 24, 1931, the test footage had been shot and ended up costing a whopping $131,690. The only reason the production didn't get shut down then and there was due to the fact that RKO had just experienced a huge hit in the form of *Cimarron*. Production would continue slowly with various sets being designed, though only a few were built. It was hoped that live-action photography with actors could begin shooting on April 23, 1931, over the course of 60 days. When it became apparent this wasn't going to happen, the date was pushed back to June with a schedule of only 41 days, plus an additional ten days, which would be shot on location in Florida. Finally, Bertram Millhauser, who had encouraged the production, was let go. In a last-ditch effort to save the project, Hoyt scaled it down considerably. For starters, only two main sets would be constructed and Hoyt cut out the ambitious sea storm sequence and replaced it with a plane crash. Also, now only Ned would fall victim to the dinosaurs, whose numbers were considerably reduced. A 36-day shooting schedule that allowed for six days of pick-up shots to begin on July 24th was proposed and subsequently rejected.

Concept art for deleted dinosaur scene where Kong was to battle several triceratops as a way of utilizing the test footage from *Creation*.

The production, which had by then tallied up $170,000 in expenses, was officially cancelled by Merian C. Cooper, who notoriously described the film as, "Just a lot of animals walking around." As far Cooper was concerned, the film lacked a central antagonist, which he felt would be better suited for his gestating ape movie. This wasn't just Cooper being selfish. The film was over budget with no end in sight.

But, thanks to the production of *King Kong*, not all of the hard work done for *Creation* was in vain. Nearly all of *Creation*'s dinosaurs, save ironically for the triceratops, made it into either *King Kong* or *Son of Kong*. The triceratops scene from *Creation* was also used as test footage for *King Kong* to help convince the RKO studio executives to greenlight the film. In this same footage is a version of the log scene where the men are trapped between Kong and the Arsinotherium. When making *King Kong*, Cooper decided he preferred the styracosaurus (also from *Creation*) to the Arsinotherium. Ironically, the styracosaurus was cut too because Cooper felt it distracted from Kong and the main action piece. Even more of *Creation*'s dinosaurs were used in other productions in later years. Portions of the Diamorphodon, a prehistoric flying reptile, were retrofitted to appear in *Witches' Brew* (1979), *Caveman* (1981), and *Q: The Winged Serpent* (1982).

In any case, it's a good thing *King Kong* was made in place of *Creation*. Though *Creation* sounds to be a wonderful dinosaur film, *King Kong* was a cultural phenomenon that *Creation* likely never would have been.

NOTES

[1] Some sources also think there's a possibility the film was meant for the Technicolor process, but considering so much money was spent on the black and white test footage this is unlikely.

[2] This is still basically in following of Burroughs's story, only in that case the crew tries to refine crude oil from Caprona to repair their sub.

[3] The idea of a battle between two monsters in a temple is repeated in *Son of Kong*.

[4] The dinosaur stampede was planned to feature into *Son of Kong* but there wasn't enough time to film it.

[5] Ralf Harolde plays Ned in this sequence, and it's unknown if he was only cast for the test footage to be replaced later, or if the role was his for the entire film.

[6] Turner and Goldner, *Spawn of Skull Island: The Making of King Kong*, p. 201.

[7] Before filming on the scene had even begun, the water proved too heavy and broke the glass tank overnight! Heavier glass then had to be brought in, which didn't react to the camera lens as well.

THE MYSTERY OF LIFE
THE LOST EVOLUTION DOCUMENTARY

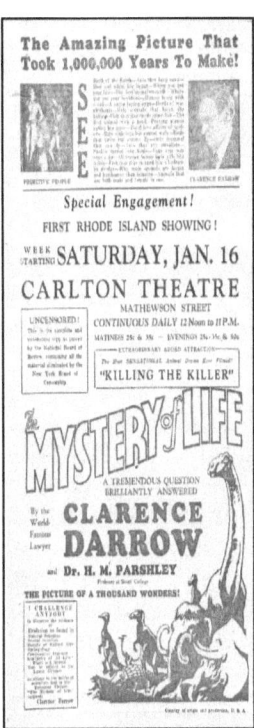

RELEASE DATE August 3, 1931

DIRECTOR George Cochrane **SCREENPLAY** H.M. Parshley **CAST** Clarence Darrow & H.M. Parshley

Academy Ratio, B&W, 62 Minutes

COMMENTARY At about the same time that *Creation* sank beneath the waves, a dinosaur-ladden documentary about evolution surfaced. It was the brainchild of lawyer Clarence Darrow. As a lawyer, Darrow was fascinated by the Scopes Trial of 1925—also known as the "Scopes Monkey Trial"— wherein science teacher John Scopes was put on trial for teaching evolution. Darrow then became determined to make a sort of evolution propaganda film, *The Mystery of Life*, which, for the most part, was his only major foray into the realm of feature films.[1] Darrow wrote of the project optimistically in his autobiography, *The Story of My Life* published in 1932, stating, "...whether it will prove to be a success I cannot say; for the present it is well received and favorably reviewed and well attended."

While Darrow's documentary was released and well-reviewed by the *New York Times*, which said that it was "excellent in the way it presents its material,"[2] the hour-long feature is today lost. Currently, most of what we know about it comes from articles of the time as well as the film's theater program booklet, reproduced on pages 61-64. Though the *Times* review was mostly favorable, even it admitted that "if the lectures seem occasionally to be proving their contentions rather blandly, that is their purpose." This is probably due to the fact that it was written by a zoologist, Howard Parshley, and not a screenwriter.

Actually, Darrow and Parshley both appear onscreen as themselves, debating the titular "Mystery of Life." The *Times* review stated that, "Professor Parshley gives most of the actual scientific material; Mr. Darrow contenting himself mainly with the whimsical, pessimistic remarks for which he is known." And what of the film's prehistoric life? From what we can tell, no new major dino-effects scenes were used, and all were lifted from past productions, notably *The Ghost of Slumber Mountain* (1918), *The Lost World* (1925) and a German documentary called *Wunder der Schöpfung* (1925). That said, *The Dinosaur Filmography* features a still from *Mystery of Life* showing a Rhamphoryncus model of some kind[3] that may have been unique to the production.

Some called for the censorship of the film due to its subject matter discussing the theory of evolution altogether, though in the end only a few scenes of animal mating were trimmed (plus a few shots of naked cavewomen). Today, no one knows where any surviving prints of the film can be found.

NOTES

[1] He appeared as an actor in the 1926 movie *Camille*.
[2] Branch, "Censoring Darrow," NCSE https://ncse.ngo/censoring-darrow
[3] At least, that's the closest prehistoric creature that it resembles but it's certainly not a dead-ringer.

FEATURE PROGRAMME

WARDOUR FILMS, Ltd.

present

THE
MYSTERY
OF
LIFE

The progress of the world from microscopic cells to modern
civilisation. The laws of nature, the urge of hunger, love and
the desire to live.

61

THE MYSTERY OF LIFE

Produced by the Educational Department of U.F.A.

FOREWORD

The Story of Life, of Evolution, presents Nature's struggle and progress, in dialogue and pictures. Herein is told, in words and dramatic scenes, how all animals fight for bare existence, for mates; and the progress of the world from microscopic cells to modern civilization. Graphic description synchronised with gripping pictures. A "talkie" of the world's greatest story—the story of the world.

THE MYSTERY OF LIFE

SYNOPSIS

Skyscrapers, aeroplanes, all the wonders of the machine are built upon the laws of nature. Through all life is the urge of hunger, the need for mates, the perpetuation of the species. Everywhere is fighting and struggle from the lowest to the highest. Each must fight for itself and its successors. On this founded all endeavour all purpose.

By the cooling and condensing of a flaming mass of gases, were the sun and worlds first formed. The world at first a ball of fire cooling slowly in the ages, cooling till solid rocks appeared, cooling till water condensed, flowing together, making seas and oceans.

Life came into this empty world. We know not how—whether brought from some other world or created in the archaic seas. At first living creatures were simple single-celled creatures, feeding by wrapping themselves round their prey, moving by flowing along, and reproducing by simple division. Several such cells by banding together form a colony, and the first big upward step is taken. Specialisation begins, sex cells are developed. So began the forerunners of the complex animals, such creatures as the jelly fish and the sea anemone.

Next arose the beginnings of a backbone. First in worm-like creatures, then fish which spread and dominated the seas. By migration on to land were formed the amphibians, the reptiles, and last the birds and mammals.

From the higher mammals arose primitive man. Living in caves, using simple stone implements he fought his battles with nature, and, aided by a brain, he fought and progressed. Later races built their homes on piles in lakes for protection. Invention began, and with them the dawn of modern humanity.

Through all the world to-day the fight continues. Animals adapt themselves to special circumstances that they may survive. Feet become paddles and wings, wings become paddles, each for the betterment of the species. In the dark caves of Dalmatia an animal has gone back, has lost its eyes, and lost its colour, gone back to the water and fish's gills; it is doomed to extinction, there is no going back in this stream of life.

So the world has progressed. Man commands every corner of the world by virtue of his brain, his skill and his inventions. The laws of nature, the urge of hunger, love and the desire to live have borne him upwards and still upwards.

THE MYSTERY OF LIFE

THE MYSTERY OF LIFE

THE LOST ATLANTIS
CREATION RE-CREATED?

PROPOSED DIRECTOR Harry O. Hoyt **PROPOSED SPECIAL EFFECTS** Fred Jackman, Edward Nassour, and Walter Lantz **PROPOSED DINOSAURS** tyrannosaurus, ceratosaurs, allosaurus, triceratops, stegosaurus, brontosaurus

COMMENTARY Though a fantastic poster exists for this film, it's hard to determine what exactly it was about—apart from the obvious—or how it came to be. The simple answer could be that it was some kind of continuation of *Atlantis* from 1925. However, this version of *Atlantis* was pitched by Harry Hoyt to Columbia Pictures sometime in the mid-1930s. It would seem that the film might have been an attempt to resurrect Hoyt's canceled *Creation* movie, with an island full of dinosaurs—in this case Atlantis—rising from the depths.

65

The camera's magic brings to vivid, spectacular life the ancient legend of a continent that vanished beneath the waters of the turbulent Atlantic! Huge beasts lash their way across the face of the earth ... great monsters stage epic undersea battles!

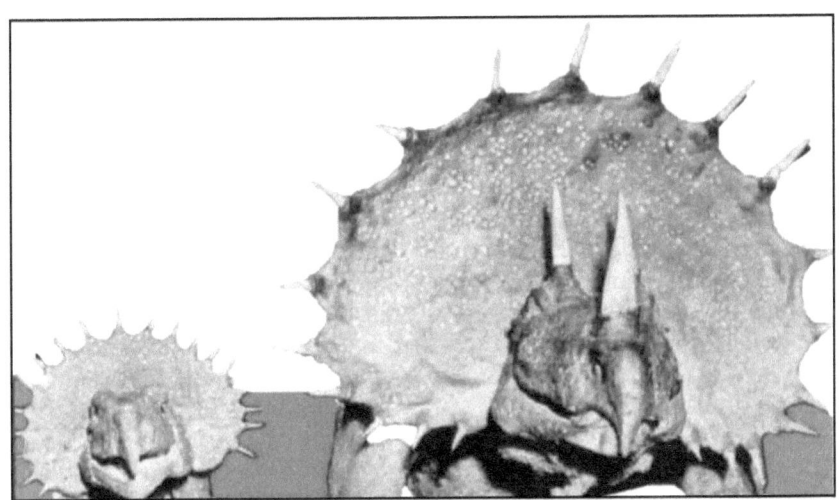

Some of Jackman's dinosaur models.

The only true indication of the plot comes from the poster presented on page opposite, which promises:

The camera's magic brings to vivid, spectacular life the ancient legend of a continent that vanished beneath the waters of the turbulent Atlantic! Huge beasts lash their way across the face of the earth ... great monsters stage epic undersea battles!

Spawn of Skull Island, the second edition of *The Making of King Kong* by George E. Turner and Orville Goldner, with additional material by Michael H. Price and Douglas Turner, implied that *The Lost Atlantis* was indeed *Creation* rebranded. The authors wrote that "another submarine would be drawn into another lost world. Once more, the villain would kill a baby dinosaur, only to be pursued and slain by the mother."[1] If I had to guess, I would speculate that Hoyt probably took the plot of *Creation*, changed the character names, and made the lost temple found in *Creation* the lost city of Atlantis itself.

In 1938, Hoyt pitched the film to Columbia alongside Fred Jackman, the former chief technician on *The Lost World*.[2] Hoyt had an in with Columbia in the form of Trem Carr, who he had known back when they both worked at Monogram. Harry Cohn, the head of Columbia, had enough faith in the Atlantis piece to invest $20,000 for two reels worth of test footage. If he liked it, they would produce the film as an A Picture with a healthy budget. If they didn't, they would use the reels in a serial of some kind. Jackman, along with a few other technicians, shot ten minutes worth of black and white test footage using some dinosaur puppets. In all, 25 dinosaur puppets were constructed, with each one costing about $600. The puppets consisted of a tyrannosaurus, brontosaurus, allosaurus, ceratosaurs, triceratops, and a stegosaurus.[3] Humorously, at least one of the props was absconded with by a pet dog.[4] However, a mistake seemed to be made in making the puppets look cutesy as opposed to menacing. This can be seen in the existing photographs of the props. Marcel Delgado, who toured the set when the test reel was being shot, noted that the dinosaurs looked "cuter than they should have been." Delgado also observed that the staff creating the dinosaurs was entirely female. Interestingly, despite their cutesy appearance, the 1939 issue of *Popular Mechanics* claimed that, "two girls who worked over a month building the creatures threatened to quit because they said the half-completed monsters crawled through their dreams."[5]

Behind the scenes of *The Lost Atlantis.*

However, the dinosaurs were hardly the stuff of nightmares, and by the time *Popular Mechanics* published that story, Cohn had rejected the project. Though the reason given was that it would be too costly, perhaps he just didn't like the cartoon-like dinosaurs.

In 1940, Hoyt tried again with two new members added to the effects crew: Edward Nassour, who would go on to do 1956's *The Beast of Hollow Mountain*, and Walter Lantz, best-known for Woody Woodpecker. This time, test footage was shot in technicolor with dinosaur models made of a special malleable plastic. In a 1973 interview with George Turner, Lantz revealed that via Nassour's animation, one reel's worth of test footage was completed and contained a fight between dinosaurs. According to him, the models were very small, and the human figurines even smaller at only two inches. Douglas W. Churchill saw this test footage back when it was produced, and wrote about it in the

November 17, 1940 edition of the *New York Times*. Churchill described the footage as smooth, and detailed a plan on Nassour's part to use the test footage in an upcoming cartoon short to see what the public's response was. The footage was never shown, and once again, *The Lost Atlantis* was shot down for budgetary reasons.

NOTES

[1] *Spawn of Skull Island*, p.221.
[2] Willis O'Brien was busy about the same time on a yet-to-be-cancelled epic called *War Eagles*. Presumably, this is why he wasn't approached for *The Lost Atlantis*.
[3] Nearly all of these animals were slated to appear in *Creation*, notably the brontosaurus, the triceratops, and the stegosaurus. The allosaurus probably took the place of the T-Rex slated to fight the stegosaurus in the temple scene that I assume was carried over from *Creation*.
[4] Lamont, "Harry Hoyt's Dashed Dinosaur Dream," *Lost Films Fanzine* #6.
[5] Quoted in *Prehistoric Monster Mash*, p.14.

RAY HARRYHAUSEN'S
EVOLUTION OF THE WORLD

·ORIGINALLY PUBLISHED IN *KONG UNMADE VOLUME I*

DEVELOPED 1938–1940

WRITTEN/FILMED/DIRECTED BY Ray Harryhausen

Academy Ratio, Color, 3 ½ minutes (completed footage)
60-90 Minutes (projected runtime upon completion)

PLOT The history of life on Earth, with an emphasis on the prehistoric age...

COMMENTARY This will probably come as no surprise, but one of beloved stopmotion animator Ray Harryhausen's first projects, *Evolution of the World*, was inspired by *King Kong's* dinosaur scenes. The project is worth discussing because, just as the ape-less *Creation* was an unmade precursor to *King Kong*, *Evolution* is, in a way, an unmade ape-less follow-up. For instance, according to John Walsh's *Harryhausen: The Lost Movies*:

> The story had many similarities with *King Kong*, by which Ray had been so enthused in 1933. Ray admitted that creating his own vision of *King Kong* had been a lifelong ambition. *Evolution of the World* featured a lost island of a ruined and ancient civilization like Atlantis, now overrun with dinosaurs.[1]

Still of *Evolution's* Allosaurus.

Harryhausen began the project in 1938 and worked on it off and on until 1940. Nor was this project a simple idea of Harryhausen's. He built sets, models, and even glass matte paintings. The way Harryhausen later described the process on *Evolution*, it almost seemed as if he was making up the story as he was building the sets. In *The Art of Ray Harryhausen,* he explains many of the alternate scenarios he came up with in his efforts to recreate *King Kong*:

> I worked on my ill-fated full-length animated dinosaur project, *Evolution of the World*, for some considerable time,

building models, miniatures, props and vegetation, painting glass jungles and generally feeling my way to a more natural flow in animated movement. At the same time, I was always trying to find a good idea for a film. Inevitably, I came up with many stories that bore more than a passing resemblance to *King Kong*, featuring lost islands, ancient civilizations, ruined temples and those ever-present dinosaurs.[2]

Harryhausen goes on to describe some of his scenarios, including the discovery of either the lost island of Atlantis or Lemuria (which he did find in the *Golden Voyage of Sinbad* in 1973), a hidden valley deep in the Sahara desert occupied by descendants of the ancient Greeks who worship living dinosaurs, and an underwater version of the lost world scenario where a professor descends into the Pacific abyss in a bathysphere. Somehow, he finds a lost land full of dinosaurs apparently hidden within some kind of huge cavern or air bubble.

Yet another, even stranger scenario for the project involved aliens as evidenced by this blurb that appeared in a 1939 fanzine:

In Los Angeles, Ray Harryhausen, nineteen-year-old dramatist, is producing a film that will out-Kong KING KONG! Putting the finishing touches on the script with the aiding abetment of [Ray] Bradbury, Harryhausen has already shot 300 feet of experimental film. Reports from Bradbury state that the work is remarkably real; dinosaurs –pterodactyls – tyrannosauri– and other horrible prehistoric monsters rant and roar in a weird tropical setting far in the Siberian interior. The plot deals with the finding of a deserted Martian rocketship in an ancient Siberian city. Huge outré statues crumble over ancient tombs and weirdly designed buildings, now empty, tell stories in hieroglyph of when the Martians, fleeing from the icy death that shrouded their planet, came to earth. It is not an exaggeration to say that the animation is as good as KING KONG. Harryhausen knows several of the animators on that picture, and consequently, knows all the tricks of the trade. Harryhausen will do the monster–building himself. All of the beasts are approximately four feet long and made of liquid rubber, steel and sponge. The same material used in the process of KONG. The picture will be silent with musical background and perhaps some speech in the most important parts. ## (Ed. note: The 1940s Chi[cago] convention should make efforts to secure this picture...)[3]

In *The Art of Ray Harryhausen,* he concluded, "None of these ideas ever came to fruition but the search for my own version of *Kong* remained a lifelong ambition..."[4]

Eventually, Harryhausen decided to abandon the idea of human characters for the most part and settled on a story more akin to a nature documentary on prehistoric life (the plan being for the film to be shown in schools for educational purposes). In his autobiography, *An Animated Life,* Harryhausen skipped over all the proto-ideas for *Evolution* and described his idea thusly,

> I planned it to encompass the very beginnings of life on earth, from the swirling gases in space, through the age of dinosaurs, to the appearance of mammals. It was to have included sequences showing various creatures, including a brontosaurus and a Tyrannosaurus rex, with the whole thing culminating with creatures and early Neolithic men being sucked into tar pits like La Brea.[5]

Now, with Harryhausen's human characters negated to that of Neanderthals, he would no longer have to worry so much about dialogue or even actors since the cavemen could be stopmotion as well. And, even though the elements of lost temples and explorers were eschewed, the dinosaur battles remained as a testament to *Kong.* Harryhausen began lensing his dinosaur footage in 1939 on 16mm after plotting out the film in his head (as such, you'll never find a treatment for *Evolution* anywhere).[6]

Naturally, the footage can't hold a candle to Harryhausen's later work, but it's still beautiful nonetheless. An early shot is very evocative of Skull Island, as a brontosaurus emerges from the ocean and walks onto the beach. In the background are high, Skull Island-like peaks, while in the foreground, several birds flock before the camera. The serene footage continues as the brontosaur wanders through the jungle until it is attacked by an Allosaurus, which literally leaps on screen. Much like the Kong vs. Tyrannosaurus fight, the animals are filmed close up during their battle. The battle scenes, including the Allosaur attacking a triceratops, will bring to mind Harryhausen's later works as well, which featured similar scenes, notably *One Million Years B.C.* (1966) and *Valley of Gwangi* (1969).

A few years later, after getting out of the army, Harryhausen revived *Evolution* as a new project called *La Brea Tar Pits*, which he had longed to make a film about since childhood. Harryhausen filmed two scenes experimenting with front and rear projection of a caveman overlooking a couple of different landscapes. After that *Evolution/La Brea Tar Pits* was finally put to rest. Above can be seen a Harryhausen drawing of cavemen attacking a cave bear, though it may have been meant for a different project.

Harryhausen never did finish *Evolution*, though. As they say, great minds think alike, and as it turned out, Walt Disney beat Harryhausen to the punch on his idea. In 1940, Harryhausen watched the "Rite of Spring" dinosaur sequence from *Fantasia*, which also depicted the birth of the world, and more importantly, dinosaur battles. "To my horror the wonderful 'Rite of Spring' sequence showed the dinosaurs and their demise, which was what I was trying to do with my project," Harryhausen said in *An Animated Life*. "I abandoned the entire project and at the same time realized that the concept of *Evolution* had been completely unrealistic for one person to try."[7]

However, *Evolution* wasn't a total wash. Though it's unfortunate the film was never completed, if nothing else, it helped Harryhausen to master his craft early on. It also provided him with useful test footage to show to potential employers.

NOTES

[1] Walsh, *Harryhausen: The Lost Movies*, p.17.
[2] Harryhausen, *The Art of Ray Harryhausen*, p.37.
[3] Hankin, *Master of the Majicks Vol.1*, p.88.
[4] Ibid.
[5] Harryhausen, *An Animated Life*, p.21.
[6] Harryhausen planned to backtrack later and show primordial life emerging from the ocean—he couldn't resist doing the dinosaurs first.
[7] Harryhausen, *An Animated Life*, p.21.

WAR EAGLES

ORIGINALLY PUBLISHED IN *KONG UNMADE VOLUME I*

DEVELOPED 1938-39

Willis O'Brien's test footage of the allosaurus battling a giant eagle.

PRODUCER Merian C. Cooper **SPECIAL EFFECTS** Willis O'Brien **OUTLINE** Merian C. Cooper **SCREENPLAY** Harold Lamb and James Creelman **PROPOSED CAST/CHARACTERS** Jack/Jimmy Matthews [pilot], Naru/Maru [chief's daughter], Victor Kovac [veteran aviator], Hiram P. Cobb [professor; final draft], Skal [Naru's grandfather], Atok [village chief] **PROPOSED CREATURES** White Eagle [largest flying eagle], Allosaurus, ape men, larger ape man chief

PLOT A marooned pilot is rescued by a tribe of giant eagle riding Vikings, who later band with him to save New York...

COMMENTARY If one were to describe a story where an explorer finds a lost land full of dinosaurs and mysterious natives which climaxes in New York, one might say that it sounds an awful lot like *King Kong*. You might even think someone was trying to replicate *King Kong's* success, which they were. However, that someone was Merian C. Cooper himself. One day Cooper mentioned a mysterious new project to Fay Wray as they saw a mutual friend off at the airport. Wray told producer Rick McCay that as they watched their friend's plane take off, Cooper had told her, "You know, I have an idea that is so much bigger than *Kong*. You thought *Kong* was big? Well, it is nothing compared to the idea I have now."

When exactly he made this statement to Wray, I'm not sure, but the project he spoke of is known as *War Eagles*. It was also in 1938, the same year that *King Kong* was seeing a successful rerelease in theaters, that Cooper got the gears moving on the project. By this time, Cooper had moved from RKO and Pioneer Pictures to MGM, which is where *War Eagles* would gestate and ultimately not come to be. Announced at first as "The Cooper-Schoedsack Show," it was later called *White Eagle*, and then finally *War Eagles*. Though there were many iterations of *War Eagles*, the basics were always the same—and they also shared a great deal with Kong. In place of Skull Island is the Valley of the Ancients, where the dinosaurs roam below and majestic Vikings ride giant eagles above. Also in the valley is a race of brutal ape men who do their best to capture the "women of the bird people" and also have enslaved dinosaurs fight it out in an arena. Like Carl Denham, the main character was based on an aspect of Cooper's personality, in this case a wild aviator (which Cooper once was) instead of a showman. And as stated earlier, it would all end with a spectacular showpiece in New York.

In Cooper's first treatment, the main character is an unnamed army pilot who gets court-martialed for a "daring foolish stunt" and gets kicked out of the military. Jilted and feeling like a man without a country, he begins a daredevil quest to fly pole to pole by himself. "All goes well until, in a hidden, unknown region over the gigantic mountain ranges in the great south polar ice fields, engine trouble forces him down into a tremendous warm volcanic valley twenty thousand feet deep," Cooper wrote.[1] Knocked unconscious in the crash landing, he is unaware as a beautiful woman riding a giant eagle descends from the sky to investigate. She lands and dismounts the eagle to take a closer look at the man. In the distance, a carnivorous dinosaur is stalking the scene. When she notices it, she takes out a reed-like instrument and blows into it, alerting others in her tribe. But, before they can arrive, the girl must fend for herself and shoots the approaching dinosaur in the neck with an arrow. Soon, others in the tribe arrive to save the girl and the crashed pilot, attacking the carnosaur with spears and arrows until it is driven away.

The allosaurus stalking through the prehistoric valley.

At this point in the treatment, Cooper ceases the immediate action to give background on the tribe of Vikings who have just rescued our hero. He explains how they live on a peaceful plateau overlooking the dangerous dinosaur valley below. Cooper details some of the scenes he'd like on the plateau, such as riders busting the eagles like broncs and says that the story is like a Western except for that they have giant eagles in place of the horses. Cooper then goes on to explain that there is no food on the plateau, hence expeditions to the horrible valley below to scour for sustenance. In addition to the dinosaurs, Cooper details the horrific ape-men and what they do to the women once they are captured:

> Twice a year, in the full of the moon, these apelike men use these captured women as human sacrifices to the prehistoric monsters, in a great, cavelike arena. These ape people are ruled by a gigantic, monstrous, semi-human figure who presides over the human sacrifices of the women. [2]

From here, Cooper explains how the captured young pilot will earn the respect of the tribe by learning to ride the eagles just as well as the Vikings. (In fact, he rides a particularly ornery one called White Eagle, which he tames.) He begins a courtship with the chief's daughter, who one day is kidnapped by the ape people. All hope seems lost, as none of the Vikings have been able to get their eagles to fly into the huge cavern-like arena in the past. Somehow our hero does and finds his lady love being dangled over an Allosaurus:

> This rescue takes place just as she is being swung like a pendulum over an Allosaurs, the apelike people laughing with high glee as the beast leaps and jumps after her body, just out of his reach in the middle of a huge natural cavern arena. The aviator kills the chief of the ape people in single combat, and escapes with the girl, bringing her back to the plateau above. [3]

Shortly after this, the chief passes away but names the young outsider as the new chief because of his daring feat. In his first act as chief, the man manages to teach the natives how to construct natural bombs out of an unnamed substance within a volcanic crater. He and the other warriors then do a scorched earth campaign on the ape men below and finally wipe them out for good. The boy marries the girl, and the two set off on their respective eagles to a secluded spot to enjoy their honeymoon. The boy brings along his plane's radio, which he salvaged from the crash, to delight his lady love with music for the first time. Instead of finding music, he hears a startling address from the President of the United States. "The enemy" (not identified as the Nazis, though that's certainly who it is) has invaded the U.S. By way of a strange new weapon, they have grounded all engines, therefore no fighter planes can take to the skies to save America.

Our pilot hero immediately rallies his tribe to help him vanquish his country's enemies since he vanquished theirs. Even though they vowed to never leave their valley, they agree. Off they go to New York on their eagles, loaded with the homemade bombs. They drop bombs on the enemy ships, making short work of them. (Remember, this is just an outline, so Cooper is only describing basic actions, there isn't much in the way of choreography or description of the enemy aircraft.) With the enemy defeated, our hero perches atop the Statue of Liberty. Though he could return to live in America as the savior of his country, he returns to the plateau to be with his wife and her people.

Though MGM greenlit the project (probably due to *Kong's* success as a reissue), from here *War Eagles'* development gets a little foggy. It's unclear what or who wrote the first actual treatment for *War Eagles* (remember, Cooper wrote an outline, not a full treatment). What we know for certain is that an 88-page treatment—closer in length to a screenplay almost—turned up in February of 1939. It was written by Harold Lamb and James A. Creelman, who had also worked on *King Kong*. Their version follows the outline, but adds in a second pilot from the outside world who serves as a mentor to our hero, now named Jack Mathews. The second pilot is an older aviator named Victor Kovac, who fought with Jack's father in the "Polish-Soviet affair", which was a post-WWI scuffle. Kovac has hired Jack to fly him over a mysterious polar region to find a lost Viking tribe, and you can guess what happens next.

Our main difference is that Kovac and Jack rescue the chief's daughter, Maru, together. After Kovac is mortally wounded, he makes a startling confession to Jack. Kovac was, in fact, an agent for the enemy, and knows of an impending attack on the U.S. from his country. He tells Jack to stay on the hidden plateau with Maru and be happy, but Jack, of course, opts to fly off and save his country. And that's all we know of this draft, of which only pieces have been found but not the whole.

The next draft came on April 17, 1939, and replaced the controversial Kovac character with a more typical, kindly professor. The character, Hiram P. Cobb, believes that somewhere in the Arctic is a hidden land of Vikings. He also thinks a species of remnant giant eagle exists there, as evidenced by a giant claw obtained from a shaman. When Cobb fails to get financing from the Museum of Natural History in New York, he simply hires a plane to take him to the Arctic. But of course, you know the dodgy old professor won't be the lead, that falls on the shoulders of the pilot: Jimmy Mathews. While flying over the Arctic, their plane is rocked by a gust of wind that sets them into a tailspin. They also catch a glimpse of a great white shape flying through the air on their way down. Jimmy manages to crash land the plane in the water, and the two men manage to get out before it sinks.

The version of the script currently being discussed has some additions in terms of the dinosaurs. It is stated, for instance, that the saddles placed upon the giant eagles are made out of triceratops hide. Most notably, there is a large scale battle between the eagles, their riders, and a group of hungry allosaurs. A few eagles perish in the skirmish (which also involves a brontosaurus), but in the end, the allosaurs are defeated when the riders throw spears down on them from the air. In yet another draft to come later, there would also be a scene of Mathews battling a pterodactyl on his eagle. In yet another, a flock of pterosaurs menaces Mathews and the Vikings on their eagles. There was also a draft by Cyril Hume in the mix, also minus the ape men and Jimmy is now named Slim. In this version is a battle between an allosaurus and a triceratops, and what sounded to be a magnificent scene where Slim somehow diverts a lava flow from a volcano into the valley which eradicates the pesky allosaurs. Above is another still of Willis O'Brien's test footage of an allosaurus for *War Eagles.*

As the two trek through the snowy wilderness, they are saved by the chief's daughter, now named Naru instead of Maru. She takes them to her village, high atop a cliff. There Cobb is elated to see that his theory about giant prehistoric eagles was right.

83

The chief, Atok, shows the two outsiders four eagles chained to posts that have been tamed. And, when he points to the great white eagle in the sky—the same one that might have played a part in crashing their plane—and says that no man can tame it, you just know that Jimmy will eventually.

And indeed, soon after he does. In an idea that surely came from the Western-loving O'Brien, Jimmy manages to lasso the great white eagle and then ride him into submission to the Vikings' shock. This, naturally, earns him the respect of the whole tribe. A bit later comes the dinosaur scenes when the party goes to a valley below to hunt for food. There they witness an allosaurus attack a brontosaurus. The carnage attracts more allosaurs, and one of them bites and kills Naru's eagle. Jimmy then saves Naru by inducing an avalanche which kills the pursuing theropod. After this, Naru's grandfather, Skal, more or less offers Naru to Jimmy as a wife, which he accepts.

The next significant plot point comes about when a curious Naru is playing with Jimmy's radio (which he managed to get from the plane before it sank). A news report comes on warning that an enemy nation is soon to invade New York. Cobb glumly says it will be the end of the world as they know it. At that, the tribe of Vikings offers to ride their eagles to the great city and defend it—hence the project's title.

Off Jimmy and the other riders go to "Flight of the Valkyrie" to New York. And what a "whiz—bang!" affair the sequence is! Had it been produced, it would have indeed topped *King Kong*. The sequence begins with searchlights crisscrossing the night skies of New York as a huge flying fortress makes its way towards the city, flanked and followed by an armada of enemy planes. As in the first draft, a super weapon (here called an "electrical neutralizing ray") has grounded all U.S. aircraft. As such, it appears that the enemy is marching on New York unopposed. But then, out of the clouds comes Jimmy on White Eagle, followed by the rest of the tribe. They drop their bombs on the enemy planes, taking them by surprise. The enemy then becomes less concerned with bombing New York and begins fighting the eagles. There are casualties on both sides, with one of the eagles sent careening right into the Empire State Building when it is hit. In an ambitious scene, Skal's eagle is shot and killed, so Skal jumps from his eagle onto the enemy's plane and begins fighting him in the cockpit! What turns the tide of the battle and sends the enemy off retreating is when Jimmy bombs the flying fortress, causing it to crash into the harbor. Jimmy, Skal, and Naru then proudly perch atop the Statue of Liberty as the citizens of New York cheer them on. Jimmy waves goodbye to his homeland and flies back to the plateau with Naru and Skal.

You might have noticed that this version didn't include the ape-men or the fantastical sequence where the hero rescues the girl from their clutches. As it was, Cooper had realized that the sequence would be too much of an expense, nor was it crucial to the story compared to the finale in New York. Cooper had still hoped this picture could out-do *King Kong*. As evidenced in the chapter on *She* and *Last Days of Pompei*, Cooper had been out to top *Kong* for some time now but had failed. In fact, he and Obie both called it the "Curse of Kong". The Technicolor *War Eagles*, they had hoped, would finally lift the curse.

Willis O'Brien was brought on as the proposed special effects director and completed 400-feet of test footage for *War Eagles* of the scene where the eagles battle the Allosaurus.[4] While O'Brien did that, Duncan Gleason drew numerous pre-production drawings to illustrate scenes from the script. More test footage was scheduled to be shot wherein the ape men would capture one of the Allosaurs, but it was never completed. Sadly, today, Gleason's drawings and a few film cells of O'Brien's test footage are all that survive of the project along with a few scripts and treatments. Ultimately, it was the real war that spelled *War Eagles* doom, as Cooper decided to quit his Vice President position at MGM to help organize the Flying Tigers to go and fight in World War II himself.

NOTES

---

[1] Cooper's treatment, p.7.
[2] Ibid.
[3] Ibid.
[4] About four hundred feet of footage was shot, though today no one knows where it is. The footage was more pain staking than usual for O'Brien, who had to animate the eagles attached to wires to keep them off the ground.

86

MAKING ONE MILLION B.C.

ORIGINALLY PUBLISHED IN *THE LOST FILMS FANZINE PRESENTS MOVIE MILESTONES* #1

The T-Rex suit (and one of the film's two non-lizard dinos) seen here was based upon a painting by Charles Knight and created by Fred Knoth. This suit was a quickly assembled prototype. Knoth had no intention of it being the final version, but once Hal Roach saw it, he loved it, so it was used.

RELEASE DATE April 5, 1940

DIRECTOR Hal Roach **SCRIPT** George Baker, Mickell Novak, Joseph Frickert & D.W. Griffith (uncredited) **SPFX DIRECTOR** Hal Roach Jr. **MUSIC** Werner R. Heymann **Cast** Victor Mature (Tumak) Carole Landis (Loana) Lon Chaney Jr. (Akhoba) Conrad Nagel (professor/narrator)

Academy Ratio, B&W, 80 Minutes

PLOT Tumak, an outcast from the Rock Tribe, is found near death by the lovely Loana of the peaceful Shell Tribe. The Stone Age lovers trek across an unforgiving prehistoric landscape and, in the end, a cataclysm causes their two tribes to band together into one.

Victor Mature as Tumak with Carole Landis as Loana behind him. Hal Roach's original choice for Tumak was Richard Denning, who would go on to star in another dinosaur picture, *Unknown Island* (1948).

COMMENTARY Today *One Million B.C.* has a somewhat dubious reputation due to the fact that not only did it use real reptiles in place of special effect dinosaurs, but said reptiles were subjected to cruel treatment during filming (namely a forced battle to the death between two starved lizards). Furthermore, the reptile footage was recycled ad nauseam in dozens of other dinosaur pictures over the years. Despite these dubious distinctions, *B.C.* is still the true grandfather of the dinosaur-caveman genre. It also could have turned out very different.

To help prep his prehistoric epic, Hal Roach (primarily a producer of comedy shorts including the Laurel and Hardy series) courted none other than D.W. Griffith, who produced many of the previously discussed caveman movies in the first chapter. Initially, the project was called *Life Begins* and Roach supposedly wanted Griffith to direct the film. It's unknown just how true this is, and more reliable sources state that Roach just wanted Griffith's name attached to the project as a producer. Rumors of Griffith as a potential director may have stemmed from the fact that Griffith helped cast the actors, and also did their screen tests and costume fittings.

"Griffith did all the tests," recalled Victor Mature in a 1966 story in the *Los Angeles Times*. "He tested for six months. I don't know what he was looking for. They'd have been better off letting the old man direct the picture. One day he just wasn't around anymore," Mature concluded after insinuating that the film might have turned out better with Griffith at the helm.

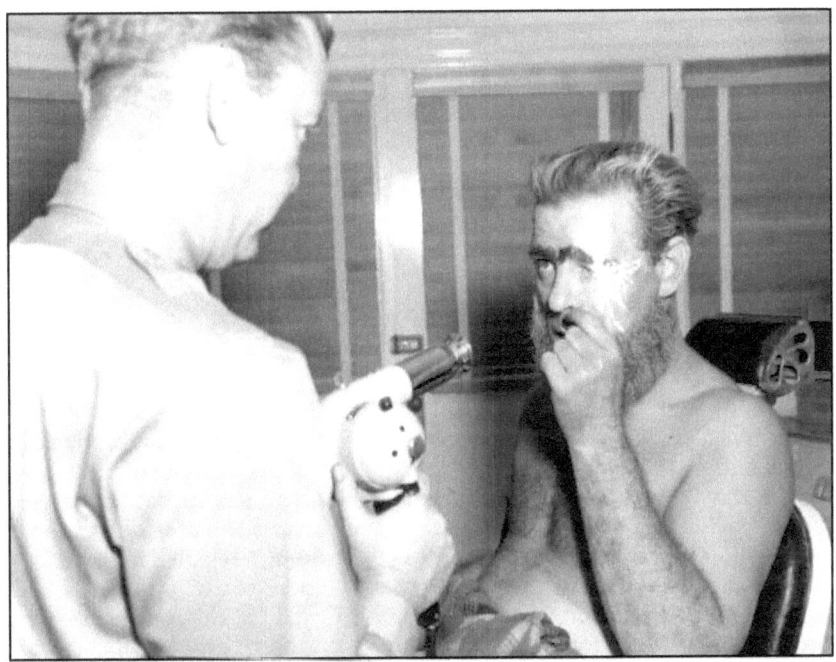

Lon Chaney Jr. in the make-up chair to transform into Akhoba. Chaney designed his own makeup for Akhoba, but couldn't use it due to Cosmetician's Union rules.

As with all completed films, there's a lost, un-shot version of *B.C.* that we'll never see. You see, Griffith left the production over arguments with Roach. One of the disagreements was that Griffith wanted to give the cavemen greater characterization.

"Mr. Roach did not feel that it was necessary to give the characters as much individuality as I thought was needed, and so I did not wish to appear responsible for the picture by having my name on it," Griffith told the *New York Times* on April 21, 1940.

The Biggest Thrill In a Million Years!

VICTOR MATURE as the "CAVE MAN"

Like most films, *One Million B.C.* was released under a few different titles. In Britain, it was released as *Man and His Mate* and was supposedly edited to remove shots of animal cruelty. Allegedly there also existed a cut of the film called *The Cave Dwellers* that removed the modern scenes that bookended the story. The film was released in Canada as *Tumak, Son of the Jungle* while in Italy it was *In the Path of Monsters*. In 1952 it was rereleased in the U.S. as *Cave Man* (shown above). Other alternate versions of *B.C.* include TV cuts, which, according to Don Glut, often removed many of the picture's exciting scenes. The baby triceratops, the cave bear, and the glyptodont were sometimes victims of time constraints. Oddly, the modern-day bookends were always retained.

What exactly would Griffith's true vision have looked like? That's tough to say, but supposedly he wrote the script based upon a French novel. However, this alleged novel by the conspicuously named "Eugene Roche" was probably just a publicity ploy made up by Roach. Eugene Roche, it is thought, was Roach's pen name for the *B.C.* story.

According to various sources, Griffith wrote several story treatments and at least one screenplay, said to run 76 pages. After reviewing these treatments, Roach handed off one of Griffith's outlines to the main scripter, George Baker, in mid-

August of 1939. At the same time, for reasons unknown, Roach also had Griffith work on his own script! Griffith's 76 page script was described by Stuart Galbraith IV (who read it) as being a "sketchy affair." In his article, "Long Ago Before Jurassic Park" in *Filmfax* #48, Galbraith wrote that the screenplay was "more akin to [Griffith's] manner of screenplay writing 20 years earlier—completely out of touch with the realities of modern film production..."[1]

Test frames of the dino-lizards.

In the absence of dialogue spoken by the main cave-characters, Griffith had scripted narration to help the audience follow the plot. Griffith also wanted the dinosaurs to be created via stopmotion, as had been done on *The Lost World* and *King Kong*. Roach did not. In fact, that "no animation" was used in *B.C.* was touted proudly by Roach in advertising as though it were an asset rather than a detriment!

Back to scripting, by contrast to Griffith's 76 page script, Baker turned in a 373-page screenplay, which he would later expand upon with Mickell Novak to 500 pages by October. The initial script also had some differences. Notably, Roach was concerned with how to introduce the picture, especially since he had done away with Griffith's scripted narration. Therefore, it was decided to bookend the film with segments set in modern times with dialogue.

Deleted Scene? Nope, just a publicity still of Landis atop the mammoth.

In the finished film, a group of hikers takes shelter in a cave. Inside they find a professor studying some ancient cave paintings. Notably, Victor Mature and Carole Landis appear as some of the hikers. The professor uses these two as examples as he interprets the cave drawings that tell the saga of Tumak and Loana. Originally, as scripted, the film was to have Mature and Landis playing young archeologist students who show up late to a cave-side dig.

The film began shooting on November 6, 1939, under the title of *1,000,000 B.C.* Location shooting was done 35 miles northeast of Las Vegas, Nevada, and wrapped within a little over a week. The rest was shot in studio until the day after Christmas. The film, now retitled *One Million B.C.,* ran before a test audience on Valentine's Day in 1940. Griffith cut several minute's worth of footage based upon the audience's reaction, though it's unknown just what these cut scenes entailed.

The film was a success at the box office, and if one were to exclude the roll-over receipts from *Gone With the Wind* into 1940, *One Million B.C.* was the highest grossing film that year. However, the critical reaction was mixed. B. R. Crisler of *The New York Times* called it "a masterpiece of imaginative fiction" while *Variety* described it as "corny." The film went on to be nominated for two Oscars, including Best Special Effects and Best Score.

As for Griffith, he had left the production before it had even begun shooting. Roach still wanted to put Griffith's name on the film (possibly as "Associate Producer") but Griffith asked not to be credited, as he was not impressed with the film.

NOTES

---

[1] Galbraith, "Long Ago Before Jurassic Park," *Filmfax* #48, p.34.

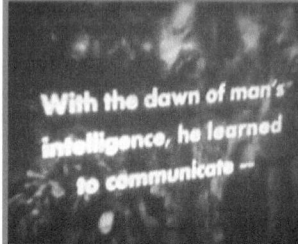

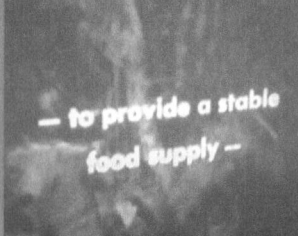

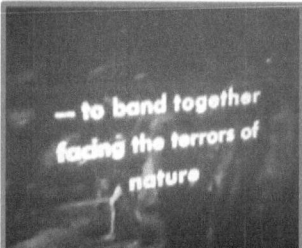

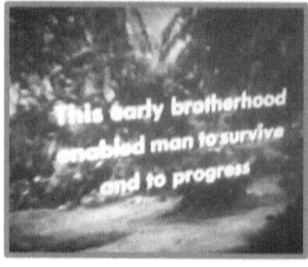

One Million B.C. received two 8-minute digest versions from Castle Films on 8mm. One focused on the "dinosaurs" and was called "Battle of the Giants." The other was called "1 Million B.C." and offered a digest version of the climax. Screengrabs of that version can be seen to the left.

MINI ONE MILLION B.C.
STOCK-FOOTAGE FILMOGRAPHY

1961's *Valley of the Dragons* resurrected not only the caveman concept, but also caveman and dinosaur footage from *One Million B.C.*

After its completion and release in 1940, *One Million B.C.* lived on for many years due to the fact that the movie's b-roll footage and alternate takes were sold off to a stock footage company. Therefore, whenever someone needed a quick dinosaur scene, they would purchase the *B.C.* footage and it was off to the races! The effects footage from the film was used in dozens of other movies. (Notably, it wasn't always the b-roll footage, sometimes it was also footage from the final release print.) It's unknown just how many films for sure the *B.C.* footage ended up in, but on the next page there's a partial filmography.

TARZAN'S DESERT MYSTERY (1943) U.S./B&W/70m. Tarzan and Boy trek through a mysterious desert full of prehistoric life to find the cure to jungle fever. This may have been the first film to use the *B.C.* stock footage in the form of the lizard fight. It occurs near the end of the film. Though Tarzan and dinosaurs may seem strange to moviegoers, in the books he tangled with dinosaurs semi-often. No new dinosaur effects were created to my memory, but a giant spider was. **STARRING** Johnny Weissmuller, Nancy Kelly, Johnny Sheffield **DIRECTOR** William Thiele

JUNGLE MANHUNT (1951) U.S./B&W/65m. Jungle Jim helps a freelance photographer find a missing WWII vet in the jungle. Though the *B.C.* footage had been used in a few Superman serials and short films since *Tarzan's Desert Mystery*, in 1951, Weissmuller again encountered the wrestling *B.C.* lizards to less excitement. An Allosaurus costume was constructed to fight Jungle Jim too, but the footage was dropped, meaning *B.C.* constitutes this film's only dino scenes. **STARRING** Johnny Weissmuller, Sheila Ryan, Bob Waterfield **DIRECTOR** Lew Landers

TWO LOST WORLDS (1951) U.S./B&W/63m. Two rival suitors must rescue the object of their affection from pirates before being stranded on an island of dinosaurs. This movie is half pirate adventure and half lost world/dinosaur movie. Even its pirate footage is taken from other films! Not only are *B.C.*'s lizards pressed into service, so is its volcano which serves as the film's climax. **STARRING** James Arness, Laura Elliot, William Kennedy **DIRECTOR** Norman Dawn

UNTAMED WOMEN (1952) U.S./B&W/70m. A pilot crashes in a land ruled over by prehistoric women. Like *Two Lost Worlds*, the amount of *B.C.* footage ran high and included the volcanic climax. **STARRING** Mikel Conrad, Doris Merrick **DIRECTOR** W. Merle Connor

ROBOT MONSTER (1953) U.S./B&W/62m. An alien invader terrorizes a family on a picnic. One of the most notorious features of all time, *Robot Monster* borrowed dino scenes not only from *B.C.*, but *Lost Continent* (1951) as well. The dinosaurs are reanimated to destroy the earth, by the way. **STARRING** George Nader, Claudia Barrett **DIRECTOR** Phil Tucker

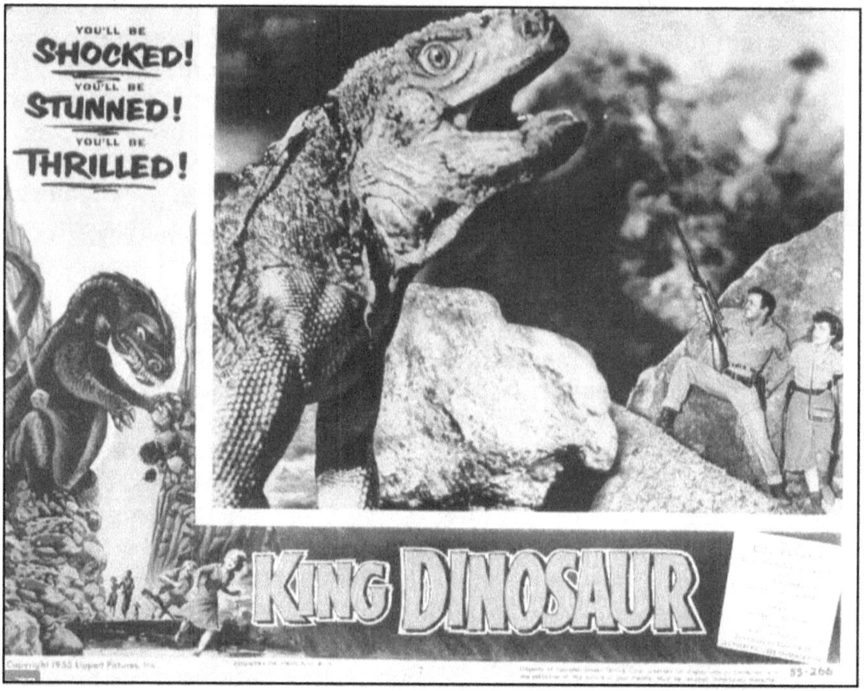

KING DINOSAUR (1955) U.S./B&W/63m. Explorers on Planet Nova encounter a tyrannosaurs rex... which is really an iguana. Surprisingly, the *B.C.* footage is minimal and makes use of the mammoth, the glyptodont, and only a few lizard shots. The iguana footage shot for the film was mostly brand new, but still awful. **STARRING** Bill Bryant, Wanda Curtis, Douglas Henderson **DIRECTOR** Bert I. Gordon

SHE DEMONS (1958) U.S./B&W /77m. Shipwrecked survivors face off against an island of deformed Nazi experiments... of which there are no dinosaurs, only the titular She Demons. In this case, a few shots of *B.C.*'s volcano/earthquake footage was used to help end the film on a bang. **STARRING** Irish McCalla, Tod Griffin, Victor Sen Yung **DIRECTOR** Richard E. Cunha

TEENAGE CAVEMAN (1958) U.S./B&W/65m. Teenage survivors encounter mutant creatures resembling dinosaurs in a post-apocalyptic wasteland. The dinosaurs in this case were again brought to life via outtakes from *B.C.*, as well as one shot from *Unknown Island* (1948). Was originally titled *The Prehistoric World* until the success of *I Was a Teenage Werewolf.* **STARRING** Robert Vaughn, Darrah Marshall **DIRECTOR** Roger Corman

THE INCREDIBLE PETRIFIED WORLD (1960) U.S./B&W/70m. Oceanic explorers become trapped in an underwater cavern with a madman. No dinosaurs in this one, but there is a volcano. This is where the *B.C.* footage, really just a few shots, comes into play. **STARRING** John Carradine, George Skaff, Sheila Noonan **DIRECTOR** Jerry Warren

VALLEY OF THE DRAGONS (1961) U.S./B&W/79m. Two men become stranded on a comet full of prehistoric life (basically). This film hinged on *B.C.*'s footage more so than any other, and not just the outtakes sold to stock footage libraries, but every piece of footage in *B.C.* (one of the producers had the rights). Therefore, this movie's climax basically is *B.C.* all over again with new actors edited into the proceedings. **STARRING** Cesare Danova, Sean McClory **DIRECTOR** Edward Bernds

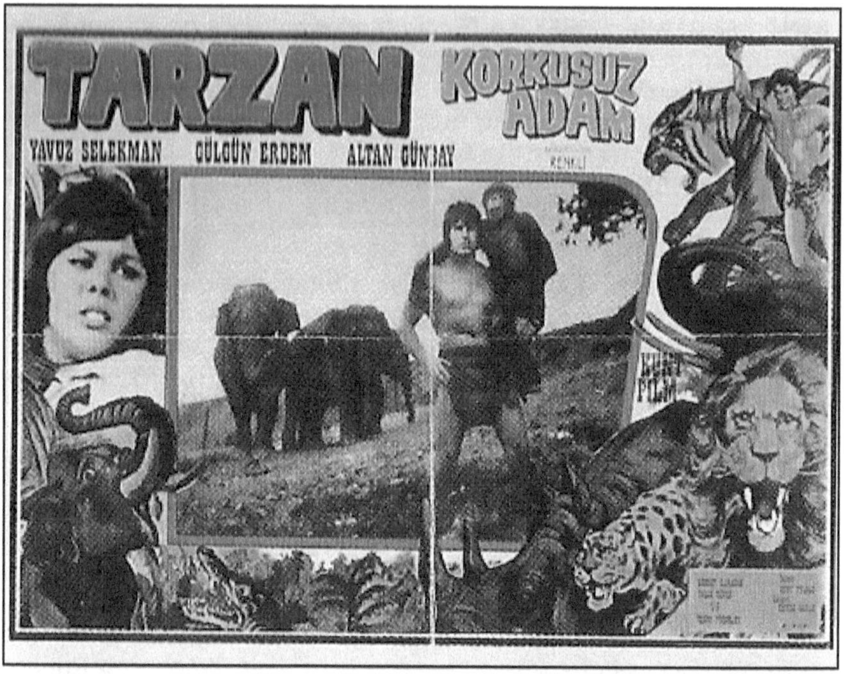

TARZAN
KORKUSUZ ADAM
YAVUZ SELEKMAN
GÜLGÜN ERDEM
ALTAN GÜNBAY

Presenta
KITTY DE HOYOS
JAVIER SOLIS
COLUMBA DOMINGUEZ
JOSE ELIAS MORENO
DAVID REYNOSO y CARLOS CORTEZ
AVENTURA AL CENTRO DE LA TIERRA

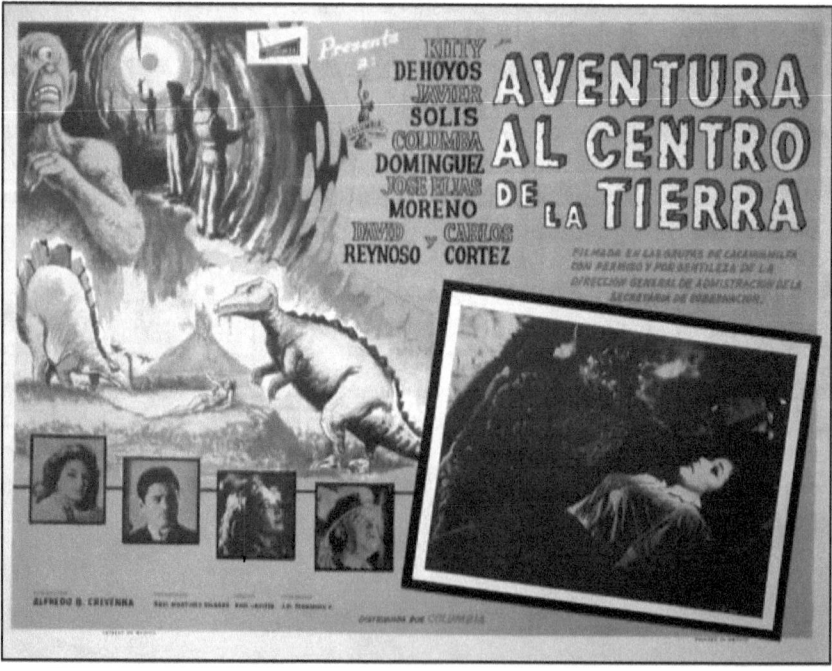

ADVENTURE AT THE CENTER OF THE EARTH (1965)
Mexico/B&W/85m. Explorers search out prehistoric life in a deep cavern. Anyone who knows *Gigantis, the Fire Monster* (1959) will recall a famous scene where the history of the world is recreated via a diverse array of dinosaur footage. The same thing happens in this film, wherein experts watch a film reel full of clips from *B.C., Unknown Island*, and *Beautiful Dreamer*. The monsters they find within the cavern are all anthropomorphic bat and lizard men. **STARRING** Kitty de Hoyos, Javier Solís **DIRECTOR** Alfredo B. Crevenna

ONE MILLION AC/DC (1969) U.S./Color/80m. This horrid soft-core porn spoof of *One Million Years B.C.* (1966) uses the infamous *B.C.* lizard scene but at least had some new (but awful) footage filmed of a T-rex (a leftover from the same year's *The Mighty Gorga*). **STARRING** Susan Berkely, Billy Wolf, Sharon Wells **DIRECTOR** Ed De Priest

HORROR OF THE BLOOD MONSTERS (1970) U.S./Color/85m. Explorers trace the source of a vampire plague on earth to a distant planet and go there to find a cure. To make use of all the *B.C.* B&W stock footage, the planet's atmosphere has a strange tint to it, so as to tint the *B.C.* footage the same color in this case. **STARRING** John Carradine, Robert Dix **DIRECTOR** Al Adamson

TARZAN THE MIGHTY MAN (1974) Turkey/B&W/70m. This unauthorized Turkish Tarzan was wisely shot in B&W, not just to reuse the *B.C.* footage but shots from numerous other films as well, like 1938's *Tarzan's Revenge* starring Glenn Morris in the role. Even Weissmuller's famous yell is used in this film. **STARRING** Yavuz Selekman **DIRECTOR** Kunt Tulgar

AADI YUG (1978) India/Color/106m. This Bollywood quasi-remake of *B.C.* was one of the last of its kind to reuse the old *B.C.* footage in all seriousness. It also illegally used some footage from *Frankenstein Conquers the World* (1965). It's the usual story of caveman looking for cavewoman, just a bit more meandering and with dance numbers. **STARRING** Mehndi Jamal, Vinay Kumar **DIRECTOR** Prasad

DINOSAUR GRAVEYARD
FROM EASTER ISLAND TO PERU

DEVELOPED 1942

CONCEPT BY Ray Harryhausen

PLOT A tunnel stretching from Easter Island to Peru contains untold dangers.

COMMENTARY Though it may seem like Ray Harryhausen had a high amount of planned dinosaur projects in his filmography alongside the completed ones, one has to remember that Ray didn't get to do his first straight-dinosaur picture until 1966's *One Million Years B.C.* As such, many of his pre-*B.C.* projects that he envisioned featured dinosaurs.

One of Ray's more interesting titles, *Dinosaur Graveyard,* revolved around a huge underground tunnel stretching from Easter Island to Peru. According to *Ray Harryhausen: An Animated Life,* a young archeologist finds an old manuscript mentioning the tunnel, and later finds the passage itself and goes to explore it, presumably with some friends and foes. In the middle of the tunnel, he discovers a graveyard for large creatures including dinosaurs and whales reminiscent of the fabled Elephant's Graveyard. Presumably, they'd run into a few living dinosaurs, though this isn't specified. For certain the characters are menaced by a race of blind cavemen that guard an unspecified hidden treasure.

Harryhausen: The Lost Movies proved to be a little more informative on the project. If one squints really hard and takes a look at the one-page handwritten treatment that appears in the book, you can make out the story thusly: the hero finds a manuscript in his father's library that speaks of a tunnel hundreds of miles long stretching from Easter Island to Peru in South America. It is noted that in the very middle of the tunnel is the dinosaur/whale graveyard. That is the introductory paragraph. In a sub paragraph marked 'A', Harryhausen describes various treasures in the cavern. First and foremost is the ivory from the whale bone, then the complete dinosaur skeletons, and lastly, the lost treasure of the Inca. Paragraph 'B' details the story's conflict, that being the hero having a half-brother who he is at odds with. This half-brother also knows of the map, and while the hero struggles to raise the funds to get to Easter Island, the half-brother plans to enter the tunnel via a sea cave which the whales use to get to the tunnel. To find this cave, he intends to harpoon a whale with a special radio transmitter and follow it in a submarine. Paragraph 'C' details a race of mole men of sorts. As opposed to blind cavemen reported in one book, this treatment describes small statured men who have no eyes at all. Notably, the page reprinted in *The Lost Movies* makes no mention of a living dinosaur. However, presumably the following pages must have mentioned one, as the book itself says that a dinosaur would be discovered in the tunnels.

The heads on Easter Island present Harryhausen's fascination with the lost empire of Mu/Lemuria, which he touched upon in *The Golden Voyage of Sinbad* (1973). The idea of the whale graveyard, coincidental or not, lines up with a discarded project from Ray's mentor, Willis O'Brien, called *Last of the Labyrinthodons*. Reports as to the plot vary, as some say it focused on a sea monster wrecking ships, while others say it centered on a graveyard of whales.

104

GWANGI
BEFORE THE VALLEY

Willis O'Brien's concept art for *Gwangi.*

PROPOSED RELEASE DATE 1943-1944

DIRECTOR Irving Reis & Willis O'Brien **SPECIAL EFFECTS** Willis O'Brien
SCREENPLAY Harold Lamb, Emily Barrye, and Jerry Cady based on a story
by Willis O'Brien **PRODUCERS** John Speaks & Willis O'Brien **MUSIC** Paul
Sawtell **PROPOSED CAST/CHARACTERS** James Craig (Tuck) Anne Shirley
(J.T.) Edgar Kennedy (Champ) George Cleveland (Mr. Carson) uncast
(Professor Zimmerman) **PROPOSED DINOSAURS** Allosaurus, pterodactyl,
triceratops, eohippus.

PLOT Cowboys in search of a race of pygmy horses find more than
they bargained for in the form of a valley of dinosaurs.

105

COMMENTARY Nearly thirty years before the release of the now-beloved Ray Harryhausen-animated *The Valley of Gwangi* (1969) was Willis O'Brien's version of the story, simply titled *Gwangi*. That's probably not new information for anyone reading this book, but the general public is mostly unaware that the cowboys vs. dinosaurs classic didn't originate with Harryhausen, and nor was it a big hit in its day. Sadly, the film was panned upon release and failed to find an audience, though it's appreciated today. The project was in fact a labor of love on Harryhausen's part as a way of finishing the abandoned project as a tribute to his mentor, Willis O'Brien. It didn't hurt that it was also a really cool idea.

As it was, O'Brien was a big fan of Westerns, so it made sense that he crafted a story idea to combine two of his favorite things: cowboys and dinosaurs. *Gwangi*,[1] named after the story's main monster like *King Kong* before it, was to be a co-production between Colonial Pictures Corporation and RKO. The story treatment that I saw was pretty similar to the final film. The main characters are present in the form of Tuck and T.J. (here called J.T.), but sans little Lope. The Professor Bromley character, meanwhile, is called Professor Zimmerman. Nor is it set in Old Mexico, but in a modern town north of the border identified as Zenith.[2] And like *Valley of Gwangi*, the first act revolves around the search for a prehistoric horse.

In the first act, we are introduced to Tuck and his companion, Professor Zimmerman, who travel from town to town following a performing circus. Tuck has something of a racket going on in that each time the circus performs, he rides their "unrideable" outlaw bronc, winning $100 every time to the chagrin of the owner, J.T. Currently, Tuck has just won the prize again in the town of Zenith. There he tells J.T. that he is rat-holing away the money he wins for a certain scheme he is willing to let her in on, though she refuses in anger.

The scheme, as it turns out, is to mount an expedition to capture a race of rare pygmy horses. Professor Zimmerman stumbled upon their tracks years ago when he was being led by a Native American tribe through the badlands outside of Zenith. Supposedly, the prehistoric horses inhabit a hidden valley just beyond a petrified forest and a river of dried lava. Tuck hires a couple of rodeo performers who specialize in roping to help him capture the horses. They run into trouble when a Native American guide named Charlie Brown Bear refuses to take them. However, Charlie more or less betrays the men to go to J.T., whom he is devoted to. He tells her of the plan to find the tiny horses, which piques her interest. Charlie also shows her a tiny hoof as proof, and so J.T. asks if he might take her to the area. He agrees, but warns that they must not go beyond something called "the Great Rock."

Storyboard from *Gwangi* of two cowboys trying to catch the Eohippus, or dawn horse.

J.T. and Charlie run into Tuck and his crew, and a fight breaks out when Tuck refuses to heed Charlie's warning about the Great Rock. The next morning, the camp is visited by one of the tiny horses, which evades capture. The tiny equine leads the group all the way to the hidden Valley of Gwangi, which the characters gain ingress to via an opening made by a rockslide. Climbing over the rocky debris, they enter the valley and find it inhabited by most of the prehistoric beasties from the final film. Notably, the pterodactyl scene is present where the flying reptile carries away a cowboy. The characters follow the flying creature only to run into Gwangi, the titular Allosaurus. Efforts are made to rope Gwangi which proves unsuccessful.

As in the film, Gwangi becomes distracted in a battle with a horned quadruped dinosaur (a Triceratops here as opposed to a Styracosaurus). Gwangi kills the Triceratops and chases the characters on their horses to the edge of the valley. There the 35-

foot dinosaur is rendered unconscious in a rockslide. Like King Kong before him, the unconscious monster is transported back to civilization.

Gwangi is unveiled in the circus to great fanfare, but a pride of lions owned by the circus escapes. In the chaos, Gwangi gets loose and battles them to the death. (In the film, it's an elephant Gwangi fights). Gwangi escapes the circus confines to "devastate Zenith" and kill many people. As opposed to burning to death in a church, Tuck forces Gwangi off a cliff in a circus truck to kill the beast. That said, the way Ray Harryhausen remembers it, Tuck only led the beast to the edge of a cliff, and it was J.T. who rammed a vehicle into it, knocking it off the cliff to its death.

Gwangi battling the lions in a storyboard.

Despite ultimately going unmade—at least by O'Brien—*Gwangi* had a fairly elaborate pre-production process complete with many pre-production drawings, paintings, and even glass matte work in addition to miniature representations of the sets. Marcel Delgado constructed what Harryhausen remembered as a "beautifully articulated allosaurus" with "wonderful skin texture"[3] though it had not yet been painted. Harryhausen added that the allosaur was later sold to Edward Nassour who "promptly dismembered it."[4] In Douglas Turner's *Willis O'Brien's Gwangi Documents* book it was revealed that Delgado constructed the skeletal frameworks of several other prehistoric creatures, too, outside of Gwangi, presumably including the triceratops and the pteranodon. Even some of the actors had been cast, such as Anne Shirley and James Craig, who had been chosen due to their good chemistry in *All That Money Can Buy* (1941).

Shooting (in Technicolor, by the way) was scheduled to begin on November 19, 1941, and conclude on January 10, 1942, as to the first unit. O'Brien would direct the second unit starting on October 15th for a planned duration of a little over two weeks. Filming locations included the RKO Ranch and Pathe. As for on location shooting, Goebel's Lion Farm would provide needed B-roll footage of the lions that would fight Gwangi, while fantastic backgrounds would be provided by Vasquez Rocks of California, plus the Petrified Forest and Painted Desert of Arizona.

Perhaps the saddest thing of all is that *Gwangi* was partially scored. Paul Sawtell began work on the score in November of 1941 with a 38-piece orchestra. He recorded about 12 minutes' worth of music including the opening and closing titles. He even recorded a total of seven western songs for the film! So far as I know, the score is lost. Supposedly some footage was shot, as Marcel Delgado made a statement implying O'Bie shot some footage with the Allosaurus.

Gwangi's last cry for help went out in early 1942 after shooting failed to commence due to studio issues. Among said issues was a stupid bureaucratic poll conducted by something called the Institute of Audience Opinion. Most everyone quizzed about *Gwangi* puzzled over the name and said that they couldn't pronounce it. But, more than anything, they claimed they just weren't interested in a movie about dinosaurs. Most likely, they were polling the wrong people. Adding insult to injury, *Gwangi* was replaced by a remake of *Little Orphan Annie* even though over $50,000 had already been spent on *Gwangi*. Sid Rogell of RKO at least tried to get the project restarted about a year later in March of 1943, hiring Ruth Rose to tweak the script a bit (although she mainly seemed to have issues with the opening segments). But it was still for naught, and Gwangi would remain in his lost valley until after his creator had passed away in the early 1960s.

Considering the 1969 iteration of *Gwangi* flopped, one has to wonder if the early 1940s version would have fared any better.

NOTES

---

[1] O'Brien told Ray Harryhausen "Gwangi" was an Indian word for lizard. While we're on the topic, the project's original name was *Bamboula*. I don't know the significance, but it was changed due to a musical of the same name to *Gwangi*.

[2] Don O. Shay apparently saw an even earlier version of the treatment which had the story specifically set in a remote part of the Grand Canyon, which also was to be inhabited by a race of prehistoric men in addition to dinosaurs.

[3] Archer, *Willis O'Brien*, p.44.

[4] Ibid.

GWANGI'S REAL-LIFE INSPIRATIONS

For years I suspected that Willis O'Brien based his *Gwangi* idea on real-life legends of remnant dinosaurs in the Southwest. There was, of course, the infamous Tombstone Thunderbird story of 1891, which alleged that two cowboys shot down a pterodactyl in the Huachuca Mountains, then dragged the body back to Tombstone, nailed it to a barn wall, and took a tintype of it. What got me more than anything, though, were stories I heard of an expedition to find pygmy horses in the Grand Canyon area in the 1930s. My suspicions proved correct when I read a rough draft of an article by George R. Turner, reprinted in *Willis O'Brien's Gwangi Documents* (compiled by Douglas Turner). Said article

revealed that O'Brien was inspired by true stories of prehistoric survivors in the Southwest. The article stated,

> There was some topicality in the yarn, in that it was suggested by news reports that a race of pygmy horses lived in certain remote parts of the Grand Canyon. There was also an Indian legend that giant monsters lived on an isolated plateau of the canyon which had never been explored. When the canyon failed to yield the hoped-for wonders, the story was changed and the valley of the tiny horses relocated to a mythical place called the Pinnacle Rocks.[1]

Everything is pretty much as said above. An expedition did seek out the prehistoric horses, and some were found (as pictured on this page), but they were not actually the prehistoric eohippus after all, just small horses. Stories of monsters on the same plateau I have never heard before, though Hava Supai canyon not far away did have pictographs of what appeared to be dinosaurs etched onto a canyon wall. So, in a very roundabout way, one could allege that *Gwangi* was a "true story".

NOTES

[1] Turner, *Willis O'Brien's Gwangi Documents*, p.7.

VALLEY OF THE MIST
ANOTHER PROTO-GWANGI

ALL NEW! NEVER BEFORE SEEN!

DEVELOPMENTAL PERIOD 1944-1950

Concept art by Ray Harryhausen, who was eyed to help with the animation on this project. Depicted above is a scene of the Indians attempting to capture the Allosaurus. If this was for *Emilio and Guloso* or the latter iteration, *Valley of the Mist*, is unknown.

SCREENPLAY Willis O'Brien

PLOT A prehistoric valley in Mexico contains giant animals, one of which is a dinosaur that is captured and brought back to civilization.

COMMENTARY Another proto version of *Valley of Gwangi* was *Valley of the Mist*. Though quite different from either it's 1941 predecessor or the 1969 film, the nine page treatment retains the essence of cowboys and dinosaurs. This one centered around a young Mexican boy and his pet bull, hence the initial title of *Emilio and Guloso* (not a great title for a prospective dinosaur movie). The story begins in the mountains of Mexico with 12-year-old Emilio being given a baby bull by some cowboys, which he raises to adulthood. (Because it eats so much, he names it Guloso, which means "greedy").

Emilio and Guloso go on many adventures in the wilderness, where Emilio rides on the bull's back. One day, a breathless Emilio returns to his parents' home to tell them of a gigantic reptile he spotted out on the open range. (Though often imagined as a dinosaur, some of O'Brien's concept art pictures it as simply a giant lizard.) No one believes poor Emilio, and the story takes another turn upon the entrance of the villain: Garzan, the operator of a bullring.[1] Garzan wants the magnificent specimen of Guloso, and Emilio's father agrees to sell him in order to buy medicine for Emilio's sickly mother. Emilio makes a deal with Garzan, though, that if he can capture the giant lizard he's seen in the wild and bring it to Garzan, he will trade Guloso for the lizard. Thinking it only a child's fantasy, Garzan agrees. Little does he know, Emilio is serious.

With the aid of some Indian friends, Emilio treks with them to a hidden valley known only to them. Said valley is shrouded in a strange mist (hence the later, better title). Not much detail is given of their adventure in the valley apart from the group being attacked by gigantic birds, one of which carries away an ox. The group wards the birds off with torches, and eventually finds the giant lizard Emilio spoke of. They lure it into a trap, and successfully begin transporting it back to the village. Emilio runs ahead to tell Garzan that he has captured the magnificent specimen, but it is too late. Not only is the bullfight about to commence, but the gigantic reptile escaped not long after Emilio ran ahead. After overturning a livestock truck full of pigs, the monster-lizard makes its way to the village. There, Emilio has unsuccessfully tried to free Guloso, and is waiting for the bullfight to begin. As the saurian makes its way through the village, it smells the livestock in the arena and heads that way. What ensues is basically a dinosaur vs. bulls scene in the arena. Eventually, Emilio lets loose Guloso and the battle between the big bull and the non-descript theropod serves as the centerpiece of the climax. Poor Guloso manages to gore the dinosaur to death, but is himself mortally wounded in the process. The bull expires as a tearful Emilio caresses him one last time.

The project attracted the attention of producer Jesse Lasky, who optioned it to the chagrin of Merian C. Cooper in 1950. Cooper was irritated not because he wanted *Emilio and Guloso*, but because he wanted O'Brien to work on his gestating *Food of the Gods* adaptation, which would also go unmade. Lasky kept both O'Brien and his protégé Ray Harryhausen on retainer for about six months. During that time, O'Brien's treatment, which had been co-written with his wife Darlene in 1946, was fleshed out into a full screenplay with the aid of Jesse Lasky Jr. The new script upped the dinosaur action, making the valley of the mist more like the Lost World with many dinosaurs plus the ruins of a megalithic civilization. The centerpiece of the new version had the Indians making camp in the valley. A pterodactyl swoops down and grabs an ox, so one of the Indians lassos the flying reptile. It takes off, dragging the man into the air. The rope snags in a tree, and the pterodactyl crashes to the ground. The Indian then jumps on the beast's back and twists its neck, killing it. The body of the dead ox attracts more pterodactyls, which begin swarming the camp. The men plant their spears in the ground with the pointy ends up and take cover. Thus the divebombing pterodactyls impale themselves on the spears. Next up, the men run afoul of a triceratops which tries to run them down. They are inadvertently saved by the allosaurus which fends off the triceratops only to be attacked by a pterodactyl. While the allosaurus is distracted by the pterodactyl, the triceratops regains consciousness and gores the allosaur to death. A second allosaur then pops up to kill the triceratops, and it is this beast that they capture and take back to the village in an oxen cart.

When Emilio shows up to inform Garza that he has his prized lizard monster, he becomes embarrassed by Emilio's very presence and sends him away in disbelief. The Indians back the cart up to the gates of the arena and set the allosaurus loose. It storms the bull ring and kills two bulls before confronting the star bull. The epic battle spills from the arena and into the streets of the village where the dinosaur is gored to death by the star bull. (Perhaps the triceratops goring the first allosaur to death was meant to foreshadow this?) Notably, the ending was changed to make the beloved survive the climactic battle. On that note, Guloso was renamed Bobito and Emilio was now Luiz, while other accounts say Guloso was now called Star. Furthermore, Obie was now calling it *El Toro Estrella* in this iteration, but the Laskys came up with the far more marketable *Valley of the Mist*.

Ray Harryhausen, having just worked with Obie on *Mighty Joe Young*, was recruited and did three concept paintings for the picture. One featured one of the Indians roping a pteranodon and being pulled off the ground, while the other two presented an allosaurus battling a triceratops. Ray was even sent to Tijuana to observe a real bullfight to get ideas for the ending, though he voiced his distaste for the brutal sport. The plan was to shoot in Mexico in Technicolor and even use many Mexican actors in the production. Basically, only the pre-production would be done in the U.S. That meant even the effects work would be done there in Mexico.

Eventually, poor Emilio and Guloso were given the boot in favor of a more adult-driven adventure where a giant dinosaur is captured in rural Mexico. (This version may have just been another stab at *Gwangi*, though.) Or, that is according to some sources. Ray Harryhausen implies that the boy and his bull hung on to the very end and were never replaced. In any case, Lasky was never able to get the desired funding from Paramount and the project was canceled. O'Brien then sold the idea to RKO, who handed it off to the Nassour brothers who produced *The Beast of*

Hollow Mountain, which is indeed about a cattle-killing dinosaur on the loose in Mexico.

The Nassours for a time seriously considered the project, calling it *Ring Around Saturn* and budgeting it at around $1 million. Paul Rader was brought in to rewrite the script. But then something funny happened. The King Brothers released a nearly identical picture (sans any dinosaurs) about a boy and his beloved bull called *The Brave One.* The Nassours naturally thought it similar enough to their story that they sued them for nearly $1 million. Adding insult to injury, *The Brave One*'s screenplay won an Academy Award. Does this mean that Obie deserved an Academy Award for his original story? Perhaps, but one also has to guess that had the film been produced with the prehistoric element, the Academy likely would have snubbed it back then. As for the King Brothers, they claimed their story had been written by an unheard of writer by the name of Robert Rich. Conveniently, they said Rich was away in Europe and could not be contacted. (The King Brothers, by the way, were said to have some ties to the mob.) The Oscar was withdrawn and awarded instead to King Brothers Productions in the absence of Robert Rich, who may have also been a blacklisted screenwriter using a pseudonym. As for the lawsuit with the Nassours, it was settled out of court in 1957.

NOTES

---

[1] He's not your typical, mustache twirling villain though and isn't all that bad. He's actually semi-compassionate with Emilio even if he does buy his beloved bull.

THE EAGLE
WAR EAGLES IN THE VALLEY OF THE MIST

DEVELOPED 1940s

PROPOSED BY Willis O'Brien

PLOT A hidden valley in the Grand Canyon is inhabited by a giant eagle and a carnivorous dinosaur.

COMMENTARY One could argue that Willis O'Brien's *The Eagle* was essentially a lower-budgeted version of *War Eagles* combined with *Gwangi* and/or *Valley of the Mist*. It is set in the Southwest with the focus again being a lost prehistoric valley, this time inhabited by only one dinosaur and the titular eagle. Unlike *Gwangi*, *The Eagle* was set in the Old West, as Obie's story treatment that I saw begins by stating that "About the time of the first stage runs, Andy Daley and Clyde Russel, friends since boyhood, came west and settled near the Grand Canyon."

Obie goes on to say that two become "good-natured rivals" each with their own ranch. Andy is described more so as the nature lover of the two and has long observed a mysterious giant eagle flying through the skies. The bird is so large that even the Indians have legends about it. When local livestock starts popping up dead torn to shreds, the big bird is blamed, and one rancher takes a shot at it when he gets the chance. The bird is clipped in the wing and has the good fortune to crash land on Andy's ranch. Andy is all too happy to nurse the bird back to health. Clyde is let in on Andy's secret eventually, and though he's more or less happy to help, he reminds Andy that eventually someone is bound to shoot and kill his beloved bird. After a while, word gets out to the other ranchers, who are still losing livestock, that Andy is harboring the enormous eagle. Though they come to "visit" with intentions of killing the big bird, it turns out to be a good thing as Andy explains the eagle has been laid up on his ranch and hasn't taken flight since. The ranchers all see the logic in this, and determine another animal must be to blame.

Eventually, the eagle flies away to Andy's dismay. He and Clyde then team up to hit the trail in the direction of a mysterious valley

117

that the eagle seems to hail from. Best that anyone can tell, the valley is also home to whatever is killing the livestock. One night, while camped at the entrance to a canyon, the men's horses become spooked by something in the bushes. Obscured in the foliage, they see a huge animal nearly ten feet tall. Its only discernable feature is a long tail, and you know what that means... a dinosaur! They fire off a few shots at it, and the beast escapes in gigantic leaps and bounds in the direction of the canyon. However, the creature disappears, and the men are able to go no further as they reach an unscalable cliff face.

When Andy returns home, he finds his old friend the eagle there waiting for him. Any has an idea. What if he can ride the eagle and fly into the canyon to track the beast? What proceeds is another staple of Obie's unmade projects wherein a man tries to lasso a monster of sorts. Basically, Andy is out to break the eagle like he would a horse by lassoing it and then mounting it. Things don't go exactly as planned. The bird takes off with Andy clutching the rope and he becomes airborne. Luckily, the eagle tires of the weight and lands, allowing Andy to put his feet safely back on the ground. When the eagle departs, Andy fears it will never return. But, the next day, the eagle is back at his barn. Andy makes himself a saddle of sorts for the bird and makes arrangements for Clyde to follow them on horseback. Things go basically to plan, with the eagle allowing Andy to ride on its back all the way to the hidden canyon. When the eagle lands them atop its nest, Andy is amazed to see a lost world made up of unfamiliar foliage, almost tropical in appearance. Below, he can even make out the form of the giant beast moving through the trees. (Perhaps Obie, now conscious of budgetary issues, was showing some restraint in limiting this lost world to only one dinosaur?)

When Andy does some exploring in the valley, he comes across a juvenile version of the beast in the form of its smaller offspring, which begins to chase him. (Obie is still noncommittal as to what type of dinosaur it is.) Lucky for Andy, his eagle comes to his rescue and is even willing to let loose of an antelope it just killed to save his friend. The eagle drops its kill, which the younger beast takes to eating, to attack the parent beast, now on the scene as well. The skirmish is short lived, and the eagle comes for Andy, who mounts the bird and they escape. From the air, Andy is finally able to determine the entrance to the hidden valley, which the beast is rushing towards as it follows the eagle. And that is where the treatment I have ends, but luckily Steve Archer also summarized the story in his book.

Picking up in Archer's *Willis O'Brien* book, Andy and the eagle soar out of the canyon and fly ahead to warn Clyde of the oncoming beast. The eagle lands at Andy's command near his friend. Andy mounts his horse with Clyde and the two ride in the opposite direction of the beast. The eagle, in an act of bravery, goes to confront the monster. The fight choreography isn't really listed, as Obie probably figured he'd make most of it up as he animated it. The bulk of the ending consists of the monster finding its way to an Old West town where it wreaks havoc. Andy and Clyde both get atop several buildings and rope it from above, holding it in place while the eagle dive bombs it. In one of its swoops, its talon pierces the dinosaur's brain and kills it. The day is saved, and the eagle flies away peacefully now proven innocent of the livestock killings.

Unfortunately, *The Eagle*, though obviously cheaper to produce, received even less traction than either *War Eagles* or *Valley of Gwangi*.

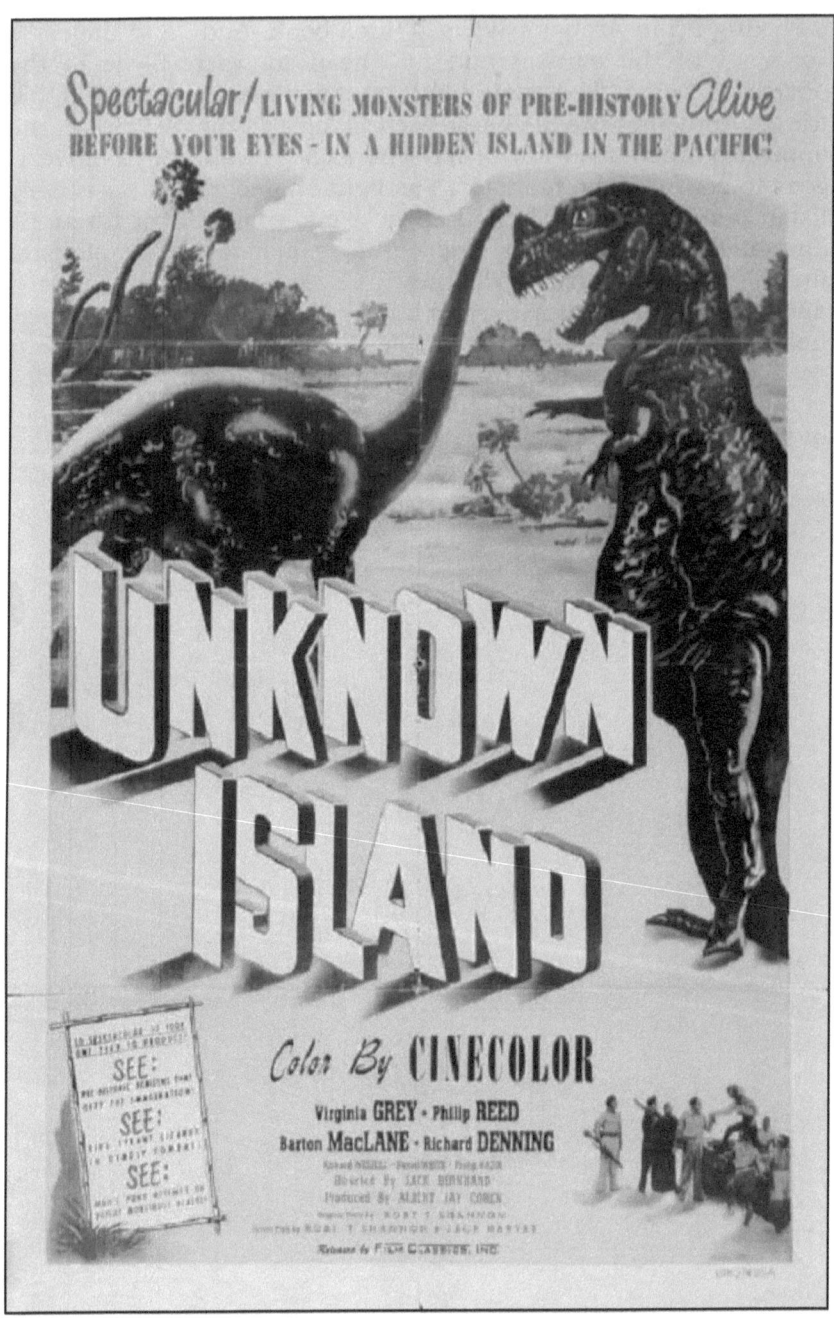

120

FILM THAT TIME FORGOT
UNKNOWN ISLAND
BY MIKE BOGUE

Due to the film having no copyright, dinosaur footage from *Unknown Island* showed up in other movies down the road, notably *Gigantis, the Fire Monster* (1959; the U.S. version of 1955's *Godzilla Raids Again*).

RELEASE DATE 1948

DIRECTOR Jack Bernhard **SCREENPLAY** Robert T. Shannon and Jack Harvey **SPECIAL EFFECTS** Ellis Burman **MUSIC** Raoul Kraushaar **CAST** Virginia Grey, Phillip Reed, and Richard Denning.

Color, 75 Minutes

PLOT One good thing about 1948's *Unknown Island* is that it uses no stock footage from *One Million B.C.* One bad thing about 1948's *Unknown Island* is...but that's not really fair. Saddled with a low budget, so-so script, and less than spectacular dinosaurs,

121

Unknown Island sports plenty of fouls on the negative side of the scoreboard. However, despite those obstacles, it somehow manages to hit a homerun in the nostalgia department.

The story explores familiar territory—there's an island in the Pacific overrun with (shock) dinosaurs. I hear you muttering, "You don't say." But I do say! I know because the alcoholic John Fairbanks (Richard Denning) has been to the atoll, where prehistoric monsters horribly killed his companions, causing him to nurse the bottle as though it were a pacifier. Also, photographer Ted Osborne (Phillip Reed) flew over the island during World War II and spotted a dinosaur. He and his fiancée Carole Lane (Virginia Grey) commission the loutish Captain Tarnowski (Barton MacLane) to take them to this South Seas island. Tarnowski drags Fairbanks along with them, despite Fairbanks' fear of the atoll (you see, he's that most despicable of adventure movie specimens, a Coward with a capital C).

The main cast of *Unknown Island.*

Once they reach the island, Fairbanks plans to stay aboard the ship and tries to persuade Carole to do the same. She replies, "I've nothing to fear, Mr. Fairbanks. After all, there's some men going along." Ouch.

However, Fairbanks changes his mind, and soon he, Captain Tarnowski, Ted, Carole, the ship's first mate, and a handful of crewmen set up camp on the island's shore. Our heroes spot two fairly convincing Brontosaurs and a not-so-convincing Dimetrodon. Shutterbug Ted snaps pictures left and right. Soon, two lurching suitmation Ceratosaurs menace a crewman, and Tarnowski shoots the man to spare him from being eaten alive by the two beasts.

Eventually, everyone, including a reluctant Ted, decides leaving the island is a swell idea. But Captain Tarnowski, aping *King Kong*'s Carl Denham, insists he won't set sail until he captures a dinosaur. This strikes everyone as screwy to the max. Although we've already seen Tarnowski is a jerk (for example, he disgustingly pawed Carole), jungle fever and whiskey morph him into that most necessary of adventure movie specimens, a Villain with a capital V.

Amid this tomfoolery, Ted (who started as the good guy) and Fairbanks (who started as the coward) change places. Tarnowski has kidnapped Carole, and Fairbanks insists on saving her, but Ted reneges, nervously saying, "Carole will be all right." Lily-livered no-count.

Despite the jungle we're told is dark (but appears well-lit), Fairbanks goes in search of Carole. After she shoots a Dimetrodon, Tarnowski sexually assaults her. Fairbanks shows up, punches out the lecherous captain, and he and Carole flee. The film's Giant Sloth (which looks more like an ape) kills Tarnowski, then clashes with a Ceratosaur. This battle of the giants blocks Fairbanks and Carole's escape, but the Sloth eventually wins, tossing its bloodied reptilian opponent over a cliff.

124

Fairbanks and Carole flee to the shore, where they and the island's other survivors escape to the ship. There, as Ted, Carole, and Fairbanks stand together, Carole in no uncertain terms gives Ted the cold shoulder and makes goo-goo eyes at Fairbanks. After all, he has become that most prized of adventure movie specimens—a Hero with a capital H.

The movie includes a number of questionable scenes. For example, after we've seen dinosaurs run rampant on the island, Carole decides to "go for a little walk." Smart. Later we see Fairbanks waste precious ammo shooting at whiskey bottles. Tarnowski, drunk as they come, douses vegetation surrounding their camp with oil and carelessly sets it aflame, where it burns everything—almost.

Despite the charred ruins, Ted searches for his photos, hitting paydirt. "At least some of my film is safe," he says.

Carole replies, "Is that all you can think about at a time like this? Your precious pictures?"

This is a subtle-as-a-Tommy-gun hint that Carole no longer has eyes for Ted. Actually, this character transformation seems

125

unfair—Ted appeared to be a stalwart guy through the first half of the movie—but he has to become a cad so we can all feel okay about Carole dumping him for Fairbanks. The originality of this conceit boggles the mind, so stunning I might have to seek psychiatric help.

The main attractions in any "lost world" movie are, of course, the prehistoric beasts themselves. Decent stop-motion animation appears to have given life to the two well-crafted brontosaurs. However, the Dimetrodon, seen several times, fails to convince, its pull-string propulsion all too obvious. The Giant Sloth, played by stuntman Ray "Crash" Corrigan, sports an adequate monster suit. As for the suitmation Ceratosaurs, they look okay in stills, but less than dynamic in the film itself. The battle between the Sloth and a Ceratosaur, though sometimes awkward and surprisingly bloody, proves entertaining.

The crewmen receive the short shrift. We see them mutiny, and considering their shabby treatment by the ship's officers, who can blame them.

As for the actors, they fare all right. Richard Denning, who plays coward-turned-hero Fairbanks, often played the bad guy, so it's refreshing to see him in a gallant turn. He's also a frequent face in fifties science fiction movies, including 1954's *The Creature from the Black Lagoon*, 1954's *Target Earth*, 1955's *Creature with the Atom Brain*, 1955's *Day the World Ended*, and 1957's *The Black Scorpion*. In 1942, Denning married "scream queen" Evelyn Ankers, who appeared in a number of 1940s Universal horror movies, most prominently 1941's classic *The Wolf Man*. Denning and Ankers remained married until her death from cancer in 1985.

Despite *Unknown Island*'s undeniable shortcomings, IMDb's "User Reviews" reveal that many who saw the movie decades ago boast fond recollections. One typical user review calls the film "an entertaining, enjoyable monster romp. Perhaps because the film has [a] 'quaintness' about it that I still find appealing today." Another review reminiscences about how the movie inspired summer play with friends, stating the film "made me long again, if only briefly, for a bag of stale popcorn, a Big Hunk candy bar, and a Captain Marvel serial."

Indeed, I didn't see the film until I was an adult, but it does bring to mind childhood "lost land" movies such as 1943's *Tarzan's Desert Mystery* and 1951's *Lost Continent*. You may be too young to remember such fare, and perhaps *Unknown Island* can only be enjoyed by Monster Kids born no latter than the sixties. But for those subject to its modest charms, *Unknown Island* can be a fun nostalgia-fest. And remember—it uses no stock footage from *One Million B.C.*

128

FILM THAT TIME FORGOT
TWO LOST WORLDS
BY MIKE BOGUE

RELEASE DATE January 5, 1951

DIRECTOR Norman Dawn **SPECIAL EFFECTS** Jack R. Glass **SCREENPLAY** Tom Hubbard (Story Adaptation by Tom Hubbard and Phyllis Parker; Narration by Bill Shaw) **MUSIC** Alex Alexander **CAST** Kasey Rogers (Elaine Jeffries) James Arness (Kirk Hamilton) Bill Kennedy (Martin Shannon) Gloria Petroff (Janice Jeffries)

1.37 : 1, B&W, 61 Minutes

COMMENTARY Near the end of 1951's *Two Lost Worlds*, the narrator tells us that for the island-stranded protagonists "the long day dragged on, seemingly without an end." The viewer may feel the same way about the film, despite its brief running time.

Two Lost Worlds is mostly done in by its conceit. The film's title and vivid movie poster suggest a lost world dinosaur movie. Indeed, the poster proclaims "Prehistoric Time's Most Awesome Spectacle!" Nothing could be further from the truth, as the film is mostly a historical 19th century action movie dealing with ships and pirates.

The film takes place in 1830. During a sea battle between a pirate ship and the Hamilton Queen, first mate and ace ship builder Kirk Hamilton (James Arness) is injured. Left to convalesce in Queensland, Australia, Arness develops romantic feelings for Elaine Jeffries (Kasey Rogers), a development frowned upon by local rancher Martin Shannon (Bill Kennedy), who hopes to marry Elaine. Before long, pirates attack Queensland and make off with Elaine, her little sister Janice (Gloris Petroff), and friend Nancy Holden (Jane Harlan). With Hamilton aboard, the Hamilton Queen attacks the pirate ship. Both sea vessels are destroyed, and a handful of survivors (Hamilton and company) take refuge on an island inhabited by prehistoric monsters. Will they live to escape from this dangerous South Seas atoll?

The main sin *Two Lost Worlds* commits is promising the viewer prehistoric thrills, but delivering precious few. In fact, dinosaurs don't appear until forty-five minutes into the film, and the dino fight we witness is from 1940's *One Million B.C.* We don't see dinos again until the island's volcano erupts, and the photographically enlarged reptiles succumbing to the resultant earthquake are also cribbed from *One Million B.C.*

Yet another lift from *One Million B.C.* is a scene in which a wall of lava swallows a female cast member. In fact, actress Jane Harlan appears to be in *Two Lost Worlds* only because she matches the hapless *One Million B.C.* victim.

As a naval action film, *Two Lost Worlds* only marginally succeeds. The actors are competent enough, and the naval battles and hand-to-hand combat with pirates fare okay. But the movie is only mediocre at best. And as a prehistoric monster film, it fails abysmally. In addition, the narrator who chatters almost non-shop through the final twenty minutes makes the viewer want to lob a George Forman grill at the TV.

Featured player James Arness (here spelled "Aurness") went on to bigger and better things, such as the depiction of the space invader in 1951's *The Thing from Another World* and the co-hero of 1954's classic Big Bug movie *Them!* Of course, his crowning achievement was his portrayal of Marshall Matt Dillon in the long-running (1955-1975) TV Western *Gunsmoke.*

Two Lost Worlds is the kind of movie that disappointed young Monster Kids during the 1960s and 1970s. Expecting from the title to see dinosaurs aplenty, they wait (and wait and wait) for mere minutes of monster stuff during the picture's finale. As a kid, I figured it might take as much as thirty minutes for the monster to appear. But forty-five minutes? There ought to be a law.

Understandably, *Two Lost Worlds* has fallen into obscurity. If you are a dino movie completist, I recommend you see it (it's only a little over an hour) for completion's sake. But if you are not a dino movie completist, I suggest you spend the movie's running time on more worthwhile pursuits, such as throwing darts at the film's misleading poster.

FILM THAT TIME FORGOT
BEAUTIFUL DREAMER

ORIGINALLY PUBLISHED IN *THE LOST FILMS FANZINE PRESENTS MOVIE MILESTONES* #1

RELEASE DATE August 29, 1952

DIRECTOR Gilberto Martínez Solares **SCREENPLAY** Juan García & Gilberto Martínez Solares **MUSIC** Manuel Esperón **CAST** Germán Valdés (Triquitrán) Lilia del Valle (Jade /Yolanda) Wolf Ruvinskis (Tracatá/Dr. Heinrich Wolf) Marcelo Chávez (Tico Tico/Don Marcelo) Juan García (Cavernario bruto)

Academy Aspect Ratio, B&W, 75 minutes

PLOT A prehistoric caveman awakens in modern Mexico.

COMMENTARY Despite being a huge hit in 1940, *One Million B.C.* oddly didn't spawn a host of imitators. But, this could have been due to WWII, which was raging at the time. Caveman pictures wouldn't begin to make a resurgence until the 1950s, when monster movies and dinosaurs in film became popular. In fact,

B.C. was part of the prehistoric wave, as it was re-released in 1952 under the title of *Cave Man*. That same year saw the release of Mexico's *The Beautiful Dreamer*. The 75 minute comedy is a bit similar to *The Flintstones*, which it predates by nearly ten years. Many of the Flintstones gags are there, such as chiseling a stone newspaper, bowling with rocks, eating dinosaurs as though they were chicken, etc.

Clearly a spoof of *B.C.*, the film mostly takes place in the prehistoric past but is bookended by modern segments where a group of archeologists finds a perfectly preserved caveman that has been sleeping in his cave for 10,000 years. The caveman doesn't tell them that, however. Somehow, much like the magic archeologist in *B.C.*, the main professor is able to perfectly narrate the caveman's story.

Two of *The Beautiful Dreamer's* dinosaurs.

Right away we are treated to shots of the prehistoric past. A volcano, another image evocative of *B.C.*, is placed in the center of the landscape. Two stopmotion brontosaurs drink from a pool in a swamp, while from a rocky overhang a stegosaurus utters an uncharacteristic growl at his fellow herbivores. The stegosaurus puppet amusingly awakens our sleeping protagonist, the caveman Triki-tran.

A tyrannosaurus comes along to terrorize the stegosaur puppet, and a nice little battle takes place. It's fake as all get out, of course, but if you like old fashioned miniatures and effects, it's a fun sequence. These aren't the last of the dinos either, they pop up sporadically throughout the rest of the film. In one scene, they even dance!

The film's story harkens back to the silent era caveman films, which often had two cavemen fighting over the same woman, which is the case here. It also precedes elements of *When Dinosaurs Ruled the Earth* (1970). In that film, prehistoric religious zealots pursue a girl named Sanna because they believe she is the cause of recent atmospheric phenomena. In this film, there are two different tribes, one of which worships fire and the other of which worships water. Naturally, they don't get along. And naturally, Triki-tran, a member of the Fire Tribe, falls in love with a girl from the Water Tribe.

The prehistoric portion of the film ends with a volcanic eruption around forty minutes in. This is accomplished partially through archival footage of a real nighttime eruption. There is also new special effects footage that shows our poor dinosaur pals getting swallowed into the earth. This all happens right after Triki-tran has been drugged by an enemy who steals his bride. It is also this magical potion that knocked him out and somehow managed to preserve him for thousands of years.

The rest of the film concerns Triki-tran's adventures in the present, learning to dance and speak Spanish. In the modern world he meets a woman who is the reincarnation of his lost love. At the picture's end, just as she is about to marry a rival suitor, an earthquake strikes. She has a flashback to the prehistoric past and remembers that Triki-tran is her true love. The two get back together, and it's a happy ending (except for the jilted fiancé).

All in all, *The Beautiful Dreamer* is a forgotten trailblazer of a film in certain, small ways. Technically, it was the first of a subgenre wherein a caveman is revived in the modern day. It's floating around online if you want to see it, though it's not subtitled. That said, it's still funny even if you can't understand the dialogue.

JUNGLE MANHUNT'S
DELETED DINOSAUR SCENE

RELEASE DATE October 4, 1951

DIRECTOR Lew Landers **SCREENPLAY** Samuel Newman **MUSIC** Mischa Bakaleinikoff **CAST** Johnny Weissmuller (Jungle Jim) Bob Waterfield (Bob Miller) Sheila Ryan (Anna Lawrence) Rick Vallin (Matusa Chief Bono) Lyle Talbot (Dr. Mitchell Heller) Tamba the Chimp

Still of deleted dinosaur scene from Jungle Jim's *Jungle Manhunt.*

PLOT Jungle Jim aids in a jungle search for a missing football player and encounters a few dinosaurs along the way.

COMMENTARY In the late 1940s, when Johnny Weissmuller got a bit too long in the tooth for Tarzan's loincloth, he traded it in for a full safari-suit and became the new adventurer Jungle Jim. Like Tarzan, the character had originated in print, in this case a 1930s era comic strip. Unlike Tarzan, the fully clothed Jim Bradley traversed the jungles of Southeast Asia for a change. In all, Weissmuller would star in 16 Jungle Jim films between 1948 to 1955.[1]

The seventh entry in the series, *Jungle Manhunt*, is notorious for a deleted scene featuring a dinosaur. Said dinosaur appears on the poster and shots of it flash by in the trailer (seen above) where it emits a hyena-like laugh. When one sees stills of the dinosaur suit, it's easy to see why it was cut as it's one of the most atrocious tyrannosaurus rex costumes ever created, done so by Ellis Burman, who had created the saurian suits for *Unknown Island* (1948). It's apparent that the dinosaur was cut late in the game, for not only does it feature as the main selling point of the poster, it was also touted in Columbia's press release: "[Jungle Jim's] latest opponent is a dinosaur! The only weapon Johnny uses on the out-sized monster is a smallish hunting knife, but when he gets through with it, the dinosaur is as dead as the fabled dodo!"

Some real dinosaurs were retained in the film at least via the by now overused *One Million B.C.* stock footage (specifically the crocodile and iguana locked in mortal combat), but that was it.

NOTES

---

[1] Technically in the last three he's playing himself and Jungle Jim isn't named.

ATOMIC DINOSAURS
1951-1965

138

THE LOST CONTINENT
THE LOST ATLANTIS RESURFACED?

Some of *The Lost Continent's* better dinosaurs.

RELEASE DATE August 17, 1951

DIRECTOR Sam Newfield **SPECIAL EFFECTS** Augie Lohman **SCREENPLAY** Orville H. Hampton, Richard H. Landau & Carroll Young (story) **MUSIC** Paul Dunlap **CAST** Cesar Romero (Major Joe Nolan) Hillary Brooke (Marla Stevens) Chick Chandler (Lt. Danny Wilson) John Hoyt (Michael Rostov) Hugh Beaumont (Robert Phillips)

Academy Aspect Ratio, B&W, 83 Minutes

PLOT A team out to recover a downed rocket in the South Pacific finds themselves stranded on a strange island on which is a plateau inhabited by prehistoric monsters.

COMMENTARY 1951's *The Lost Continent* is something of an anomaly amongst the dinosaur pictures of its day because it actually utilized original stopmotion dinosaurs as opposed to recycled lizards from *One Million B.C.* However, this "new" footage may have actually been linked to *The Lost Atlantis*.

139

For some reason, this triceratops from *Lost Continent* showed up on the poster for *Panther Girl of the Kongo*. Was stock footage from *Lost Continent* planned to pop up in *Panther Girl*? If so, it was cut.

The great dinosaur filmographer Mark Berry said himself that "little is known about the stop-motion animation in *Lost Continent*," and that "The identity of the animator, as well as the maker of the models, seems to be lost to history."[1] Though the effects work is indeed credited to a technician named Augie Lohman, film historians like Berry agree it's highly unlikely he did the stopmotion as he was never known for that process. This is why many have come to believe that the dino-models may have come from *The Lost Atlantis*.

The dinosaur designs are what one might call rather "cutesy" which is odd when the two triceratopses are goring each other to death. Later, the same triceratops also charges and kills one of the expedition members. (No, it's not really all that similar to the scene from *Creation* for those no doubt wondering.) Though the triceratops is probably the picture's best remembered dinosaur, it also sports a brontosaur and a pterodactyl and that's it.[2] Also, all scenes on the dinosaur-laden plateau are tinted green,[3] which was done to mimic the red-tinted footage present in *Rocketship XM* from around the same time, which used a red filter when the characters were on Mars.

The live-action footage with the actors was shot in just 11 days in April of 1951 at Goldwyn Studios, while the effects footage was finished in only six weeks. This is another reason why some think that test footage from *The Lost Atlantis* was utilized. Lohman himself told George Tuner that he did not construct the models. More notably, the models included dinosaurs slated for both *Creation* and *The Lost Atlantis*. The authors of *Spawn of Skull Island* put it best in terms of their argument that these could very well be the dinosaurs from *Lost Atlantis*, so there's no sense in paraphrasing them:

This animation is smooth, but the creatures *are* rather "cute" and lacking in intimidating presence (consistent, perhaps, with Delgado's description) and are seen mostly in long shots—a give away that the models were very small.[4]

Regardless of whether or not he made the model dinosaurs, Lohman did construct a monster plant meant to menace the heroes. However, after constructing it, the carnivorous plant was removed from the script. Perhaps it was for the best, as the big plant prop was malfunctioning as it was.

Allen Debus's *Prehistoric Monster Mash* also offers some good evidence for this hypothesis:

In *Film Fax Plus* (no.105, Jan/March 2005, p.122) William Fogg mentioned rather suspicious circumstances surrounding stop-motion animation witnessed in *The Lost Continent*. Fogg states "750 feet of 35 mm black and white film featuring prehistoric animals would be completed in six weeks and delivered to Lippert Productions for the sum of $9,000." And according to the contract, "The animation in this film is to be compared to some of the footage of prehistoric monsters that was seen a few weeks ago in the

141

screening room at the studio..." Hmmm—six weeks is a suspiciously short time to produce high-quality stopmotion animation scenes.[5]

Mark Berry has also pondered whether or not *The Lost Continent*'s dinosaurs may have really come from *The Lost Atlantis*, speculating that perhaps the footage was a mix of old and new animation in *Prehistoric Times* #79. Though no definitive proof has emerged, a strong case has certainly been made.

The Lost Continent has what you might call a spiritual sequel in the form of the simply titled *The Jungle*. Released in 1952, it also stars Cesar Romero (as a different character, mind you). The film was shot in the jungles of India, and ended with a stampede of mammoths in the form of the redressed elephants seen above.

NOTES

[1] Berry, *Dinosaur Filmography*, p.237.
[2] Despite a tyrannosaurus depicted on the poster, none show up on film.
[3] The green-tinted footage was not used in TV broadcasts, and so was lost until it was restored for home video in the 1980s.
[4] *Spawn of Skull Island*, p.222.
[5] Debus, *Prehistoric Monster Mash*, pp.14-15.

THE BEAST FROM OUTER SPACE

A few frames of mysteriously unused Beast footage turned up in the trailer for *The Black Scorpion* seen here.

RELEASE DATE June 13, 1953

DIRECTOR Eugène Lourié **SPECIAL EFFECTS** Ray Harryhausen **SCREENPLAY** Fred Freiberger, Eugène Lourié, Louis Morheim & Robert Smith **MUSIC** David Buttolph **CAST** Paul Christian (Professor Tom Nesbitt) Paula Raymond (Lee Hunter) Cecil Kellaway (Dr. Thurgood Elson) Kenneth Tobey (Colonel Jack Evans) Donald Woods (Captain Phil Jackson)

Academy Ratio, B&W, 80 Minutes

PLOT Atomic testing awakens a dinosaur that devastates New York.

COMMENTARY In 1951, Ray Bradbury published his short story "The Beast from 20,000 Fathoms" in *The Saturday Evening Post*.[1] It told of a lonely remnant dinosaur that hears a foghorn in the distance and mistakes it for one of his own kind. In a rage, the monster tears down the lighthouse that the noise emanated from. Film lore states that this short story was fleshed out into a full screenplay, but that isn't exactly true.

143

144

Concept art by Ray Harryhausen for the Beast.

What really happened was that Jack Dietz and Hal E. Chester, two film producers, were looking to make three low-budget thrillers in 1951 via their company Mutual Films. One of the pictures, actually the only picture at all to be finished, dealt with an atomic bomb awakening a slumbering monster and was titled simply *The Monster from Under the Sea.*

How exactly the gestating *Monster from Under the Sea* became conflated with Bradbury's story is still debated to this day, and everyone gives a different account. Some say that when director Eugène Lourié came onboard he took note of Bradbury's story, and suggested buying the rights to it even though *Monster from Under the Sea* already had a working outline. Supposedly, they added the lighthouse scene as an excuse to put Bradbury's name, then popular, on the project.[2]

Others say that Bradbury was hired to do rewrites on the script and suggested it himself. Whatever the case, *Monster from Under the Sea* was gestating long before anyone saw Bradbury's famous story, as Ray Harryhausen confirmed that he saw an outline prior to the story's publication. Notably, Harryhausen said that just what the beast was, or what it looked like, was as yet undecided. As Harryhausen put it in *The Art of Ray Harryhausen*, "[N]either producer had a clear idea of how the Beast should look on the screen, so the challenge for me was to find a creature that fit the bill."[3] In *Ray Harryhausen, An Animated Life*, Harryhausen gave yet another account of the design process, stating that the producers didn't know if it "should be a man in a suit or an alligator dressed up."[4]

Harryhausen said that his initial Beast sculpt had a rounded head that appeared too gentle, so he made it more angular and reptilian. Also, according to IMDB's trivia page, "The film's original release prints were processed in sepia tone. Some prints also had the underwater sequences tinted green."

In that same book, Harryhausen also revealed just how different the original premise really was and all but confirmed it most certainly was not based upon Bradbury's story in any way. The first outline Harryhausen saw was written by G.J. Schnitzer and had scientists piercing the Earth's crust and releasing "an alien monster that was trapped there before time began."[5] Not a brainless brute by any means, the giant alien declares to the world that it will soon take over the planet. And so, one of the scientists builds a giant robot in secret to battle the alien menace. The robot successfully destroys not only the alien but its own creator. Something apparently went wrong, and humanity then has to destroy the giant robot with an atomic bomb. "It sounds like something written for a cartoon series," Ray concluded.[6]

This is probably why Harryhausen's own sketches of the monster are so interesting, as some are not the least bit dinosaurian. One shows a beaked, bipedal menace rising from the ocean. Yet another gave it a strange, shelled head, and another made it look like a triceratops sans the three horns. Even stranger sketches envisioned the Beast as a single-eyed multi tentacled monster befitting of the alien concept. Another was dragon-like and gave the Beast six legs as opposed to four. Another gave it two heads. In *The Art of Ray Harryhausen,* the man himself also revealed that some strictly aquatic menaces were considered in the forms of a giant shark, octopus, and a leviathan.

A second fourteen-page outline given to Ray, now titled *The Monster from Beneath the Sea* (as opposed to *Under the Sea*) read a little better. Though he found the opening scenes where an A-bomb is tested in Arctic to be a little too wordy, he felt he could work with the story for the most part. In this one, a giant monster identified curiously as a minotaur is found in a block of ice that eventually melts. The monster swims away and later attacks a lighthouse on Lake Michigan, shades of Bradbury's story. It also destroys the Statue of Liberty and is defeated when it is refrozen by use of special freezing jets attached to helicopters. It is then taken out to sea in its frozen form and nuked. Thus, the atomic age awakened the beast and it also destroyed it.

Minotaurs and aliens aside, eventually an all-original dinosaur was created by Harryhausen that has since been dubbed the Rhedosaurus, basically a quadrupedal T-rex in some ways, just with proportional forearms, obviously. Apparently, the brontosaur-like look of the *Saturday Evening Post* illustration that accompanied Bradbury's story was considered but dropped because it was "too familiar" to audiences according to Harryhausen after *The Lost World* (then only about 25 years old). However, a theropod was out of the question due to the swimming scenes, and so the creature became a sort of theropod sauropod hybrid. As for other dropped ideas, there was a flirtation with having the beast shoot flames from its nostrils, which you might notice that it still does on the poster.

The music of the *Beast* is also worth discussing, as Harryhausen had hoped that Max Steiner, *King Kong's* composer, might score the film but he was too busy. Other sources claim that originally Michel Michelet did the film's score. But, when the picture was sold to Warner Bros for distribution, they disliked it and replaced it with a new score by David Buttolph.

Ultimately, *The Beast From 20,000 Fathoms*' marriage of dinosaurs and atomic weapons proved to be a fateful one. When *Beast* turned into a huge hit, it spawned a whole subgenre of mutated dinosaur movies, the biggest and longest lasting of which would be Japan's Godzilla series.

NOTES

---

[1] It was later retitled "The Foghorn" by Bradbury in short story collections.

[2] This is just my own conjecture, but Bradbury said he was inspired to write the story when he saw the ruins of an old rollercoaster. Considering the film ends with the monster demolishing a rollercoaster, perhaps that was an element that came from Bradbury?

[3] Harryhausen, *Art of Ray Harryhausen*, p.73.

[4] Dalton & Harryhausen, *An Animated Life*, p.49.

[5] Ibid.

[6] Ibid.

THEM!
IN COLOR AND 3-D

Red title card for *THEM!,* one of the only vestiges of the planned color/3-D production.

RELEASE DATE June 18, 1954

DIRECTOR Gordon Douglas **SPECIAL EFFECTS** Ralph Ayres **SCREENPLAY** Ted Sherdeman & Russell Hughes based on a story by George Worthing Yates **MUSIC** Bronislau Kaper **CAST** James Whitmore (Sgt. Ben Peterson) Edmund Gwenn (Dr. Harold Medford) Joan Weldon (Dr. Pat Medford) James Arness (FBI Agent Robert Graham) Onslow Stevens (General O'Brien) Sean McClory (Major Kibbee)

Academy Ratio, B&W, 94 Minutes

PLOT Giant ants irradiated in the New Mexico desert begin spreading across the United States.

150

COMMENTARY No, this picture does not belong in this book. But you can blame *Fantastic Dinosaurs of the Movies* for corrupting me as a kid as it lumped giant monster trailers in with the dinosaur ones. Besides, this movie was at least inspired by a dinosaur movie...

After the big success of *The Beast from 20,000 Fathoms*, other producers and studios became interested in seeing what atomic terrors they could conjure up themselves. George Worthington Yates immediately came up with a concept for a giant ant movie, wherein the insects are mutated by radiation. (Actually, script dates would indicate Yates was working on the idea before *Beast*.) Yates first shopped his idea to George Pal, who was already doing a movie with a big big-ant scene in the form of *The Naked Jungle*, and so he passed, though he was polite enough to suggest Yates go to Warner Bros. He did, and thankful this began *Them!*'s journey to the big screen.

Yates was clever enough to set his story in the vicinity of White Sands Missile range near the Trinity Site where one of the first atomic bombs was tested. Or, at least, that was the locale settled on for the final draft. That said, all of the story treatments were set in the desert Southwest. Appropriately, Yates' first draft contained several Native American characters, none of which survived the numerous script revisions to follow. Yates first protagonist was a Native American, Juan, and his sidekick, Jack Weed, was an officer from the Office of Indian Affairs. The duo investigates strange happenings in Arizona, among them a store that has been destroyed.

During the night, Weed and his family are disturbed by strange creatures that they can only hear, not see. The next day, he and Juan follow the animals' tracks up a ravine where they first discover mutated plants, and then ants the size of horses. Things are quasi-similar to the final film: the military wipes out the nest in the desert but the queens have already flown elsewhere. In this case, one goes to Manitoba where a scene was written for one of the queen ants to fight and kill a bear. Rather than Los Angeles, the climax was slated for New York, where ants take over the subway system. Notably, Juan would die while rescuing Weed's son, Peter.

Actually, what I described above was something of a pastiche of the first few drafts. Some did away with the Indian agent, but kept Juan, who teamed with a tourist whose family had become endangered by the ants. Notably, Juan also changed from draft to draft, sometimes appearing as a young man, and in others, as

151

an older shaman or medicine man. In his shaman iteration, Juan spoke of evil spirits coming up from the earth after the great "fire blossom" or atomic test. One of Yates early drafts also featured an amusing scene in a Los Angeles amusement park where the giant ants abduct a girl from the Tunnel of Love. In King Kong style, they don't harm her and just seem to inspect her before she flees into a funhouse pursued by one of the giant ants.

According to the authors of *Keep Watching the Skies*, who read the treatment, it was apparent that Yates was envisioning the ants to be brought to life by real ants photographically enlarged as opposed to the large props used in the film. However, since optical effects were impossible to accomplish in 3-D, scale props, like the one seen above, had to be used. Had the film been filmed in color as planned, we would have seen greenish purple colored ants, as that's how the actors described their color on set.

In January of 1953, Russell Hughes took over writing duties on the project and by September, Ted Sherdeman joined the fray. By December, the idea of 3-D was being flirted with, as script notes indicated that the ants' antennae should reach out over the audience. The film was also planned to be shot in Warner Color Widescreen, the plan being for it to outshine even 1953's *War of the Worlds* as a huge, color epic. Test footage of some sort was shot during pre-production. However, when it came time for test

152

footage featuring the big ant props, the "All Media" 3D camera rig malfunctioned. Supposedly, repairing it would prove not only costly, but would also delay shooting. Only a day later, Warners decided to scrap the color 3-D aspect. Still vestiges of the idea remain. One might notice in the final print that certain shots are framed for 3-D such as the military shooting the flamethrowers towards the camera. The title lettering is presented in a bold red that still looks 3-D-ish. Even the film's director, Gordon Douglas, was chosen because he had just finished the 3D Western *The Charge at Feather River* (1953). Reportedly, Douglas was quite angry with the studio for not completing the project in color 3D as planned. But perhaps it was for the best, since many feel that *Them!* was a film that actually played out better in black and white for a number of reasons.

GODZILLA IN THE LOST WORLD
BRIDE OF GODZILLA?

ORIGINALLY PUBLISHED IN *JAPANESE MONSTERS UNMADE VOLUME I*

Third Draft Date June 17, 1955

SCREENPLAY Hideo Unagami **PROPOSED CAST/CHARACTERS** Dr. Zenji Shida [scientist], Foster Daughter Riko [artificial human], Yoshi Shida [brother of Dr. Shida/manager of Kyushu mine], Dr. Yanai [scientist/former friend of Dr. Shida], Eve [wife of Dr. Shida/artificial human], Suzuki, Yamamoto [reporter], Riko Yanai [wife of Dr. Yanai] **PROPOSED MONSTERS** Godzilla, Anguirus, Archaeopteryx, Robot Daughter, Chameleon, Sea Serpent, Mammoth, Giant Fleas, Giant Octopus, Mermaids

PLOT Godzilla is rediscovered in a hollow earth inhabited by dinosaurs.

COMMENTARY Some hardcore American dinosaur fans tend to have a love it or hate it relationship with Godzilla. On the one hand, he is a very charming giant dinosaur. On the other, he's a man in a suit. It didn't help that Ray Harryhausen was not a fan of the Big G. After all, his debut outing was clearly inspired by his own *Beast from 20,000 Fathoms*, and unlike the Beast, Godzilla spawned over 30 sequels and counting. Godzilla began life as a project titled *The Big Monster from 20,000 Leagues Under the Sea* until becoming *Gojira*. The film was a huge hit, spawning a quickie sequel where the theropod-like Godzilla fought an ankylosaur-like opponent in *Godzilla Raids Again* (1955). Though succesful, it was clear that the film in no way lived up to the original. As such, Toho, Godzilla's parent company, was content to let the monster take a break, or perhaps never return at all. However, a bit part actor at Toho wasn't content to let the monster sit.

In 1955, aspiring screenwriter Hideo Unagami took it upon himself to write a sequel to *Godzilla Raids Again*. Unagami delivered his unsolicited script to Toho President Iwao Mori, who passed it along to Tomoyuki Tanaka.[1] Though it was never made, Tanaka clearly liked the screenplay as the script was reportedly found in Tomoyuki Tanaka's desk drawer after his death in February of 1997.

The story begins at the Godzilla Countermeasures Center located in Tokyo. There Dr. Zenji Shida is giving a lecture on his theories regarding Godzilla and Anguirus, namely that they sprung from a prehistoric hollow earth cavern. As reporters watch Dr. Shida point to various prehistoric pictures on the wall, he also explains that an Archaeopteryx and a giant chameleon could also live in a cavern deep under the earth. This, of course, is all shameless foreshadowing for later in the script where said creatures all appear. The same is true of Shida's somewhat random theory that mermaids were a step in the evolution of the human race and could also live in said cavern.

To return to Shida's talk, there is also discussion of Godzilla being frozen in the ice as seen in the previous film in keeping with the continuity.[2] This leads into the topic of a need for new weapons to kill the beast should he escape. It is at this point that Dr. Shida reveals he has created a giant artificial human to combat the monster he calls the Bride of Godzilla. In addition to the giant robot, Shida has also created a normal-sized robot in the form of a beautiful woman, whom he calls Eve and which he unveils to the reporters. The robot is completely life-like and has an artificial brain that allows it to carry on intelligent conversations with the reporters.

The action switches to Kyushu, where Dr. Shida's brother, Yoshi Shida, oversees a mining corporation. The following scenes, as it turned out, served as the inspiration for Toho's 1956 pteranodon horror thriller *Rodan*. As in that film, a small village is attacked by a giant bug, in this case a blood-sucking flea. Yoshi and some other men manage to kill the flea, which sheds blood everywhere. As they ponder its prehistoric attributes, they consider calling in Yoshi's brother but decide against it in favor of another scientist: Dr. Yanai.

As it turns out, Yanai is an old colleague of Dr. Shida. The two are no longer friends, however, as Yanai married Shida's sweetheart, Riko. A further wedge between the two is the fact that Yanai is a Christian, which opposes Shida's worldview—it would seem that author Unagami is trying to make a comparison between Dr. Shida and his robot and Dr. Frankenstein and his monster in that both are trying to 'play God'. Yanai and his wife do not believe in Shida's meddling. To further complicate matters, Shida has built the robot Eve in Riko's image! Dr. Yanai and Riko are surprised to learn of this fact when one of the reporters who was at Shida's talk interviews Yanai and tells him of his wife's resemblance to Shida's robot.

This fact prompts Riko to go to Dr. Shida's house, which is described as a luxurious mansion with a large, mad scientist laboratory. As *Bride of Godzilla* was meant to be filmed in color—more on that later—Unagami goes out of his way to describe the multi-colored beakers in Dr. Shida's lab in his script.

At the mansion, Riko comes face to face with her robotic double and faints. When she awakens, she also finds out that Dr. Shida even has a robot foster daughter named Riko after herself. This information is too much for the real Riko to handle, who runs out of the house crying. Suzuki, a supporting reporter character, convinces Riko to go back to Dr. Shida's. There she receives a proper introduction to the robot foster daughter—nicknamed "robo-sume" by fans. Riko finds out her namesake is actually quite charming and exudes a certain innocence.

From here, we transition back to the Kyushu plot, where we find more elements similar to *Rodan*—namely miners becoming lost underground. The discovery of the lost cavern is well handled as several miners walk down a shaft discussing Godzilla's battle with Anguirus in Osaka. As the men jokingly begin to imitate the monsters' cries, the real call of Anguirus reverberates through the walls. An opening appears before the men revealing a lost world full of mountains, deserts, lakes, and even its own orange-colored sky. The men explore the cavern, calling it the womb of the earth. As they do so, they are attacked by a giant bat. Next, they spy a trio of beautiful mermaids in a pool: a mother, a father, and an infant. The men spy Godzilla emerging from another lake and decide to make a run for it. As they do, Anguirus passes by and shakes off one of the giant fleas from his back.

The men all escape back to the surface and tell Yoshi Shida what they saw. It is at this point that Yoshi finally decides to call in his older brother and his robot foster daughter to investigate the cavern. Similar to a scene in *Rodan*, the office suddenly shakes during a sudden, surprise earthquake. In this case, the quake seals up the entrance into the cavern, meaning another opening will have to be found. When a helicopter spies a mermaid swimming in the ocean, it is concluded there must be an underwater passage into the cavern. Therefore Dr. Shida takes a boat on behalf of the government out to sea, and the robotic foster daughter Riko dives in and follows the mermaids. In a sequence that was surely too ambitious for the time, Unagami has the mermaids fight off a giant octopus!

After the octopus is defeated, Riko follows the mermaids into the cavern. To befriend the shy creatures, she performs a dance (also the method in which she won over the real Riko and Suzuki). It works, and she and the mermaids become friends. Riko then goes out to explore the lost world where she not coincidentally observes all of the creatures that her father predicted would live there: a giant archaeopteryx, a giant chameleon, and Godzilla. Initially, Riko regards Godzilla with friendship as he approaches her. But, in keeping with his villainous identity of the 1950s, Godzilla responds by hitting the rocky cliff that Riko stands upon, causing her to tumble into the waters below. She is then saved by the female mermaid. When the mermaid tries to take the damaged Riko back to the ship, she is confronted by a sea serpent. A military diver is able to drive the serpent away with an underwater weapon and Riko is reunited with her father. Shida decides to return to Japan to prepare to bring his gigantic robot daughter online to battle Godzilla.

It is at this point that the author will insert some of his own conjecture on the part of the story. Translation issues being what they are, it would seem that the damaged Riko's consciousness is "downloaded" into the giant robot daughter. This robot daughter is creepily described as being naked (likely in the Barbie doll sense) with Eve's body (or, in other words, the real Riko's body) with the face of the Foster Daughter Riko (who would presumably resemble the real Riko as a child). That part is not conjecture, by the way, all translations seem to agree that this is indeed the description!

Anyhow, as final preparations continue on the giant Bride of Godzilla, a power plant is used to charge it up. The robot Riko is recuperating in bed when news comes that Godzilla has surfaced in Kyushu. The monster tramples Wakamatsu Port at night and is followed by Anguirus and a giant chameleon. Then, a giant Archaeopteryx emerges from the mines in Kyushu. Keep in mind here that Rodan was initially designed as an Archaeopteryx until the monster was changed to better resemble a pteranodon. The similarities won't end there, but we'll get to those later.

During Godzilla's rampage, Dr. Yanai and others take solace in a church where they are all killed. Only Riko Yanai escapes. Some suspense occurs as Godzilla approaches the power plant charging the Bride, who becomes fully charged just before Godzilla destroys it. Again, author conjecture here, but considering the robot Riko isn't seen again at this point, it is my belief that her consciousness is within the giant Bride.

As the Bride sets out to battle the monsters, the four-way monster assault on Kyushu continues. So far, the self-defense forces have only managed to kill the giant chameleon while the giant Archaeopteryx battles a fleet of jet fighters in the skies à la *Rodan*. It is also stated the bird would peck through the windshield of a crashed plane to eat its pilot! In a show of monster humor predating *King Kong vs. Godzilla* (1962), Godzilla sets aflame a fighter jet that the Archaeopteryx is chasing and then seems to "laugh" or show some form of amusement at the bird's consternation. Soon after that, this particularly vindictive Godzilla roasts a group of refugees running across a bridge.

A detailed scene also describes a jet fighter squadron attacking Godzilla and glimpsing the monster's giant head through the POV of the pilot inside the cockpit. Godzilla plucks one of the planes from the sky and then plays with it like a child with a toy, tearing the wings off and then prying out the unfortunate pilot and "smiling" as he screams. Script notes, by the way, implied that this new Godzilla suit should be capable of a wider range of expression and "smiling"!

Finally, the Bride shows up on scene and begins attacking the monster. The script describes some of the fantastic final battle maneuvers, such as the Bride defeating Anguirus by breaking his jaws apart and ripping out his throat. In another scene, she was to swing Godzilla by the tail King Kong-style. After tussling with Godzilla for a while, the Bride seems to earn his respect and infatuation after his ray fails to phase her. The Bride then catches the Archaeopteryx and breaks its neck. Godzilla roasts the bird in her hands, seeming to imply he is now on her side. Oddly, Dr. Shida and his cohorts say that a "wedding" between the two is imminent and that, "It is the foreplay of love to be beaten."

The two wrestle their way into the bay and swim to the ocean bottom together where Godzilla fires his atomic ray underwater to reveal another opening into the hollow earth cavern. Dr. Shida then announces to everyone that it is time for the wedding ceremony to commence—he has hidden a hydrogen bomb inside of the Bride! This leads to the most awkward aspect of the whole script where Godzilla takes the Bride back to his cave where the duo hug before the Bride (presumably along with Riko's consciousness) detonates herself forever destroying the lost world.

Like the previous two Godzilla films, *The Bride of Godzilla?* features a tragic ending involving Shida and Riko Yanai. As Dr. Yanai has perished in the church, Riko Yanai is on the observatory boat over the underwater passage with Dr. Shida when the Bride detonates. After this Shida tries to reconcile with her but she refuses. As she runs to look over the bow of the ship, she sees the sweet mermaid family. The female mermaid frightens a military crew member on the boat. He opens fire on the mermaid, and her small child is killed. Thus ends the script as she swims away weeping—the dead child still clutching the bouquet.

Despite it not being produced, it was clear that Tomoyuki Tanaka liked some aspects of the script, as evidenced in the production of *Rodan* shot the next year in 1956. Though written by Ken Kuronuma and Takeshi Kimura, the fact that *Bride of Godzilla?* and *Rodan* are both set primarily in Kyushu, have giant murderous insects, lost miners, a frightening underground world, and a giant flying prehistoric menace clearly indicates a connection between the two even if Hideo Unagami gets no credit on *Rodan's* screenplay.

As to why *Bride of Godzilla?* itself wasn't produced, the main factor is undeniably the budget. Had the script been filmed as it was written, it would have cost Toho a fortune in the form of the hollow earth set alone. Bringing the half-human mermaids to life in addition to all of the inevitable underwater filming would no doubt also have been a considerable undertaking. Notes also indicated the production would have pre-dated *The Mysterians* (1957) as Toho's first color Tohoscope production, another additional expense. The technicolor would have been put to good use, as Unagami describes the Pellucidar-like roof of the cavern as changing color every 23 seconds—seven colors in all. In the story, Yoshi Shida speculates this "underground sun" is likely a massive wall of uranium. During the city destruction scenes, the sky was described as being a burning red. Whatever their reasons for aborting the production, Toho had to be serious about the script considering it got as far as three major drafts. And, considering scripts usually get trimmed down for the sake of the budget as the various drafts progress, one also has to wonder just how much wilder the first two drafts were?

NOTES

---

[1] Considering that there were three script drafts, it's possible Tanaka was brought the first draft and encouraged Unagami to keep working on his idea.
[2] However, later in the script we will find Godzilla living in the cavern, it is never addressed how Godzilla goes from being frozen in the ice to popping up underground, so perhaps it's a third Godzilla? Furthermore, some sources also attest that there are multiple Godzillas living in the cavern, though I personally did not get this impression.

FROM THE DIM DAWN OF HISTORY...
A MONSTER BEYOND BELIEF!
GUY MADISON · PATRICIA MEDINA
in
"THE BEAST OF HOLLOW MOUNTAIN"
And introducing the new REGISCOPE Process
Screenplay by ROBERT HILL · From an original story by WILLIS O'BRIEN
Produced by WILLIAM and EDWARD NASSOUR · Directed by EDWARD NASSOUR
CINEMASCOPE · COLOR by DE LUXE · Released thu UNITED ARTISTS

WILLIS O'BRIEN'S
BEAST OF HOLLOW MOUNTAIN

RELEASE DATE August 1956

DIRECTORS Edward Nassour & Ismael Rodríguez **SPECIAL EFFECTS** Jack Rabin, Henry Sharp and Louis de Witt **SCREENPLAY** Robert Hill, Willis O'Brien (story) & Jack DeWitt (dialogue) **MUSIC** Raúl Lavista **CAST** Guy Madison (Jimmy Ryan) Patricia Medina (Sarita) Carlos Rivas (Felipe Sanchez) Eduardo Noriega (Enrique Rios) Julio Villarreal (Don Pedro) Mario Navarro (Panchito) Pascual García Peña (Pancho) Lupe Carriles (Margarita)

Cinemascope, Deluxe color, 79 Minutes

PLOT A dinosaur terrorizes the ranges south of the border.

COMMENTARY Though *Valley of Gwangi* is often thought of as the first Cowboys vs. Dinosaurs movie, it was actually *The Beast of Hollow Mountain*. That said, it's likely that *Beast of Hollow Mountain* was part of the evolutionary chain that began with Willis O'Brien's 1940 *Gwangi* and concluded with Ray Harryhausen's 1969 version. As such, the origins of *Beast of Hollow Mountain* can be somewhat nebulous. Some think that it might be tied into the development and purchase of *Valley of the Mist* by the Nassour brothers from Willis O'Brien. However, the only similarities the stories share are a villainous allosaurus loose in Mexico. In any case, *Hollow Mountain's* story does stem from O'Brien, and the Nassours purchased this concept as well. Reportedly they bought it from Obie cheap, too, under the condition that they would let him animate it. They didn't, and poor Obie was betrayed again.

In addition to lacking Obie's animation, the final film lacks his original vision for the story as well. Obie's outline for *The Beast of Hollow Mountain* would have featured more dinosaur action than the final film, where the titular monster's screen time is a bit limited. In O'Brien's treatment, a cattleman named Hank Oliver is found murdered. Specifically, Oliver's men find some fences trampled which leads them to some mangled cattle, and then to Oliver's mutilated body as well. The prime suspect becomes

161

Oliver's main rival, Jim Larkin, who denies that he did it. Incredibly, Larkin claims the culprit is a giant reptile.

GUY MADISON in "THE BEAST OF HOLLOW MOUNTAIN"
PATRICIA MEDINA   REGISCOPE   CINEMASCOPE   COLOR by DE LUXE

As a publicity ploy, the Nassours claimed that the picture had been brought to life via a brand-new process, called Regiscope, where, according to the *New York Times,* a "machine predetermines every movement of any inanimate objects to be used in the motion picture and records it on a tape. The 'actor' is then electronically controlled in all of its motion. To insure complete fidelity of movement, the Regiscope operator can rehearse the 'actor' in its motions in front of him before filming begins. The director can select the best of the 'performances' in the rehearsals and, from that moment, there is no deviation because of the electronic controls." This was just a marketing ploy though, and no such method was used.

The Oliver cowboys prepare to lynch Larkin, but he is saved by the deputy sheriff, Dean Roberts, and his Native American tracker, John Longtooth. Together, the trio tracks the dinosaur, which has absconded with a cow, to its cave lair. The men hide among the strewn bones, and Roberts tries to rope the creature which proves to be a mistake. The three men escape and come back with some of Longtooth's fellow tribesmen. Essentially, the planned scene for *Valley of the Mist* where Native American trappers catch the allosaur is reprised here. The monster is captured and transported to the village in a big wagon as the monster will prove Larkin's innocence. The wagon breaks and the beast escapes to a nearby village where it raises whatever havoc Obie and the Nassours could afford. Roberts gets to play the hero and lures it into a sharpened pole which it impales itself upon, while in the final film, it is lured into quicksand and drowns.

The film was not a hit upon release, and has since been overshadowed by 1969's *The Valley of Gwangi.*

It is thought that the armature the Nassours built was based upon the one Obie had Marcel Delgado build for his version of *Gwangi.* As one last aside, in *Keep Watching the Skies,* mention is made of a neat publicity photo of actress Irish McCalla in her *Sheena Queen of the Jungle* costume from her TV series posing next to a life-size dinosaur model which doesn't appear in the final film. Try as I may, I was unable to find it.

MARK OF THE CLAW
THE GIANT CLAW TAKES FLIGHT

Poster for *The Giant Claw*. Notice how the monster is described as prehistoric, and nor can its face be seen.

RELEASE DATE June 1957

DIRECTOR Fred F. Sears **SPECIAL EFFECTS** Ralph Hammeras, George Teague and Larry Butler **SCREENPLAY** Samuel Newman & Paul Gangelin **MUSIC SUPERVISOR:** Mischa Bakaleinikoff **CAST** Jeff Morrow (Mitch MacAfee) Mara Corday (Sally Caldwell) Morris Ankrum (Lt. Gen Edward Considine) Lou Merrill (Pierre Broussard) Edgar Barrier (Dr. Karol Noymann)

Academy Ratio, B&W, 75 Minutes

PLOT An interdimensional space vulture terrorizes North America.

Reportedly Producer Sam Katzman bragged to star Mara Corday about how fantastic the monster would be. The cast envisioned it as a monstrous eagle rather than the goofy space buzzard they got.

COMMENTARY *The Giant Claw* will forever live in infamy as one of the worst creature features of all time due to its comical, muppet-like monster. It didn't have to be that way, though. The strange tale of the giant space bird isn't so bad on story alone, it's predominantly the effects that sink it. Development on the film started innocently enough, with the germ of an idea gestating off of recent news detailing discoveries in the realm of particle physics, specifically in terms of matter and antimatter.[1] Regarding the monster, *Rodan* was an obvious influence, having just been a massive hit on both sides of the pacific. But the producers couldn't do another supersonic pterodactyl. To differentiate their avian horror, they settled on the myth of *la Carcagne*, the flying bird-like banshee of French-Canadian folklore. Actually, though in the final film the big bird is said to come from an "antimatter galaxy," some taglines implied it was a

FLYING BEAST OUT OF PREHISTORIC SKIES !

JEFF MORROW · MARA CORDAY

Written by SAMUEL NEWMAN and PAUL GANGELIN
Technical Effects Created by RALPH HAMMERAS and GEORGE TEAGUE
Produced by SAM KATZMAN · Directed by FRED F. SEARS · A CLOVER Production
A COLUMBIA PICTURE

dinosaur, screaming, "Winged Monster from 17,000,000 B.C.! Big as a Battleship! Flies 4 Times the Speed of Sound! Atomic Weapons Can't Hurt It!"

The feature was pitched under the working title of *The Mark of the Claw*. Producer Sam Katzman wanted to hire Ray Harryhausen to bring the big bird to life. He had, after all, worked with Ray on *Earth vs. the Flying Saucers*. Constraints of time and budget forbade this— though *Harryhausen: The Lost Movies* says Ray turned it down— and so Katz farmed out the effects work to a small studio in Mexico City. Perhaps they misunderstood that the movie was meant to be played as serious? Some even say this marionette amounted to a mere $50! Nor does the finished space buzzard resemble the poster's rather vague monster.

The cast, in particular, was horrified when they saw the monster months later at the film's premier. They were essentially just imagining the creature during production, and presumably any of the pre-production drawings they saw couldn't prepare them for the horror of *The Giant Claw*. Star Jeff Morrow in particular was embarrassed as he listened to the audience laugh at the monster and went home early to have several drinks.

Overall, *The Giant Claw* represents a big missed opportunity at the time, though, ironically enough, today the film might actually be better remembered for just how bad the monster is.

NOTES

[1] According to Richard Harland Smith of Turner Classic Movies, at least.

THE BLACK SCORPION & THE SPIDER PIT

ADAPTED FROM MATERIAL ORIGINALLY PUBLISHED IN *KONG UNMADE VOLUME I*

Horrific scene from *The Black Scorpion's* cave of horrors, which many feel is similar to *King Kong's* lost "Spider Pit" scene.

RELEASE DATE October 11, 1957

DIRECTOR Edward Ludwig **SPECIAL EFFECTS** Willis O'Brien **SCREENPLAY** David Duncan and Robert Blees based upon a story by Paul Yawitz **MUSIC** Paul Sawtell **CAST** Richard Denning (Dr. Hank Scott) Mara Corday (Teresa Alvarez) Carlos Rivas (Dr. Arturo Ramos) Mario Navarro (Juanito) Carlos Múzquiz (Dr. Velasco)

Academy Ratio, B&W, 88 Minutes

PLOT An erupting volcano lets loose a horde of giant scorpions in Mexico.

COMMENTARY *The Black Scorpion* is included in this book due to two cases of lost footage. Firstly, it is said that *The Black Scorpion* was born of test footage created between Willis O'Brien and Pete Peterson. The test footage came in two parts. The first had a huge

 scorpion smashing into a truck, and then plucking a man from a telephone pole and stinging him to death. The other is of either an alien ape of some kind or a radioactively mutated baboon. Either the footage was for two separate ideas, or maybe Obie and Peterson were thinking of a film where various animals become mutated. In any case, the scorpion footage was chosen as the basis for another big bug movie following *Them!*, and the ape footage evolved into a project called *The Las Vegas Monster* that eventually died.

As to the second set of lost footage[1] that is tangentially related to this piece, I am referring to the infamous lost "Spider Pit" scene from the 1933 *King Kong*. As every stopmotion fans knows, a horrific sequence was animated of the sailors falling into a chasm in Skull Island and being devoured by a cascade of creepy crawlies. Merian C. Cooper felt the scene stopped the film's pacing and removed it. He also quite likely let the footage be destroyed. Some have since speculated that some of the big bugs in *The Black Scorpion*, notably the giant spider seen above left, are actually the leftover armatures from the Spider Pit scene.

In *Keep Watching the Skies*, Bill Warren sung the spider's praises, stating,

> The spider, however, may be the triumph for the film for all its brief appearance. It rockets across the cave floor in a comically frightening manner, seeming altogether and astonishingly spider-like. When it's shot, it flops over on its back, and its slender legs quiver satisfactorily in its death throes. This model was constructed for use in *King Kong*, but footage with it was removed before the feature was released. It doesn't seem to have been the star of *King Kong*'s famous missing "spider-pit" sequence, but was a planned supporting critter for making the background nicely crawly.[2]

However, it has since been debunked that the spider seen in *The Black Scorpion* was the same armature from *King Kong*'s

Spider Pit scene. That said, *The Black Scorpion*'s cavern of horrors sequence is the closest one can get to seeing O'Brien's Spider Pit scene. In his book *Willis O'Brien: Special Effects Pioneer*, Steve Archer even says, "This sequence is effectively staged in the cavernlike subterranean depths of the volcano, evoking images of what the unseen 'spider pit' scene in *King Kong* might have looked like."[3]

Even if Willis O'Brien never got to animate cowboys vs. dinosaurs south of the border like he wanted to for *Gwangi* and *Valley of the Mist*, perhaps it's a small consolation that he did at least get to animate giant bugs on the loose in the Southwest. And, overall, *The Black Scorpion* is also a solid 1950s monster movie despite being written off by some as a *Them!* rip-off.

According to Kris Yeaworth on his audio commentary for *Dinosaurus!*, which Willis O'Brien worked on, *Black Scorpion* had a deleted scene of a scorpion battling a steam shovel.

NOTES

[1] Actually, there is a third piece of lost footage associated with this film, since the trailer for The Black Scorpion utilized a deleted shot from *The Beast of 20,000 Fathoms.*

[2] Warren, *Keep Watching the Skies*, Kindle Edition.

[3] Archer, *Willis O'Brien*, p.66.

WILLIS O'BRIEN'S
LAST OF THE OSO SI-PAPU

DEVELOPED
Late 1940s-1950s

CONCEPT BY Willis and Darlyne O'Brien

The Oso Si-Papu confronts a movie crew in one of Willis O'Brien's beautiful paintings.

PLOT A legendary creature seen once every hundred years resurfaces in the Southwest.

COMMENTARY Perhaps the oddest of Willis O'Brien's "Lost World" in the Southwest scenarios was this one, entitled *The Last of the Oso Si-Papu*. O'Brien got the strange name from the Native American portals to the underworld, called Si-papu, and added the Spanish word for bear to the front making Oso Si-Papu. According to Obie's wife, Darlyne, she got the idea from an old issue of *Arizona Highways* magazine that told of a mythical creature known to the Native Americans. Though no description of the beast was given, Obie imagined it as a cross between a Gila monster and a bear. With *Gwangi*, *Valley of the Mist*, and *Umbah* (about a Native American giant who fights a dino-sized Gila

170

monster) all going unrealized, perhaps Obie decided to try his hand at something completely different in the form of *The Last of the Oso Si-Papu.*

Obie's treatment begins with Tom Mederson, a talented young cowboy proficient with a bow and arrow looking for adventure. He gets more than he bargained for when he answers a wanted ad looking for someone with just his skill set. Upon arrival in the small settlement of Haden, Arizona, he finds things to be in a state of excitement as much of the local Native American population seems to be in a hurry to leave the area. The daughter of Professor Haden, who filed the want ad, arrives to pick Tom up in a jeep. (Naturally she is very beautiful and will serve as Tom's love interest as the story progresses.) Jean, as she is called, informs Tom that her father and his associate, Dr. Thaddeus Brown, believe there's some truth in a Native American prediction that claims a prehistoric monster called the Oso Si-Papu is soon to emerge from the underworld. The monster is described as looking something like a reptilian bear of sorts. The locals claim it emerges once every hundred years to kill everything in sight. Tom finally learns the purpose of his visit will be to shoot the creature with arrows laced with hypodermic needles to knock the monster out, and the story takes off from there.

Obie had a good sense of visual flare for the story, as he envisioned a pueblo atop a mesa as one of the main locations. He may have been thinking of the real-life Acoma Pueblo in New Mexico, which was built atop a mesa. Or, he may have been thinking of something more along the lines of a cliff-side pueblo, such as Montezuma Castle of Arizona. Whatever locale he had in mind, the scene at the pueblo is reminiscent of *King Kong* as the tribe awaits thc monster's arrival and beat on some drums. Eventually they see its silhouette sauntering along the horizon and the drums cease.

Dr. Brown and Professor Haden then proceed to lure the beast on horseback towards a steer tied up as bait. The plan is for Tom to shoot the monster as it feasts on the steer. But we all know nothing can go to plan, especially not this early in the story. When the beast begins its feast, Tom's arrow is unable to penetrate its thick hide. The situation intensifies when another Oso Si-Papu comes on the scene and fights the other over the carcass. The battle of the behemoths shakes the whole pueblo until one kills the other. When the survivor takes a victory stance, Tom shoots its soft underbelly and successfully penetrates the hide. The Oso Si-Papu eventually succumbs to the sedative and becomes unconscious. As King Kong before him, the monster is tied up and prepared for transport. And like King Kong, there's also a would-be Carl Denham waiting in the wings.

Perhaps more so than Carl Denham, though, the character of Joe Kane is more a parody of the movie makers of Obie's day, as he is described as a producer of "cheap monster movies". This, perhaps, shows that it was one of Obie's later treatments, as cheap monster movies weren't quite yet a thing back in the 1930s and didn't truly become prominent until the 1950s. Kane had expressed interest to Professor Haden in filming the capture but was barred from doing so. Therefore, when he sees some ranch hands hauling the beast through the desert on a tractor trailer, Kane devises a plan to hijack it. He does so by having his men distract the cowboy in charge, knocking him out, and then taking the trailer away to a lonely wash out in the desert. There they set up cameras along the ravine, planning to shoot footage of the monster as it awakens. Notably, it doesn't seem that Kane is out to make a documentary. As I said, Kane seems to be a parody of sorts, and plans to write his monster movie around whatever footage he manages to capture, similar to the producers who made films around the *One Million B.C.* footage during the same decade.

Like Kong, the monster is too much to handle and breaks free of its chains. Though this is what he wanted to see, the monster naturally comes after Kane and his men. Lucky for them, the hero and heroine arrive to shoot arrows at the monster, attracting its attention. Tom and Jean then lead the monster on a horseback chase towards a field of oil derricks. Notably, Obie points out that the oil pumps may resemble prehistoric monsters to the oncoming Oso Si-Papu. Indeed, the Oso Si-Papu views the derricks as foes to be vanquished and begins its attack. After demolishing a derrick, Kane and his men arrive on the scene in a station wagon and the chase is on yet again when the monster sees them.

The men drive to a chasm that leads to a bat guano mine via cable car. The men board the cable car to escape the beast across the deep ravine. It's a bad decision, as it turns into a Southwestern version of the Skull Island log scene from *King Kong*. As the men are midway across the chasm in the cable car, the monster begins tugging on the cable. As the car violently wobbles back and forth, men plunge to their death much like the sailors of Skull Island. Not long after, Tom comes on the scene and fires another doped-up arrow into the monster, which topples into the ravine to its death. (Perhaps that's just coincidental, but one could compare the beast's fall to its death to Kong, too.)

As a revisional note, Obie also added in that perhaps the female lead, rather than being Professor Haden's daughter, could be a motion picture starlet brought along by Joe Kane. This would make her more like Ann Darrow, meant to be the pretty girl in the monster picture. Obie also noted that to make Kane truly villainous before he plunges to his death, that maybe he doesn't wait for Jean to board the cable car.

The Oso Si-Papu chasing Kane and his men to the cable car.

Obie had a lot of faith in the project as he completed 90 watercolor storyboards plus seven larger, more elaborate production paintings. An animation model of the titular creature was even constructed, as it was later found in the belongings of the late Pete Peterson, one of Obie's apprentices.

Sadly, *The Last of the Oso Si-Papu* was just another of Obie's projects that should have been realized by a studio if they had the good sense to do so.

173

OBIE VS. THE MARX BROTHERS
TILDA AND THE ISLE OF WOMEN

CONCEPT BY Willis O'Brien with Jerry Cady

PLOT Two men become stranded on a deserted island ruled over by savage women and a gigantic brontosaurus.

COMMENTARY The last of Obie's unmade dinosaur projects was a comedy, and possibly an attempt at reviving an unmade spoof of *The Lost World* to star Charlie Chaplin as it sounds similar. It is thought that the Marx Brothers were the templates Obie was thinking of as he wrote the treatment, though he also had his eye on a comedy duo known as Lum and Abner as a either a more realistic choice or a backup. The two main characters comprise of country bumpkin Elmos Grubb and city slicker Horace Pie. As Horace watches Elmos feed his pigs some garbage, he thinks back to the new invention of garbage disposals in the big cities. He pitches the idea of Elmos using his pigs as a rural form of garbage disposal and renting them around the country. For what it's worth, Obie's attempt at comedy isn't bad by any stretch. Elmos and Horace "install" three pigs beneath a woman's kitchen sink, and all seems to go well until the pigs break out and stampede through the house.

The somewhat episodic story continues with Elmos inheriting a circus from his uncle and taking it over with Horace. During their tour of the carnival, the duo board a hot air balloon for a test flight, only the carnies sever the rope and send their unwanted new owners into the skies. Off the duo go *Mysterious Island* style until they drift over the sea and the balloon crash lands in the trees of a desert-isle. The duo watch in amazement as a brontosaurus emerges from a nearby lake and walks towards them. They are horrified as the animal bites the balloon carriage and then lifts it from the tree. Over a course of misadventures, one of which involves a log over a ravine à la Skull Island, the two men figure out that the brontosaurus looks at itself as Elmos' pet and they name it Tildy, after Elmos' old girlfriend.

The story makes its next big development upon the discovery of an inhabited settlement across the lake. The two men board the brontosaurus and use it as a prehistoric ferry. (As they do so, a nondescript water monster of some sort stalks them, but it's played only for comedic effect.) Upon safely crossing the lake, the men cautiously avoid the village in favor of exploring a huge wall that borders it—shades of Skull Island. Eventually the inhabitants make themselves known, and they are all women. The two men are tied up like animals and paraded through the village until brought before their queen. That night, the men are treated as esteemed guests in a celebration which employs and makes musical instruments out of prehistoric bones (dinosaur ribs make a harp, while a mammoth tusk is used as a horn). Eventually, the men discover the fate of the last man on the island, who is buried in a grave with a marker distinguishing him for having "entertained" the queen for three years before expiring along with four others. Figuring out that they will be made into exhausted love slaves, the two men plot their escape.

To do so, they make friends with the women in the dinosaur bone band, promising to take them to a land rife with men who will adore them. It's not necessarily a lie, as Elmos and Horace imagine the girls would be great carnival performers along with their pet dinosaur. The duo constructs a howdah (the type of carriage situated on the back on an elephant in India) and places it upon Tildy. With the girls, they lead Tildy out to sea and set sail for San Francisco. Upon arrival there are the expected traffic pile ups and other chaotic incidents. However, they make it safely to the carnival where Elmos teaches Tildy the usual circus tricks. The animal act becomes a huge hit, but it's not enough for Horace, who pitches a grand parade through the streets. Naturally, we get back into *King Kong* territory when things go awry during the parade. Tildy gets spooked and goes on a comical rampage. To catch the dinosaur, Horace and Elmos board a cable car and go chasing after her. (Notably, Obie also planned a cable car sequence for *Mighty Joe Young* which also went unrealized.) The car races past the dinosaur and goes crashing into the bay. So does Tildy, who jumps in and decides to swim back home and away from civilization while Horace and Elmos must deal with the chaos they've caused.

In many respects, the proposed picture was more or less a parody of *King Kong* with a brontosaurus in place of an ape. Unlike most of Obie's projects, no pre-production drawings survived as Obie loaned them out and they were never returned.

CHARLES GEMORA'S
THE BIG THAW

ORIGINALLY PUBLISHED IN *KONG UNMADE VOLUME I*

DEVELOPED
Late 1940s-1957

CONCEPT BY Charles Gemora

Some of Charles Gemora's sketches for *The Big Thaw.*

PLOT A polar shift causes Ice Age monsters to thaw, including a giant ape...

COMMENTARY Throughout the 1930s all the way up into the 1950s, if you saw a movie with a man in an ape suit, chances are it was the great Charles Gemora playing the gorilla, which he did in films such as *Murders in the Rue Morgue* (1932) among many others. But Gemora was so much more than just the man in the gorilla suit. In addition to being a talented artist and makeup technician, he had many ideas of his own for full-blown feature films, one of which was *The Big Thaw.*

The Big Thaw was an ambitious idea that would have seen Ice Age monsters thawing out in the present day. Among them are some mammoths and a giant ape. Like the 1925 *Lost World*, the plan was probably to use stopmotion for the mammoths and the suitmation technique for the ape. (Would Gemora have played the creature? Who knows?) The story was to be set in Siberia during a reversal of the North and South Poles. During the shift, creatures frozen during the Ice Age begin to thaw. As stated before, the only creatures planned for the film that we know of were a herd of wooly mammoths and one giant ape. One of the mammoths would have a playful relationship with the protagonists, while the ape was to be an antagonist who would try to abduct the girl as in *King Kong*.

Overall, *The Big Thaw* was ahead of its time in terms of its concept, which is comparable to *The Day After Tomorrow* (2004). The main inspiration for the story was likely the frozen mammoth found in the Beresovca River in Siberia, which was so well preserved that it still had grass in its mouth in 1901. Gemora's treatment makes mention of people in Siberia eating the meat of frozen mammoths:

It has been known to science that millions of years ago, the axis of the earth - the North and the South Poles were not

177

in their position. The far north was once a tropical region. Time and time again large animals such as the mammoth elephant, the Mastodon has been discovered buried in the ice of the great Glacier of Siberia. It is known too that some of the people who live in that remote region of Siberia are actually mining fresh meat from the well preserved bodies of these tropical animals. They have found undigested vegetation in the stomachs of these animals - vegetation that can only be found in tropical countries. These animals had been frozen evidently in quick-freeze manner and are perfectly preserved.

As far as the production's timeline, many sources imply it was to be a feature film in the late 1940s. Gemora's relatives imply it was developed later, in 1957. Via Facebook, Jason Lee Barnett (producer of the documentary *Charlie Gemora Uncredited*) told me, "I believe [*Big Thaw*] is from circa 1957 and Anne Baxter was a possible lead (Gemora last working with her on *The Ten*

Commandments)." Barnett also spoke to the effects, saying that since Gemora created the ape-man for *The Lost World,* that the giant ape would probably be a man in a suit while the mammoths would be stopmotion. Asked if any other ice age creatures besides Mammoths or giant apes would appear, he replied, "That's all of the creatures I know of." And, as to the rumors of the lead actress, he also added, "And Anne Baxter is a guess as the character is named Ann Baxter."

Had the film been produced, it would have been unique for putting the spotlight on Ice Age mammals rather than prehistoric reptiles for once.

CinemaScope

The Land Unknown

BEHIND A BARRIER OF ANTARCTIC ICE...
A PARADISE OF HIDDEN TERRORS!

A Universal-International Picture starring
JOCK MAHONEY • SHAWN SMITH • WILLIAM REYNOLDS
with HENRY BRANDON • PHIL HARVEY • DOUGLAS KENNEDY
Directed by VIRGIL VOGEL • Screenplay by LASZLO GOROG • Produced by WILLIAM ALLAND

THE LAND UNKNOWN
AS A BIG BUDGET A-PICTURE

RELEASE DATE October 30, 1957

DIRECTOR Virgil W. Vogel **SCREENPLAY** László Görög based on a story by Charles Palmer & William N. Robson **MUSIC** Henry Mancini, Heinz Roemheld, Hans J. Salter & Herman Stein **CAST** Jock Mahoney (Commander Hal Roberts) Shirley Patterson (Margaret Hathaway) William Reynolds (Lt. Jack Carmen) Henry Brandon (Dr. Carl Hunter) Douglas Kennedy (Capt. Burnham)

Cinemascope, B&W, 78 Minutes

PLOT A military expedition discovers a prehistoric oasis in the Antarctic.

COMMENTARY *The Land Unknown* was announced four years before it came out in 1953 by Charles "Cap" Palmer. Tom Weaver detailed Palmer's 51-page story treament on his excellent commentary of *The Land Unknown* on the Blu-Ray from Shout! Factory. It is structurally similar to the finished film but with completely different characters.

The treament begins with Commander Burnham and two other men, Pat Carmon, the pilot, and Hal Thurber, a geologist, flying over the South Pole on the way back to their base located at the Ross Ice Barrier. As their fuel begins to run low, they are forced to fly low through a strange cloudbank in their plane. Hot, gray gasses gust against them, and the brawny pilot has to fight the controls to get them through it and back to base. Over dinner, they discuss the strange cloud mass and how it was clearly hovering over a huge chasm worthy of exploration. An expedition is put in place on which will also go Commander Burnham's daughter, Ann, due to the fact that she is a skilled cartographer. Considering that Ann is a stuffy academic-type interested in Hal, the geologist, you just know she'll fall for Pat, the pilot, eventually. The excursion determines that the abyss is twenty miles across and a mile deep. As such, Pat refuses to land in it. However, as the group flies over, Hal parachutes out, which forces Pat to land in the abyss in order to rescue him.

181

Both the original treatment and the finished film had the tyrannosaurs rex menacing the heroes in their aerial craft twice, once in the midlle and once at the end, though the treatment used a plane instead of a helicopter.

As in the film, in which a pterodactyl buzzes the helicopter, in the treatment's case, the pterodactly dive bombs the plane and is injured by the propeller. The radio has also been damaged in the crash landing. They soon find Hal tangled up in a fern-like tree and get him down. Pat and Commander Burnham focus on fixing the plane while Ann and Hal go off exploring in the tropical oasis. Hal, not wanting to leave, later removes the plane's ignition coil and hides it under some rocks. Obviously, Hal is a rather troublesome character and it will only get worse from here. At one point, when Ann is about to be attacked by a "huge serpent", Pat fires a flare into its mouth saving her. (Likely this influenced the flare fired into the mouth of the Elasmosaurus in the finished film.) After this, their perfunctory romance begins. Next, Pat figures out that Hal hid the ignition coil, and Commander Burnham orders Hal to bring it back. When he goes to retrieve it, he's shocked to see that it's gone.

That night, a tyranosaurus comes calling. It somehow wounds Commander Burnham, though it doesn't kill him, and all the

182

characters take shelter in the plane. Pat fires up the propeller, which the T-rex loses one of its tiny arms to and flees. (In the film, the characters seek solace in the helicopter, also damaged. The pilot fires up the blades, and they cut into the tyrannosaur's throat, causing it to retreat as well.)

The huge Elasmosaurus was built when the project was still a big-budgeted A-Picture. Actually, its construction ate up too much of the project's budget and the T-Rex, the pterandon, and the human cast all suffered as a result.

The next dino-sequence has Pat saving Ann again, this time from an amphibious creature of some sort. This ends with a kiss and an embrace. Hal apparently witnesses this, for later he tells Ann that she shouldn't be falling for Pat as there's a good chance they will be stranded there for life. As such, Hal plans to kill Pat and tells Ann as much, his excuse being that she must produce offspring with him because he is of a superior intellect and only children born of their union will prosper in the lost world! As Ann walks back to the plane with Hal, she picks up a rock and considers bashing him over the head with it. Before she can, a large red-beared caveman comes along and abducts her. (As it turns out, this is the treatment's more primitive version of Dr. Hunter, the plane crash survivor in the film who has gone a little feral.)

Pat and Hal build a raft out of the plane's skis to cross a tropical lake in pursuit of the caveman, who took Ann away on a raft. Back in the primitive man's cave, in true King Kong style, he begins to fondle Ann. The desperate woman indicates she needs food as a distraction, and so the caveman departs to hunt some up for her. As soon as he leaves, Ann looks for a way out, and is dismayed to see she's being kept high off the ground in the side of the cliffs that make the abyss and the only way down is a vine rope. Eventually, Hal and Pat arrive at the cave, where Ann immediately embraces Pat. The caveman bursts back in, and a fight ensues between Pat and the primitive man. Hal probably hopes one will kill the other, but Ann intervenes by bashing the caveman over the head with a rock. When Pat goes to kill the caveman, Hal argues that he should be preserved for scientific study. Hal injects him with a sedative, which suddenly puts what they thought was a primitive neanderthal into an altered state of mind. The caveman is really a survivor of the Nordon Expedition of 20 years ago. His name is Butch, and he was the pilot of the expedition. Over the last twenty years, surviving in the strange land has turned him savage, and when the drugs wear off, he goes back to being a caveman.

The group spends the night in the cave with Butch/the caveman tied up in the corner, and Ann confesses her love to Pat. He brushes it off, stating that when they return to civilization she'll lose interest in him. Luckily, the next morning they discover the missing ignition coil, which the caveman stole. (Maybe being a former pilot he recognized it?) They hurry back to the plane, straighten out the damaged propeller, and reinstall the coil. However, the plane can no longer handle their combined weight with Butch along. Someone will have to stay behind. A guilty Hal offers to do so since he intended to murder Pat earlier. However, Commander Burnham is too weak to be transported, and Ann won't leave him. As such, Pat and Ann stay behind with her father while Hal pilots the plane out to get help along with Butch in the cargo hold. As he does so, the tyrannosaur returns, and Pat and Ann must flee towards the cliffs to get away.

In the air, Butch emerges from the cargo hold. The altitude, plus the familiar noises of the plane, have returned him to sanity. However, Butch thinks that Hal is leaving the others behind and insists they go back and being the more experienced pilot, comandeers the plane. It's a good thing they did, too, as they observe that the T-Rex has trapped the remaining trio in a cliffside cave that is crumbling away. Hal parachutes out to aid them, while Butch does some daring maneuvers to distract the dinosaur. One proves too close, and he accidentally crashes the plane into the T-Rex. It's chest bursts into flames, and so does poor Butch, who runs into the jungle screaming. But not all is as lost as it seems. A rescue plane soon descends into the lost world to rescue them. Hal is happy to load the plane with prehistoric specimens, while Pat is happy to have the girl. They fly back to civilization, and a happy ending is had by all (except for poor Butch).

Universal-International snatched up Palmer's idea when they were having a period of success with sci-fi films. They had big plans for the project, to be shot in color and in Cinerama. They also courted the likes of Cary Grant and Veronica Lake to star in it under the direction of Jack Arnold, Universal's top sci-fi director at the time, having helmed *Creature from the Black Lagoon*. The plan was for *The Land Unknown* to be the biggest science fiction spectacle of its time. It was also to be shot outdoors on the large Universal backlot at a nice location called Fall's Lake, surrounded by big, rock cliffs as opposed to the interior studio as in the finished film.

The production reportedly turned on a dime when Universal lost faith in big-budgeted sci-fi spectacles and downgraded the feature into a B-picture, at which point Jack Arnold left the project. With Arnold went the idea of any big stars, too.

"By the time Universal-International stopped fantasizing about big stars and actually hired some actors, *The Land Unknown* was inhabited by the cast unknown," Mark Berry humorously noted in *The Dinosaur Filmography*.[1] That said, it's still a great dinosaur picture and fairly well-polished when compared to other creature features of the era.

NOTES

---

[1] Berry, *Dinosaur Filmography*, p.215.

GODZILLA IN AMERICA
THE VOLCANO MONSTERS

·ADAPTED FROM MATERIAL ORIGINALLY PUBLISHED IN *JAPANESE MONSTERS UNMADE VOLUME I*

Newspaper ad for the film's eventual release as *Gigantis, the Fire Monster* in 1957.

INTENDED RELEASE DATE 1957

SCREENPLAY Ib Melchior & Ed Watson Proposed **CAST/CHARACTERS** Dr. Roy Carlyle [scientist], Marge [Dr. Carlyle's assistant/scientist], Commander Steve McBain [Navy Commander] **PROPOSED DINOSAURS** Godzilla/"Tyrannosaurus", Anguirus/ "Ankylosaurs"

PLOT Two dinosaurs found in a Japanese volcano come back to life to wreck San Francisco.

COMMENTARY *Godzilla Raids Again* (1955) almost had what would surely have been one of the most notorious Americanizations in the series' history. Whereas *Godzilla, King of the Monsters!* (1956) merely edited Raymond Burr into the original *Godzilla*, what was planned as *The Volcano Monsters* would have taken things a step further by completely eliminating the entire Japanese cast of *Godzilla Raids Again*! Not only that, Godzilla and Anguirus would be retrofitted to become a

186

tyrannosaurus rex and an ankylosaurus, respectively, who run amuck in San Francisco's Chinatown.

This was orchestrated in part by Paul Schreibman, Harry Rybnick, Richard Kay, and Edmund Goldman, all of whom had a hand in the Americanized *Godzilla, King of the Monsters*. Ib Melchior, the future writer of films such as *Reptilicus* (1961) and *The Angry Red Planet* (1960), wrote *The Volcano Monsters* script with Ed Watson revolving around Caucasian actors.[1] An ad was even placed for the film in *Variety* in their May 7, 1957, issue with a starting date of June 17th.

Toho, eager to get a foothold in the American marketplace, agreed to the idea and, although the script meshed well with the actual footage,[2] Toho actually constructed new suits of Godzilla and Anguirus to fill in the gaps of *The Volcano Monsters* script,[3] and photos of these suits exist taken by Toho. Among the new scenes that would need to be filmed were the discovery of the dinosaurs, their trip across the ocean on a Navy Destroyer, and the Tyrannosaurus destroying a university building (There are other mentions of the Navy bombing the monster, but these scenes could have very well played out as exposition).

It's worth noting that around this time a deal was struck with AB-PT Pictures to help finance the film, which also (presumably) led Toho into working on the project that eventually became *Giant Monster Varan* (1958) with AB-PT. This division of the television network ABC that specialized in TV movies later collapsed in July of 1957, which meant the cancelation of *The Volcano Monsters*. As to what happened to the new Godzilla and Anguirus suits shipped to America, their fate is still a mystery. Blogger Ken Husley writes, "A few years ago I looked into the matter some and discovered that the old AB-PT studio property and structures became part of Desilu Studios, which then became part of the Paramount lot."[4] In *Japanese Science Fiction, Fantasy and Horror Films,* Stuart Galbraith IV writes, "*Markalite* reported that effects man Bob Burns remembers seeing Gigantis and [sic] Angilas suits Toho presumably shipped to the United States for the new effects footage."[5] This quote refers to Bob Burns during the shooting of 1957's *Invasion of the Saucer Men*. As he and the effects crew were preparing to blow up one of the alien saucers, they needed something to hide behind. They chose a large crate with curious Japanese writing on it. They opened it up to find the Godzilla and Anguirus suits, one of which Burns tried on.

Photographic evidence exists in the form of a remarkable color photo of the Godzilla suit posing with the Phantom of the Opera. Sources think it was taken at Universal Studios, though this has never been confirmed. The two new suits had some interesting differences compared to the Japanese originals. Godzilla, most notably, lacked ears and had only three toes compared to the original's four. Interestingly, these modifications would carry over to the suit for *King Kong vs. Godzilla* in 1962, which *The Volcano Monsters* suit somewhat resembled. As for Anguirus, it would seem to have fewer teeth, and the overall appearance is more bulky and awkward in general.

As to scripting, apparently, the writers weren't even aware that they were more or less adapting an existing film until late in the game. In an interview, Melchior said:

> "Ed and I were asked to...basically Americanize the Godzilla movies. I think the producers had seen the Japanese version of *Gigantis*, figured it would be released in the U.S., took the screenplay and said to Ed and I, 'Do this story.' Up until now, I had no idea that we might be redoing a Japanese script for an already completed movie."[6]

In another interview with Brett Homenick, Melchoir talked about the film's collapse:

> "Our final script was dated 5/7/1957 and was accepted by Rybnick, Barison, and Schreib-man. These three producers had a production/ distribution deal with a company called AB-PT when, in July of 1957, that company closed down. Now, for whatever reasons that I have no idea why, they did not replace the production/distribution company, and *The Volcano Monsters* bit the dust. I don't know if a copy of the script still exists somewhere. It's possible that I have it somewhere, but (laughs) I have no idea where."[7]

After the collapse of *The Volcano Monsters*, Paul Schreibman, Edmund Goldman, and Newton P. Jacobs decided to merely dub *Godzilla Raids Again* into English and release it through Warner Bros with whom they had a distribution deal. Strangely, it was not billed as a Godzilla sequel even though *Godzilla, King of the Monsters!* had been an enormous hit in the United States. Back in the days before sequels were big business, Schreibman, Goldman, and Jacobs thought a new monster film would fare better and, as such, created the *Gigantis, the Fire Monster* name.

As to *The Volcano Monster's* complete script, it is par for the course when it comes to 1950s sci-fi in terms of its lead characters. (Elderly scientist, check! Attractive female assistant, check! Chauvinistic military romantic lead, check!) At one point, the military hero, McBain, even punches the assistant, Marge, across the face to knock her out and rescue her from the Tyrannosaurus when she refuses to vacate her lab! However, that all being said, the duo of screenwriters did a commendable job of crafting a new storyline around the existing footage.

To digress, the story opens excitingly in the aftermath of a huge eruption that occurred at the fictional Noshiro volcano in Japan (if said eruption occurs onscreen or off is unknown to this author). A cavern is then discovered containing various fossils, among them a perfectly-preserved Ankylosaurus and Tyrannosaurus Rex. We then meet our stereotypical leads in the form of Dr. Roy Carlyle, along with assistant Marge, who surmises that the larger than normal dinosaurs were kept in their current state by the volcanic gasses.[8]

When Carlyle plans to have the monsters transported to San Francisco, a Japanese resident warns him that the dinosaurs are the fulfillment of an ancient prophecy and will cause destruction if awakened. After a press conference announcing the discovery in Tokyo, the U.S. Navy hauls the carcasses onto an aircraft carrier for a long voyage across the Pacific. During the journey, Marge develops feelings for Navy commander Steve McBain (our other stereotypical lead) who is somewhat resentful of his assignment. When it is learned the monsters are not only perfectly-preserved but also in a state of suspended animation, McBain wants to throw them overboard in fear they could awaken.

Of course, McBain's prediction comes true when, during a storm, a cable holding the Tyrannosaurus snaps and it tumbles into the water and is lost. The Ankylosaurus is delivered safely to San Francisco. In celebration, Marge and McBain go out on the town while at the same time, the Tyrannosaurus surfaces in the bay. This disturbs the Ankylosaurus who breaks loose to battle its opponent. Eventually, the duo's struggle takes them to Chinatown (really the city of Osaka in *Godzilla Raids Again*).

A guilt-ridden Carlyle has a stroke (this idea would be repeated by Melchoir in *Reptilicus*), and when Marge and McBain visit him in the hospital, he implores them to destroy the dinosaurs. However, in a melodramatic turn, Carlyle's doctor tells the duo that if this happens, Carlyle will lose his shot at the Nobel Prize and will likely become so depressed that he will die!

Meanwhile, the Tyrannosaurus kills the Ankylosaurus and then marches on through the mainland. Marge and a team of scientists work tirelessly at her university to create a recreation of the volcanic gas to put the dinosaur back to sleep. As the monster approaches their campus, McBain arrives to rescue Marge, and when she refuses to leave, knocks her out with a punch to the face. McBain carries Marge to safety as the dinosaur destroys the building (this would have been one of the new scenes the Godzilla suit was used for) and then slips off into the sea.

The Navy attacks the Tyrannosaurus with bombs and depth charges to no avail (possibly off-screen, it's not clear). McBain and Marge follow the creature on a Navy destroyer and eventually deduce it is heading for a tropical island in the polar region shielded by ice caps where it will lay eggs. For one, this idea is rather funny, as there is no hint that there's a hidden tropical oasis hidden within Shinko Island in *Godzilla Raids Again.* Second, this author has always wondered where Ian Thorne (author of the Crestwood House Monster Series) got his misinformation that the second Godzilla in *Gigantis the Fire Monster* was a female. Perhaps *The Volcano Monsters* had something to do with it?

But, back to the story, nuking the monster is considered but a plan is hatched to bury the dinosaur in an avalanche instead (so as to use footage from the original film's climax). The plan works and Dr. Carlyle's prized possession is rendered harmless but still left alive in a state of suspended animation. Meanwhile, back at Noshiro volcano, a claw bursts from the cave from an unknown monster...

It is thought that some of Melchoir's ideas in this script eventually found their way into *Reptilicus* (1961), which is highly likely as the similarities are certainly there. First off, the main trope of characters is similar (but then again, aren't they always?) with the iron-jawed military man, an elderly scientist, and his attractive daughter (or daughters in *Reptilicus's* case). Said elderly scientist suffers a heart attack when he is unable to stop an attack on Reptilicus which would do the world more harm than good. As far as the idea of finding a preserved dinosaur, or in this case the preserved tail of a dinosaur-like creature, that was a fairly common convention by this time. The other main similarity is that both scripts feature a scene where the female lab assistant makes some type of anti-monster biological weapon at a university when the monster is in close range. *The Volcano Monsters* ends with another dinosaur emerging from the volcano, and *Reptilicus* ends hinting that the titular monster will regenerate again. So, in a strange roundabout way, if nothing else *The Volcano Monsters* ended up influencing the writing process for the most famous Danish monster movie of all time.

NOTES

[1] This and the English dub of *Gigantis, the Fire Monster* was Watson's only screenplay credit.

[2] All scenes of Godzilla's atomic ray would be removed though.

[3] Toho had already done something similar in the case of the American version of 1955's *Abominable Snowman,* which needed an additional scene to be filmed before it became the John Carradine vehicle *Half Human* in 1958. In this case, Toho sent the young Snowman suit to America for the filming of new scenes (though in the finished film, it's merely a corpse lying on a table).

[4] kensforce.wixsite.com/viewobscura/single-post/2017/02/11/Godzilla-Anguirus-and-the-Case-of-the-Missing-Monster-Suits

[5] Galbraith, *Japanese Science Fiction, Fantasy and Horror Films,* pp.16-17.

[6] Shapiro, *When Dinosaurs Ruled the Screen,* pp.33-34.

[7] Homenick, "The Imagination of Ib Melchior," Vantage Point Interviews. vantagepointinterviews.com/2017/05/18/the-imagination-of-ib-melchior-a-conversation-with-the-danish-monster-movie-maker/

[8] Actually, the script probably doesn't even address the fact that the dinosaurs are incredibly large compared to real life dinosaurs.

191

FILM THAT TIME FORGOT
SON OF THE VOLCANO
BY LEE POWERS

ORIGINALLY PUBLISHED IN *THE LOST FILMS FANZINE* #4

RELEASE DATE September 7, 1959

DIRECTOR Emmanuel I. Rojas **SCREENPLAY** Jose Flores Sibal & Jose Domingo Karasig based on ideas by Cirio H. Santiago & Emmanuel I. Rojas **MUSIC** Tito Arevalo **CAST** Fernando Poe Jr. (Arturo) Edna Luna (Julia) Ronald Remy (Ramon)

Academy Ratio, B&W, 117 minutes

PLOT A giant bird awakens from a volcano.

COMMENTARY *Anak Ng Bulkan,* or *The Son of the Volcano,* is a 1959 giant monster movie from the Philippines. Considering the year in which it was released, and also due to many of the plot points, it was probably inspired by Toho's *Rodan* (1956). If anything, one could consider it a cross between *Rodan* and the Gamera movies, as the main character is a young boy who befriends the monster. It was shot in black and white and runs at a lengthy 117 minutes. Very little is known about the film other than that it was well-remembered enough in its native country to receive a remake in 1997.

The movie begins when a small eruption occurs on an island in the Philippines. It releases an egg which a small boy finds along with his friend (a girl that looks to be his same age). He opens the egg and finds a small baby bird (an actual chicken) inside. The boy has an abusive father at home who wants the boy to be all work and no play. Even though he knows he wouldn't like it, the boy sneaks the baby monster home. He names him Anak, and the bird grows bigger and bigger each day until the local villagers catch it in a wooden cage. The boy's father wants to kill Anak with his machete, but the boy intervenes and his father kills his dog instead! Eventually, the monster bird breaks out of the wood cage and escapes. The boy continues to spend time with Anak and even convinces his friend to go for a ride on the bird with him as time goes by.

The villagers are terrified of the bird and sightings begin to flood the authorities' office. Reports are even being broadcast on the radio. The children make it back home safely after fighter pilots are deployed to chase them as Aank flies over the islands. Time goes by and Anak continues to grow even larger. He gets so big that the wind gusts from his wings create giant waves and sink ships. The young boy confronts Anak hoping to convince him to hide or at least to not cause trouble. The sightings and news of the large bird continue to escalate causing the local military to respond. Eventually the military pinpoints the origin of the bird to the little boy's island. The military evacuates the island and observes the volcano where Anak had originated from.

Anak emerges and now looks to be the size of the monster from *The Giant Claw*. Military planes are deployed to battle Anak. The little boy finds a way back to his island (despite having been evacuated) and calls to Anak in the middle of the battle. Anak continues to battle planes and ships as the volcano begins to erupt. The little boy and Anak seem to share some sort of psychic connection, as both think about each other as the boy is injured from debris and Anak from the attack. Both are bleeding from their wounds. At the same time, the villainous father meets his demise from volcanic debris as he's trying to rape a young woman! What exactly happens in the end is unclear, as Anak dives into the volcano either to end his life or maybe just return to where he came from while the little boy is rescued by the military. The boy is on a military ship with his wounds being tended to and is reunited with his mother on the ship. A local authority gives a few closing remarks and the film ends.

THE LOST WORLD'S
LOST POTENTIAL

RELEASE DATE July 13, 1960

DIRECTOR Irwin Allen **SCREENPLAY** Irwin Allen & Charles Bennett **MUSIC** Paul Sawtell &Bert Shefter **CAST** Michael Rennie (Lord John Roxton) Jill St. John (Jennifer Holmes) David Hedison (Ed Malone) Claude Rains (Professor Challenger) Fernando Lamas (Manuel Gomez) Richard Haydn (Professor Summerlee)

2.35 : 1, Color, 97 Minutes

PLOT Modern day explorers led by Professor Challenger head to a lost world in the Amazon.

COMMENTARY By 1960, poor Willis O'Brien had fathered quite a few unfinished projects between *Gwangi*, *Valley of the Mist*, and others. Unbeknownst to him, the worst was yet to come, as he was not only about to be swindled out of his burgeoning *King Kong vs. Frankenstein* feature, but also a looming *Lost World* remake. Twentieth Century Fox had recently had a big success in the form of *Journey to the Center of the Earth* (1959) and wanted to do a similar picture. They landed on a gestating remake of *The Lost World* via producer Irwin Allen, and Willis O'Brien was approached about the effects work. To O'Brien's disappointment, doing effects work really just meant doing storyboards, as Twentieth Century Fox was already set on using lizards to bring to life the dinosaurs as they did on *Journey.*

Lobby Card for *The Lost World,* which was initially going to be another Allied Artists release from Irwin Allen, but the success of *Journey to the Center of the Earth* attracted Twentieth Century Fox to the project instead.

To backtrack a bit, while Allen was in New York in June of 1959 on a publicity tour for *The Big Circus,* he told the *New York Times* that he had bought the rights to film *The Lost World* from the Conan Doyle estate for $100,000 and planned to shoot the picture as "a $3,000,000 production in either the Todd-AO or Technirama wide screen process." The *New York Times* article also stated that "Willis O'Brien has been engaged to create mechanical counterparts of some of the prehistoric giant monsters such as dinosaurs, pterodactyls and brontosauruses."

As for other grand plans, Allen wanted to bring back Gilbert Roland, who had been in the 1925 film, and to feature *One Million B.C.* star Victor Mature in the production. Also attached in some early capacity were Robert Mitchum, Trevor Howard, Clifton Webb, Orson Welles, Robert Morley and Peter Ustinov. None of them appeared in the picture, just like O'Brien's planned dinosaurs.

One of *The Lost World's* better-remembered giant lizards. The film does have one deleted scene of note worth discussing, which was to have involved a pterodactyl. It was likely cut because, how would one make a pterodactyl out of an iguana? Glue wings to it and flit it about from some wires? There is a mention of the scene in the official synopsis, which states, "The explorers are attacked by a flying dinosaur, a pterodactyl. The bird-like creature has leathery, 20-foot long wings, and it is finally driven off with rifle fire." As stated before, it was probably too difficult to film and thus what could have been the picture's one true dinosaur not portrayed by a lizard was dropped.

One reason was that Irwin Allen didn't like the time-consuming nature of the stopmotion effects work which he experienced firsthand on *The Animal World*. (Coincidentally, on that project, Obie had been encouraging Allen to remake *The Lost World* in color.) It would almost seem as if Obie was brought onto the

196

project as a publicity ploy, since he was the reason the original had been a success. Had stopmotion been used, it probably would have taken at least six months, which was too long for Twentieth Century Fox's liking. Even Todd-AO cinematography was dropped in favor of the more usual CinemaScope.

To some degree, it could be argued that the 1960 *Lost World* was essentially a cash grab, resting on the laurels of the famous book, its previous film adaptation, and the recent success of *Journey*. The story was retrofitted to take place in the current day of 1960, and several new characters were created like Jill St. John's Jennifer Holmes. (The last name was given to her because it was felt audiences would expect a character named Holmes to pop up in a Conan Doyle movie!) It doesn't even set a monster loose in London at the end. That said, the ending, where Professor Challenger captures a dinosaur egg that hatches a baby T-Rex (just another lizard), is truer to the book in a way. However, this occurred not out of concern for being true to the novel so much as keeping the budget down, I suspect. In addition to the lizards portraying dinosaurs, another way in which the 1960 *Lost World* copied *Journey* was via the inclusion of a lost city that didn't exist in the book. Since *Journey* had inserted Atlantis, *Lost World* included the South American equivalent of El Dorado. Though not part of the book, it did at least adds some exciting scenes to the remake.

Despite its shortcomings in the effects field, Allen's *Lost World* was still fairly polished and entertaining. Allen wanted to follow the feature film with a *Lost World* TV series, which never materialized. Instead, he would make good use of his stock-lizard-footage in his TV series *Land of the Giants, Lost in Space, The Time Tunnel,* and *Voyage to the Bottom of the Sea.*

197

GOLIATH AND
THE ADDED DRAGON

ORIGINALLY PUBLISHED IN *THE LOST FILMS FANZINE* #8

The mightiest adventure of them all!

GOLIATH AND THE DRAGON in COLORSCOPE

MARK FOREST · BRODERICK CRAWFORD · ELEONORA RUFFO AND A CAST OF THOUSANDS · A JAMES H. NICHOLSON & SAMUEL Z. ARKOFF Presentation

RELEASE DATE November 1960

DIRECTOR Vittorio Cottafavi **SCREENPLAY** Marcello Baldi, Duccio Tessari, Mario Ferrari, Nicolo Ferrari, Fabio Carpi, Ennio De Concini & Franco Rossetti **MUSIC** Alexandre Derevitsky **CAST** Mark Forest (Hercules/Goliath) Broderick Crawford (King Eurystheus) Sandro Moretti (Hyllus) Gaby André (Ismene) Philippe Hersent (Androclo) Leonora Ruffo (Deianira) Giancarlo Sbragia (Tindaro)

2.35 : 1, Color, 87 Minutes

PLOT Goliath battles a multitude of monsters across ancient Greece.

198

COMMENTARY Oh what a tangled web these lost films weave sometimes. Tracing their lineages can be maddening, and now we will do our best to unravel the tangled web that extends between an unmade Hercules movie to star Steeve Reeves, a Hercules movie that was made but didn't star Reeves, and an unmade sequel to *Goliath and the Barbarians* which starred Steve Reeves—but not as Hercules.

Let's start at the beginning. In the late 1950s, Joseph Levine, the same man who brought *Godzilla, King of the Monsters!* to America in 1956, hit paydirt on another foreign import. That film was 1958's *Le fatiche di Ercole,* or *The Labours of Hercules,* which Levine simply shortened to *Hercules* for its U.S. release. The film had gestated in the mind of director Pietro Francisci since the early 1950s. His main holdup was finding the right man to play Hercules. Eventually, he saw Mr. Universe Steve Reeves in action in 1954's *Athena* and cast Reeves immediately, ending a five year search for his perfect muscleman. The film was shot in the summer and fall of 1957 and was released in Italy on February 20, 1958.

Joseph Levine sensed an exploitable property in the film and paid $120,000 for distribution rights and then spent another million promoting it. The investment paid off and he managed to make a $5 million profit. Considering the film was a hit on both sides of the Atlantic, it should come as no surprise that an equally profitable sequel followed in the form of *Hercules Unchained* (1959 in Europe, 1960 in the U.S.).

If both of those films did boffo box office, then why wasn't there a third Steve Reeves Hercules film? Thanks to the efforts of dedicated Peplum blogger Peplum TV, it was learned that there was a third Reeves Hercules film planned. It was to be titled *Ercole Contro gli Dei,* or *Hercules Against the Gods.* Peplum TV's proof in the pudding was found in the form of a collection of publicity photos taken on October 30, 1959. In the photos, one can see Steve Reeves and others at a cocktail party to announce the production.

Peplum TV elaborates that, "Unfortunately, and according to Facebook friend Pasquale (who met and chatted with Reeves), director Pietro Francisci wasn't going to direct it and Steve wanted ONLY Pietro. Because of scheduling issues (Pietro was filming SIEGE OF SYRACUSE and SAPPHO VENUS OF LESBOS during that period) Pietro wasn't going to direct it, most likely writing and/or producing it."[1]

The original Hercules, Steve Reeves (above), compared to the new Hercules, Mark Forest as he appeared in *Vengeance of Hercules* (1960) on page opposite.

After this, Reeves unfortunately pulled out of the project. However, had *Hercules Against the Gods* been produced it would have provided a fairly epic trilogy capper for the Reeves Hercules saga. I say this not because I have seen the script, but because I have seen the film in alternate form: *Goliath and the Dragon*. And this is where the web gets tangled.

What was put out in the U.S. as *Goliath and the Dragon* was released in Italy as *La vendetta di Ercole,* or *The Vengeance of Hercules* starring Mark Forest as the title character. After Reeves' departure, it was decided not to let a good script go to waste, and so Hercules was merely recast with a new actor and the film went from being called *Hercules Against the Gods* to *The Vengeance of Hercules.* Presumably Joseph Levin could have purchased it for U.S. distribution but, curiously, he didn't. American International Pictures did and retitled it *Goliath and the Dragon* for reasons I will discuss later. Before getting into that, let's discuss the Italian *Vengeance of Hercules* some more.

The film gets off to a heck of a start, with Hercules braving the underworld to steal a mythical jewel, thus completing the last of his 12 labors. The rest of the plot is a confusing mess that I can't even begin to try and describe in great detail. But, the gist of it is this: Hercules returns home to his wife and fully grown son, Illo, who is set to wed a certain king's daughter. Shenanigans ensue, Illo is turned against his father, Hercules turns against the gods in anger and has to rescue his wife and son from multiple dangers throughout the film. By the time the picture comes to an end, the evil king has been defeated and all is well with the Hercules family.

And why was the film's story such a mess? I can only guess that the exit of Reeves from the project altered the development process as a new actor was sought out. Stranger yet, even though this was meant to be the third Hercules movie, the character of Iole, the hero's wife in the past two films, does not return. As it stands, in the photos to surface of the cocktail party from 1959, Iole actress Sylva Koscina is conspicuously absent. Had she been recast? Was Iole not going to be in the third Hercules? We don't know, but it's certainly strange that we find Hercules married to a different character named Deianira in *Vengeance of Hercules*. And yet, despite the new wife, the son's name of Illo seems to be derived from Iole. Perhaps the writers merely forgot the name of Hercules's wife in the previous two pictures? Who knows. In any case, we'll let Peplum TV weigh in on the disjointed script: "...there were apparently at least 7 people who worked on the script. This tells me that a lot of last minute changes were made while they were shooting, many changes which were illogical."[2]

Continuity errors and plot holes aside, the fact that one of the film's most important scenes has Hercules turning against the gods does more or less confirm that this started out as *Hercules Against the Gods*. And had it gone before cameras with Reeves, perhaps it would have kept Iole in place of new wife Deianira. Heck, as I was watching it, I halfway wondered if in the original script that perhaps Hercules's fully grown son Illo was originally Ulysses, Hercules's younger trusty sidekick in the previous two flicks. As it stands, Hercules doesn't look old enough to be Illo's father in the film.[3]

Even if the film is a mess, it's still fun to watch. One of the main reasons for this is that the movie features a multitude of monsters when compared to the previous two Hercules pictures. The first film included Jason confronting a dragon (which Joseph Levine dubbed with Godzilla's roar for his version!) while the second Hercules featured no giant monsters at all. Within the first act of *Vengeance*, Hercules encounters two monsters: a three-headed Cerberus dog and a strange man-bat creature. As the film progresses he also battles a bear (or a guy in a bear suit at least) and an elephant. The elephant scene is quite impressive, as it was indeed a real elephant that Hercules brings to its knees! A bit later, a centaur even appears in the film.

However, if you watch the U.S. version, there are even more monsters in the form of the titular titan of *Goliath and the Dragon*. And why did AIP add in a dragon? Well, that's another long story related to another unproduced sequel...

Before he passed on his third Hercules feature, Steve Reeves had played another Peplum hero in *Il Terrore dei Barbari*, or *Terror of the Barbarians*, released in the summer of 1959. The film was loosely based upon the Lombard invasion of Italy in AD 568. When American International Pictures (AIP for short) saw this exciting Reeves actioner, they wanted to capitalize on *Hercules* and so snatched up the rights. And though they might have considered retitling the film "Hercules and the Barbarians," at the time, Levine held the rights to the Hercules name regarding U.S.

theatrical releases. As such, AIP created their own hero in the form of Goliath, and retitled the film *Goliath and the Barbarians*. (They also rescored it with music by Les Baxter.)

The film was a huge hit for AIP, who wanted a sequel. Instead of waiting for the Italians to produce one on their own, AIP commissioned writers Lou Rusoff and Debra Paget to write a sequel called *Goliath and the Dragon*. Whether they actually wrote the script or not is unknown, but the project never went before cameras. AIP had a problem though in that they had already announced the film. As such, they quickly snatched up *Vengeance of Hercules* and rebranded it as a Goliath movie via the dubbing process.

The titular dragon from *Goliath and the Dragon*.

In the book *American International Pictures: A Comprehensive Filmography*, author Rob Craig states the following:

After the smash box office success of *Goliath and the Barbarians* (1959), AIP's response to Joe Levine's smash hit *Hercules* (U.S. release 1959), they purchased a "new" Hercules movie from Italy called *The Vengeance of Hercules*. As Levine had dibs on the Hercules title in theatrical situations, AIP followed up their first "Goliath hit" with a sequel of sorts, turning the Hercules film into *Goliath and the Dragon* via clever dubbing, additional footage, and a new score.

The dragon was said to be animated by Jim Danforth, though this has never been confirmed. Furthermore, outtakes of the dragon were later used by David Hewitt in his King Kong homage *The Mighty Gorga* (1969).

The additional footage Craig speaks of is the titular dragon. In *Goliath and the Dragon*, during the scene where Goliath trapses through the underworld, in addition to Cerberus and the bat monster, he also catches a glimpse of a dragon. Your first clue that this is new footage is that Peplum monsters were always either suitmation creations or full-sized marionets. In long shots, the dragon was created via stopmotion, which was not a Peplum method. The dragon later pops up again towards the end, when Goliath fights it to save one of the female characters. In this case, stopmotion is used only for the long shots, and a goofy-looking scale head fights Goliath in close ups. And though Mark Forest looks a little different in the footage, it does appear to be Forest battling AIP's dragon and not a body double. While it wasn't unheard of for co-productions between AIP and other studios outside of the U.S. to film alternate footage for their respective versions, to my knowledge AIP bought this film after it was completed. Typically by then, new footage would not be shot. So I have to wonder, was AIP actually tied into the preproduction process of *Vengeance of Hercules*? Considering that Hercules was in the title, this seems unlikely since AIP would not be able to use

204

that name without the cooperation of Levine in some way. So the real mystery here is when was this new footage shot and under what circumstances?

This then leads into a bigger question, which is, why didn't Jospeh Levine want *Vengeance of Hercules*? Typically one dumps a franchise after it stops making money. And, as established, even if Reeves was no longer in the role, this film was meant to be the third entry in that continuity.

Clearly, there are a lot of mysteries still left to be solved when it comes to the nebulous origins of *The Vengeance of Hercules* and its acquisition by AIP. Hopefully one day we can learn the answers.

NOTES

---

[1] www.peplumtv.com
[2] http://www.peplumtv.com/2012/12/featured-film-goliath-and-dragon.html
[3] In fact, *Goliath and the Dragon* changed the relationship from father and son to brothers.

FOUR BOYS
LIVING THE
EXCITEMENT
EVERY BOY
DREAMS
ABOUT!...

Suddenly you are plunged into
an age when gigantic monsters
roamed the earth ...when flying
lizards ruled the skies ...when man
discovered fire...in
THE MOST FANTASTIC
ADVENTURE OF ANY AGE!

JOURNEY
TO THE BEGINNING OF TIME

JOURNEY TO THE BEGINNING OF A CLASSIC
BY NEIL RIEBE

One of *Journey to the Beginning of Time's* standout stopmotion sequences.

RELEASE DATE August 5, 1955 (Czechoslovakia) Dec 1960 (U.S.)

DIRECTOR Karel Zeman **SPECIAL EFFECTS** Arnost Kupcik, Jindrich Liska & Karel Zeman **SCREENPLAY** J.A. Novotný & Karel Zeman **MUSIC** E.F. Burian & Frantisek Strangmüller **CAST** Josef Lukáš (Petr / Doc) Petr Herrmann* (Toník/Tony) Zdeněk Husták (Jenda/Ben) Vladimír Bejval (Jirka /Jo-Jo)

1.37 : 1, Color, 93 minutes (Czech)/84 minutes (U.S.)

PLOT Four boys follow a river backwards through time to the age of dinosaurs, or just have a dream in the Museum of Natural history depending upon which version you watch…

COMMENTARY Back in the pre-internet days—or as you might put it, "back in my grandfather's day"—children who loved dinosaurs received dinosaur books and toys from their parents.

207

And then that was it. That was their connection to these "really cool" and wondrous animals. They had to rely on their imaginations to figure out how dinosaurs behaved. Of course, they watched movies like *Valley of Gwangi* and *The Land Unknown*. Saturday mornings, during the 70s, the networks aired the live-action series *The Land of the Lost* and the animated series *Valley of the Dinosaurs*. And then in 1974, Amicus Productions released *The Land That Time Forgot*. The trailer promised to reveal the "secrets of evolution." Aside from the fact all of these shows were great fun, the portrayal of the dinosaurs were little different from their monster-on-the-loose cousins, like the Rhedosaurus from *The Beast From 20,000 Fathoms*, and for the record we never did learn the secret of evolution in *The Land That Time Forgot*.

This is where *Journey to the Beginning of Time* stands heads and shoulders above its peers. The portrayals of the animals felt authentic. After reading the books, a person could look at the movie and say, "Yes, this is what the dinosaurs were like." This was the element, its authenticity, which welled up a sense of wonder in a child that no other motion picture from this time could do. Today, *Jurassic Park* and other big-budget Science Fiction franchises have elbowed this golden oldie from the online conversation. It is only fitting we dedicate a chapter to this classic of the genre.

Journey to the Beginning of Time was derived from a Czechoslovakian film called *Cesta do pravěku*, which means *Journey to Prehistory*. Its creator, Karel Zeman, was an accomplished artist. He was a graphic designer, puppeteer, animator, screenwriter, and film director. "Why do I make films?" he said of his objective in life. "I'm looking for No Man's Land, an island where no filmmaker's foot has yet set foot, a planet where no director has yet raised the explorer's flag, a world that only exists in fairy tales." He was an inspiration to others, such as Terry Gilliam, who was a member of the Monty Python troupe. If you recall, he produced the animations for their show, *Monty Python's Flying Circus*. Even Zeman's daughter, Ludmila Zemanová, followed in his footsteps, becoming an illustrator, animator, screenwriter, and film director. Tim Burton and stop-motion master Ray Harryhausen are counted among his admirers.

Karel Zamen was born on November 3, 1910. He graduated from business school in Kolin. He then enrolled in a school for advertising. After completing his military service, he worked as the head of advertisement at a business called Dům služeb, or

"The House of Services" in English. His work impressed film director Elmar Klos. Klos offered him a job at Zlin film studios, which Zeman accepted. Thus his career in the film industry began.

A Christmas Dream (Vánoční sen) and Inspiration (Inspirace) were two of his standout features. These were released to theaters in 1945 and 1949, respectively. Both combined stop motion puppetry and animation with live action actors, techniques he used for Journey to Prehistory. In A Christmas Dream, a girl pitches her old doll on the floor after seeing the much nicer toys her parents had placed under the Christmas tree for her. That night, the discarded doll comes to life, dances for her, plays the piano, and performs a number of other tricks, proving he can still bring her joy. The girl wakes up to find that the whole escapade was a dream. Yet the dream taught her not to turn her back on an old friend. She retrieves her raggedy doll from the floor and puts it with her other toys. In Inspiration, an artist struggles to come up with an idea for his next project. Frustrated, he sits at the window, staring outside while rain pours down the glass. The camera closes in on a single rain drop until it fills the screen. Inside we see fish swimming among the seaweed and bubbles popping out from the mouth of a clam. One bubble forms a ballerina on the surface of the water. Later a dandelion seed falls onto the rain drop and forms into a clown. The clown becomes enchanted by the ballerina and tries to make her acquaintance, but circumstance keeps them apart. Did he ever find her? We never know. Not that it matters. The point is this: we can draw inspiration from the simplest things. The artist learns this lesson and returns to his bench to begin his next project.

During this same period of time Karel Zeman wrote and directed the Mr. Prokouk series. These short films averaged ten minutes in length. They were similar to the animated Rankin/Bass Christmas specials where the characters were played by stop-motion puppets. The protagonist, Mr. Pokouk, was a man in his late middle years with a mustache and deeply receded hair. He wore glasses and a straw hat. In each of his episodes he gets embroiled in a new adventure, each with its own theme. In one he repurposed a hand-cranked musical instrument into a camera and becomes a filmmaker. In another he was a factory worker puzzling over how to improve his working conditions. Zeman left the series in 1955 to finish Journey to Prehistory, which was already in production since 1953.

According to the CSFD website, Karel Zeman originally wanted to make a movie about going to the moon. The title would have been *Journey to the Moon*. But after seeing the paleo artwork of Zdenko Burian, he changed his mind and wanted his picture to go back in time rather than out into space. Hence *Journey to the Moon* became *Journey to Prehistory*.

The protagonists were four boys—Petr, who kept a log of their expedition, Jirka, the youngest in the troupe, Tonik, who was the group's photographer, and Jenda, who was just one of the gang. The actors who played these roles were, respectively, Josef Lukás, Vladimir Bejval, Petr Hermann, and Zdenek Husták. Vladimir Bejval (Jirka), who was the youngest of the four actors, had the most experience. He was ten years old with nine films under his belt at the time Zeman filmed his part for this movie. After his role as Tonik, Petr Hermann's career expanded into theater and television. Josef Lukás' character, Petr, was the film's narrator, but he did not voice the narration. Sixteen-year-old Bedřich Šetena performed the narration. This was Bedřich's first dubbing role. (Later in life he dubbed Mr. Burns from *The Simpsons*, Mack from the movie *Cars*, and Eugene Krabs from *Spongebob Squarepants*.)

Jirka is the impetus for the story. He finds a trilobite fossil at a cave where there is a river flowing into its mouth and a cross etched in the rock face. Fascinated by his find, he wants to see a living specimen. Of course there are no trilobites alive today. They are extinct. So the three older boys take him to a museum where he sees a wide assortment of fossilized animals. This fails to satisfy him. Later, after reading Jules Verne's *Journey to the Center of the Earth*, Jirka hypothesizes that they could journey back through time if they sailed into the cave where he found the trilobite fossil. Since almost everything else Verne wrote came true, Petr, Jenda, and Tonik figured Jirka's idea might work. The characters in *Journey to the Center of the Earth* encountered prehistoric monsters in the caves in their search for the Earth's core, so maybe the boys would find prehistoric animals in their cave.

They fetch a row boat, enter the cave and come out on the other side in the middle of the Ice Age where the river is frozen solid. The boys drag their boat across the ice until they reach warm waters. Here they spot their first prehistoric animal—a wooly mammoth. Exploring inland, they find a cave. Inside are the remains of a campfire, a mammoth tusk, a *Megaloceros* antler, a stone axe, and cave paintings.

The boys encounter a mammoth on their *Journey to the Beginning of Time.*

After exploring the cave, the boys continue downstream, going further back in time. Their next stop is the Tertiary Period where they see a *Deinotherium,* an ancestor to the elephant, the terror bird *Phorusrhacos,* and the knobby-faced *Uintatherium.* There are also familiar animals such as giraffes, bison, and flamingos.

After the Tertiary they arrive at the Mesozoic Era, the Age of the Dinosaurs. The lineup includes the *Pteranodon, Styracosaurus,* and *Trachodon* from the Cretaceous Period; and the *Brontosaurus, Stegosaurus,* and the carnivorous *Ceratosaurus* from the Jurassic Period. Like junior paleontologists, Petr jots down notes of their encounters while Tonik records them in photographs with his camera.

Zeman employed cartoon animation, stop-motion models, and full-sized puppets. In some cases, like the Brontosaurus, he combined a matt painting of the animal's body with a stop-motion neck and head. The animation is crude but blends in well with the live action elements. The stop-motion creatures are the highlight. The beautifully sculpted wooly mammoth, especially, makes a stunning first impression. Combined with its elephantine sound effects, the wooly beast projects strength and majesty.

The furthest extent the boys go is the Silurian Period, five hundred million years from their starting point. The land is rocky and bleak. There is no life on land but it is abundant in the sea. It is here Jirka finds a living trilobite. He holds it side by side with his fossil. His wish is fulfilled and the film comes to an end.

Journey to Prehistory had many of the same touches Karel Zeman had put in his previous movies. For instance, the four boys lost their fear of the caveman when they saw his paintings on the cave wall. Likewise, the little girl in *A Christmas Dream* took back her doll after it proved it could still make her happy. In both cases the characters learn to find value in others. In another instance the *Ceratosaurus* tried to prey upon the *Stegosaurus*. The *Stegosaurus* fended off his attacker, but he limped away with open wounds in his neck and succumbed to blood loss. His head was framed by the setting sun as his life drained away. No sound effects, such as growling and stomping of feet, were used to juice up the fight. Instead Zeman used the absence of sound to heighten the drama, relying on the character's performance and music. This was the same approach he used with the clown in *Inspiration.* He used the actions of the clown and music to express the clown's struggle to get the attention of the ballerina.

According to online sources, *Journey to Prehistory* sold to 72 countries. No other Czech movie has received that much distribution outside of its native country. Communists saw this film as a useful tool to steer youngsters into accepting "Soviet science" over the Biblical explanation for the origin of the Earth. *Journey to Prehistory* would go on to win a number of awards. Starting in 1956, it won the award for the Ideal Film for Young People at the School Film Working Community Conference in Gelsenkirchen, Germany. In 1957, it won a Special Gold Medal in the International Competition of Professionals, Amateurs, and Film Schools, which was held at the 6th World Youth and Student Festival in Moscow. In 1969, it won the children's award at the Exhibition of Czechoslovak and Foreign Films for Children, which was held in Ostrov, Czechoslovakia.

The boys inspect a dead stegosaurus, in this case a full-scale prop as opposed to a model.

William D'Arcy Cayton produced the U.S. version of *Cesta do pravĕku*, the version dinosaur fans in the United States know as *Journey to the Beginning of Time*. He is an unlikely figure in the American importation of Zeman's film. William graduated from the University of Maryland in 1937 with a degree in engineering, but instead of pursuing a career in this field he founded an advertising agency called Cayton, Inc. This occurred in 1945.

213

Three years later he produced the television program *Greatest Fights of the Century*, which featured vintage footage of boxing matches. From then on boxing dominated his career in one form or another, including as a promoter. Mike Tyson was his most high profile client. This career extended into the 1990s. For ESPN2 he worked as a boxing coordinator for *Friday Night Fights*. His influence on the show has been credited for a resurgence in its ratings. Go to his bio on the International Boxing Hall of Fame website and you will see no mention of *Journey to the Beginning of Time* in his list of accomplishments. He founded, or co-founded, several companies, such as Big Fights, Inc., Cayton Sports, Inc., Radio and Television Packagers, Inc., and Reel Sports, Inc. According to the Insider Peeps website, his net worth totaled $1.7 million dollars.

As something of a side gig, William collaborated with Fred Ladd in dubbing Russian and European animated features for American audiences via Cayton's Radio and Television Packagers, Inc. Anime fans may remember Fred Ladd as the man who brought *Testuwan Astromu*, aka *Astro Boy*, to NBC-TV. For Karel Zeman's *Cesta do pravěku*, they dubbed the film and serialized it into six-minute chapters. The names of the boys changed from Petr to Pete, aka "Doc", Jirka to Jo Jo, Tonik to Tony, and Jenda to Ben.

Fred Ladd reshot a new opening for their version of the movie with new actors to stand in for the originals. They were filmed with their backs to the camera or from a distance to hide the fact these were not the same child actors who played the characters in the Czech version.

Just as in Zeman's version, the boys visit a museum before embarking on their trip down the river, however the original took place in an unnamed museum in Europe and is presented in a montage of photographs taken by Tonik (Tony). In the American version, the scene takes place at The American Museum of Natural History. The first exhibit Pete and the gang view is a display of Native Americans rowing a war canoe. They then proceed to the dinosaur exhibits before circling back to the war canoe where they take a seat on a bench to rest their feet. Amongst the wooden mock-ups of the Indians is a medicine man. The intense stare on his face makes Jo Jo feel as though they are being hypnotized. After their tour of the museum they go canoeing on the lake and spot a cave with an Indian hex sign on the cave's opening. The boys explore the cave and come out on the other side to a river choked with ice. At this point the American footage switches to the original Czech. A new matt painting of the cave with the hex sign replaces the original painting with the cross.

In the original, Petr, Jirka, Tonik, and Jenda entered their cave with the intent of going back in time. In Cayton's version, Peter, Jo Jo, Tony, and Ben are unaware they have gone into the past until after they spot the Wooly Mammoth. Instead of returning to the cave, they decide to push on to see how far they can go. Slight cuts are made to the main body of the original Czech, primarily to the rowing, camping, and journal entry portions of the narrative. There are also alterations in the music and sound effects. For example, roars were added to the battle between the *Stegosaurus* and *Ceratosaurus*.

Some of the film's non-dinosaurian life-forms.

The most noticeable difference is the change of attitude in the characters. Peter and his friends did not gain respect for the unseen Stone Age hunter after finding his cave paintings. Instead, Tony cautions the others, saying, "Just because he can paint doesn't mean he's friendly." Peter is as knowledgeable as his Czech counterpart, Petr, in paleontology but he, Jo Jo, Tony, and Ben are more interested in seeing how far they can go back in time than studying the plants and animals. So instead of stopping in the Silurian period, they push on to the Precambrian. The last portion of Zeman's movie we see is of the boys climbing down from the bluff and stopping at the shoreline to gaze out at the sea. Cayton cut the part where Jirka finds the trilobite and brings his

215

version to a climax with the creation of the Earth itself. Stock footage of flowing, spewing lava is used to represent this event. The scene morphs from oozing molten rock to a colorful mosaic of lights. Peter then quotes verses from Genesis chapter one of the Bible, the chapter which famously begins with, "In the beginning, God created the heaven and the Earth." The boys reached their summit. They arrived at the beginning of time.

Journey to the Beginning of Time ends with Peter, Jo Jo, Tony, and Ben waking up back in The Museum of Natural History under the watchful eye of the Indian medicine man. Peter wonders if their journey had been a dream, but then he notices that his journal shows the wear and tear it had gone through from their trip. We are led to believe the wooden statue of the medicine man did indeed transport them into the past.

Journey to Prehistory has the reputation for being scientifically accurate, but dated by today's standards. But even when this factor is taken into account Zeman's movie is both accurate and inaccurate in many ways. The battle between the *Stegosaurus* and *Ceratosaurus* is an example of where Zeman got it right, unlike Hammer's *One Million Years B.C.* which paired the *Ceratosaurus*, an animal from the Jurassic period, against the *Triceratops*, which lived during the late Cretaceous. *Stegosaurus* lived during the Kimmeridgian through the Tithonian stages of the late Jurassic, which, in total, lasted from 154 million years ago to 145 million. *Ceratosaurus* lived during this time, too. Not only that, their fossil remains have been found in the same rock formation, that being the Morrison Formation in the United States. The likelihood of these two prehistoric beasts encountering each other is very high.

The most significant example of where Zeman got the science right is the inclusion of modern day animals in the Tertiary period. Few books available to the public point out this fact. Flamingos, leopards, vultures, antelopes, and giraffes, all of which were featured in the movie, lived during the Pliocene. The Pliocene, in case the reader is unfamiliar, occurred during the late Tertiary, which spanned from 5.33 million years ago to 2.58. Think of that the next time you see those pink flamingo lawn ornaments. Those birds' great-great-great-great-great-great grandparents shared the Earth with the mastodons, the massive glyptodonts, and saber-tooth cats. They may even had seen these exotic animals with their own eyes.

A small error in the movie was in the order in which the boys encountered the *Uintatherium*, the knobby-faced mammal which resembled a hippo, and the terror bird *Phorusrhacos*. The *Phorusrhacos* should have been seen first because the *Phorusrhacos* lived during the Miocene epoch of the Tertiary period and the *Uintatherium* lived during the Eocene epoch. The Miocene occurred in the middle of the Tertiary, 5.33 million years ago to 23 million, while the Eocene came later, 34 million to 55.9 million years ago. To put it in simpler terms, the *Uintatherium* came on the scene about ten million years after the extinction of the dinosaurs while *Phorusrhacos* showed up forty million years after the extinction, and in between the two time periods, the *Uintatheriums* died out 14 million years before the first generation of the *Phorusrhacos* was born.

Zeman, for whatever reason, completely botched the placement of the trilobites in the geologic timeline. This is astonishing because locating a live specimen was the movie's objective. What's more, Dr. Josef Augusta served as Zeman's advisor. Dr. Augusta was an accomplished paleontologist whose initial studies involved sea life during the Paleozoic era, the era in which the trilobites had lived. Here's the problem. In the film Petr states that the trilobites existed exclusively during the Silurian period, which occurred during the Paleozoic. This is false. Trilobites first appeared in the fossil record dating back to the Cambrian period, which was the first chapter of the Paleozoic. They thrived throughout the era and became extinct at the end of the last chapter, the Permian period. So, Petr and the gang could just as well have gone back to the end of the Permian, about 255 million years or so, rather than five hundred, as stated in the film.

Another problem is the placement of the Silurian period itself. Back in the 1950s, the five hundred million year mark, which was the pivotal point in the movie's plot, fell during the prior period, the Ordovician. Today, the five hundred year mark falls during the Cambrian. To help the reader, the Paleozoic is broken up into six periods. This is the list starting with the most ancient to the least: The Cambrian, Ordovician, Silurian, Devonian, Carboniferous, and the Permian. Geologists update the duration of these periods as per advancements in their science. For example, in 1962 the Silurian period ranged from 425-405 million years ago (source: *Fossils: A Golden Guide*, copyright 1962). Today the duration is 443.8-419.2 million years ago (source: United States Geologic Survey publication, August 2018).

The description of the Silurian period is also incorrect. There were terrestrial plants during this period. They were scraggily compared to today's foliage, but nevertheless they were present. The land was not barren and rocky as shown in the movie, although the movie is correct in saying there were no land plants five hundred million years ago.

The problem could have been solved by saying the protagonists had to go back five hundred million years to the early days of the Ordovician period, and then say they needed to locate a specific specie of trilobite which was endemic to that time period. Why this was not done is hard to say. Perhaps the error was a deliberate artistic license on Zeman's part. "Silurian" rolls off the tongue more eloquently than "Ordovician" and he may have thought by placing the trilobites exclusively at the five hundred million year mark made it easier for moviegoers to follow the story. Just as the occurrence of the *Phorusrhacos* scene may have been done for entertainment purposes as that scene is more exciting than the scene with the *Uintatherium*.

The errors were even more inexplicable in the US version of the movie. Did William Cayton tap a paleontologist's expertise? He sure did—Dr. Edwin H. Colbert. At the time Dr. Colbert was the chairman and curator of the Department of Vertebrate Paleontology at the American Museum of Natural History and had authored more than two hundred scientific papers and several books, including the popular *Dinosaurs: Their Discovery and Their World.*

Cayton and Ladd's script said the *Brontosaurus* was the largest dinosaur that had ever lived. Incorrect. The *Brachiosaurus* was even larger. Also according to the script, the *Stegosaurus* lived a hundred million years ago. Incorrect. According to the geologic timeline in Dr. Colbert's book, *Dinosaurs: Their Discovery and Their World,* the time should be about 140 million years ago. Dr. Colbert's book lists the lizards as a separate lineage of reptiles from the dinosaurs while in Cayton's version of the movie the lizards are said to be the direct descendants of the dinosaurs. All of these errors pop up during the scene at the American Museum of Natural History, 'the very same museum Dr. Colbert held his position as chairman. One cannot help but wonder how much involvement Colbert had in Cayton's project.

Cayton's version did correct Zeman's geologic timeline error by moving the last scene with the boys from the Silurian to the Precambrian. The land was indeed barren during this time. Plant and animal life was confined to the sea. Despite these flaws, both Karel Zeman's *Cesta do pravěku,* aka *Journey to Prehistory,* and William Cayton's *Journey to the Beginning of Time* still rank as the most scientifically accurate movies in their class. Only purists would take issue with the errors. After all, the *Brontosaurus* may not have been the largest dinosaur, but he was a sauropod, just like the *Brachiosaurus,* and the sauropods were the largest land animals that had ever walked the earth.

For further reading, Martin Arlt published an article about *Journey to the Beginning of Time* in issue #32 of his magazine *Mad Scientist.* Derrick Davis dedicated a video about both versions of the film on his Youtube channel, Jurassic Time. Lastly, the Criterion Collection has released both the original Czech and American versions of the film on their *Three Fantastic Journeys by Karel Zeman* DVD\Blu Ray set.

SOURCES

Karel Zeman's Wiki page, both Czech and English

Journey to the Beginning of Time Wiki page

Cesta do pravĕku Wiki page

William Cayton & Fredd Ladd's Wiki pages

Vladimir Bejval's Wiki page

Petr Hermann's Wiki page

Bedřich Šetena's Wiki page

All other online sources are noted in the body of the text

BIBLIOGRAPHY

Colbert, Dr. Edwin. *Dinosaurs, Their Discovery and Their World.* New York: E.P. Dutton & Co., Inc., 1961.

Rhodes, Frank H.T. and Herbert S. Zim & Paul R. Shaffer. *Fossils.* Racine, Wisconsin: Western Publishing Company, Inc., 1962.

* Astute readers will notice that the actor listed for Tonik in the Czech version is Petr Hermann while in the American version the actor named for the same character is Peter Hermann. The likelihood Fredd Ladd and William Clayton hired a child actor with the same name as the Czech actor for their reshoots is highly unlikely. Perhaps it was an error. In any case, the names shown in this chapter were taken from the cast list as shown in the film credits of both movies.

KURU ISLAND &
GORGO'S WORLD TOUR OF DESTRCUTION

ORIGINALLY PUBLISHED IN *THE LOST FILMS FANZINE PRESENTS MOVIE MILESTONES* #4

Beautiful concept paintings by Edgar Kiechle, some of which depict Ogra attacking Paris and also London. Before Paris, the King Bros also considered having the monster attack Australia. However, they decided against it because "there are no monuments in Australia, and besides, who cares if a monster destroys Australia?" According to Eugène Lourié, Rome and Madrid were also considered for a time.

RELEASE DATE March 29, 1961 (U.S.)

DIRECTOR Eugène Lourié **SPECIAL EFFECTS** Tom Howard **SCREENPLAY** Robert L. Richards, Daniel James & Eugène Lourié (story) **MUSIC** Angelo Francesco Lavagnino **CAST** Bill Travers (Captain Joe Ryan) William Sylvester (Sam Slade) Vincent Winter (Sean) Christopher Rhodes (Harbour Master) Joseph O'Conor (Professor Hendricks) Bruce Seton (Professor Flaherty) Martin Benson (Dorkin)

Spherical, Technicolor, 78 Minutes

PLOT While searching for treasure off the coast of Ireland's Nara Island, Captain Joe Ryan and his ship barely survive a volcanic eruption at sea. Ryan and his friend/first officer, Sam Slade, come ashore to make arrangements for repairs. There they meet the harbor master and his young ward, Sean. Not long after, an enormous sea monster surfaces and attacks the village before

223

being driven away. Ryan and Slade make a deal to capture the creature in return for a share of some of the hidden treasure found in the area. Slade and Ryan capture the monster via a huge net, and then transport it back to London, where it is slated to be sold to Dorkin's Circus. Unbeknownst to the men, Sean has stowed away to keep the monster company. As such, when they arrive in England, Sean becomes the two men's ward. The monster is given the moniker of Gorgo and becomes a popular attraction at the circus. It's eventually learned that little Gorgo is only an infant, and his mother, Ogra, is on her way to London. The even more massive Ogra surfaces and destroys most of London on her way to the circus. Meanwhile, Sean is lost in the chaos and rescued by Ryan, while Ogra rescues Gorgo. Despite the best efforts of the military, the mother monster and her infant make their way safely back to the sea and disappear.

Beautiful concept paintings by Edgar Kiechle depicting the monster in a quadruped stance.

COMMENTARY In an era of stop motion monsters, 1961's *Gorgo* always stood out in the west because the monster was brought to life through the distinctly Japanese suitmation technique. Perhaps it shouldn't come as a surprise then that *Gorgo* actually has some roots in Japan. It all started with the King Brothers' very successful U.S. distribution of *Rodan*. As a result, they wanted to create their own giant monster. They also had a unique angle to their idea, that being that the giant monster be captured by a circus. The King Brothers made a deal with an unnamed Japanese studio, which was most likely Toho since they had worked with them to distribute *Rodan*. From what we can piece together, they secured a deal with the mystery studio in Japan sometime in 1958 (which makes sense, since *Rodan* was released in the U.S. in 1957 and had generated huge profits). With the U.S.-Japan co-production secured, the King Brothers next needed a director.

Concept painting by Edgar Kiechle showing Gorgo loose in Paris.

Due to his success directing *The Beast from 20,000 Fathoms* (1953) and *The Giant Behemoth* (1959), the King Brothers approached Eugène Lourié. Lourié wasn't exactly itching to make another such film, and was actually working on another project that would ultimately go unmade. He told Paul Mandell in *Fantastic Films* that, "This type of picture was not in my mind at the time—I had hoped to realize an ultra-modern science fiction story called *Moonwreck* which I had adapted from a British SF novel. But after some reflection, I saw many possible variations on the same theme—a helpless sea monster against a city. I also remembered, quite vividly, the incident with my daughter and *The Beast From 20,000 Fathoms*. Here was the occasion to repair my wrongs against the sea monster species!"

225

Lourié's concept drawing of Gorgo. Take note of the fact that the man holding the spear appears to be a pearl diver, and certainly doesn't look like a Nara Islander from Ireland.

A closer detail on the head by Lourié.

The incident that Lourie speaks of with his daughter involved a promise he had made to her after her disappointment in *The Beast's* ending. She had apparently told her father, "You are bad, Daddy! You killed the big nice Beast!" Lourié told Mandell that, "I knew that someday I would have to write a story in which the creature does not die—it just goes away!"

The story, which was mandated to be set in Japan, was co-written with Lourié's friend and collaborator Daniel James (under the name David Hyatt) and was titled *Kuru Island*. It is similar to *Gorgo* but with a huge difference in location being set in Japan and the South Pacific. Paul Mandell described his recollection of the story as being set on "a fictitious atoll in the South Pacific where cultured pearls were the main export. After a tremendous storm and an underwater eruption, the baby creature surfaces and adheres [sic] to the island. Tidal waves and other phenomena mark the unbalancing of the environment. The beast was to have been captured and brought to a Tokyo zoo for observation when the mother beast surfaces to rescue it." The only other details known about the script was that it had a reverence for nature, a few of the main characters would be pearl divers, and the opening volcanic eruption seen in *Gorgo* was also present in *Kuru Island*. Bill Cooke's *Gorgo* book also offers a similar synopsis: "...an oceanic earthquake unleashes a sea monster that is captured by a couple of pearl divers off said island and brought to the Tokyo Zoo for study. But in a surprising plot development, the creature's much-larger parent soon surfaces, trampling through the city in search for her stolen offspring."

Gorgo, or rather, Ogra, on the loose.

Lourié was keen on making a "poetic" non-violent monster film. He told Mandell, "I wanted the creature to confront human beings but there were no scenes of the military shooting at it and not being able to destroy it. That concept is really ridiculous... The

228

creature was not supposed to destroy the town, and there were no stock shots planned of military intervention." The basis for Lourié's story was centered instead on motherly love over conflict with the military. He was sure the idea would appeal to the King Brothers, whom Lourié said, "I believe they had a bit of a mother complex." However, later when it would come time to shoot, the King Brothers made sure to add in plenty of city destruction and military battles.

Other than the previous statements, we unfortunately don't know much about more specific details of *Kuru Island*. It is said that the first treatment was ten pages long, and that it was approved by the financers in Japan. In August of 1958, they began work on a full *Kuru Island* script and were allotted two months to complete it. In November of 1958, just as the duo were finishing up the last pages of the script, the deal fell through with the mystery Japanese studio and the King Brothers were on their own.

Once the Japanese studio was out, the King Brothers no longer had any interest in setting or shooting the picture in Japan. Lourié remembered to Paul Mandell that, "After living intensely with my Japanese and Pacific native characters for two months, it was impossible for me to do a rewrite and change the locale to some European country." Or, in other words, *Kuru Island* was culturally tailored to Japan, and retrofitting the story wouldn't be as simple as switching the locales to another country. (I don't know of any pearl divers off the coast of Ireland, do you?)

Rather than Lourié, it was the King Brothers who started brainstorming ideas for alternate locations. Specifically, they had their sights set on Paris. In an interview with Art Buchwald in his column on May 18, 1959, Maurice King told him, "We're going to destroy Paris like it's never been destroyed before. Frank's dying to because of the prices. But Paris has something. Tokyo's already been destroyed [on-screen and in real life], and so has Berlin. And King Kong wrecked New York." King also added that, "In trying to find her baby, [the mother monster] wrecks the Eiffel Tower, the Arc de Triomphe, the Louvre, the Opera, the Grand Palais and two bridges on the Seine."

However, only Lourié thought through the realities of the scenario. Lourié said, "During my meetings with the King brothers, they expressed their desire to have the climax happen in Paris. 'Think, Gene,' pleaded Frank King, 'how spectacular it would be if the monster were to climb the Eiffel Tower!' When I told him that Paris is at least 250 miles from the sea, he doubted my words."

In searching for a new location, London was the one finally slated for demolition. Elsewhere, a new writer, Robert L. Richards under the alias of John Loring, was hired to overhaul *Kuru Island* to match the new characters and settings. Many of the ideas were retained, such as opening with a volcanic eruption, the mother and baby monster, and so on. What differed was the removal of Lourié's theme of imbalance of nature. The new theme inserted by Loring was the peril of humanity's greed. The new writer also inserted exactly what the King Brothers had wanted from the beginning: military on monster action, which Lourié had been reluctant to include. Upon reading the new script, Lourié almost wanted to reject it. "It was enough to make me lose heart over the project. But I wanted to direct the film," Lourié told Mandell.

Though it's unknown what the monster's name had been in *Kuru Island*, now it was Gorgo, so named after the Gorgosaurus ("a gigantic carnivore saurian that lived during the Upper Cretaceous and resembled the Tyrannosaurus Rex", according to a Dr. J. Augusta in a book on prehistoric animals).

Lourié said of the finished *Gorgo* script, "The story as originally conceived was far more poetic. But the King Brothers butchered the idea entirely." Lourié also cut the film together to his liking, and then had to go on to work another job in early 1960. During this time, the King Brothers recut the film the way they wanted, adding in a multitude of military stock shots. "[Depth] charges were being dropped, planes crisscrossed the skies, explosives were added! When I expressed my doubts to the King brothers, they assured me that they knew the taste of audiences better than me... maybe they knew?"

Lourié was so disappointed with the additions of graphic city destruction and military conflict that in later years, he even edited his own version of *Gorgo*. He told Mandell, "I recently acquired an old print of *Gorgo*...and made a 35-minute version by taking out all those unnecessary scenes. Everything was so much better." This cut was created during the year 1980 (or possibly sometime prior), but no one knows if it was ever shown in any official capacity.

GORGO'S DELETED SCENE *Gorgo* had several ambitious scripted scenes that were never filmed such as a scuffle with a giant octopus that may have been present in the *Kuru Island* script. The scene was to have Joe and Sam diving amongst a graveyard of Viking ships only to be pursued by a killer whale. As the duo hides out in one of the ships, they find it to be home to a giant octopus, which naturally attacks them. After struggling in the grasp of the beast's tentacles, baby Gorgo makes his entrance shrouded by a cloud of ink from the octopus:

BACK TO SCENE - ANOTHER ANGLE - THE TWO   59
as Joe charges in, CAMERA MOVING with him. Sam has dropped
his flare, and it now lies a little distance below on the
rocky bottom. As Joe comes in, another tentacle whips out
for him, and now we can see the huge, dirty-green body of
the thing and its great, staring, saucer-eyes. But Joe
does not make the mistake of trying to avoid the tentacle.
He fights only to keep his arms and gun free, and rides
in with the snake-like arm, Intent only on getting in
close enough for a killing shot. Sam by now is almost
help-less. With a half-Imprisoned arm, he is trying to
cut through a truck tire with a Jackknife. Another
tentacle has coiled around Joe, but he drives in.

And now, straight between the eyes of the thing, he fires.
There is a dull, muffled explosion (the exploding tip of
the harpoon). The great octopus shudders violently, its
color changes rapidly from the dirty-green to a reddish-
brown, its tentacles loosen and become limp, and, as the
two men struggle free, in its death agony, it emits a
great, jetting cloud of black ink, all but obliterating
the scene.

Joe and Sam pull back a little, close together.

CLOSE SHOT - JOE   60
his anxious face seen through his face plate, looking at
Sam.

TWO SHOT   61
as Sam, exhausted, nevertheless gestures that he's okay.
Now the two look around, looking upward through the murk,
the killer whale not forgotten.

WHAT THEY SEE: 62
dimly through the darkly clouded waters, a shadow passing
over. The whale has not forgotten them.

Other unfilmed scenes included baby Gorgo scuffling with a circus elephant and Ogra destroying a lighthouse.

BACK TO SCENE   63
as Joe gestures caution. They are in no shape for another
fight at the moment. From his belt, Joe gets another
charge for the harpoon gun, loads it. Prom somewhat below,
the flare glows dimly. Then suddenly there is a
tremendous, thrashing turmoil in the water above them.
They look up quickly, SEE:

WHAT THEY SEE: 64
Through the murk and the wildly turbulent water, they can
see only something fantastically big and vague, like a
great thundercloud. The water is whipped to fury. Then
all at once there is a great jetting gush of blood that
crimsons the water all around, blotting out everything in
a swirling red haze.

BACK TO SCENE   65
as the two cling to the rook formation, staring up-wards,
staring at each other.

Fantastic Films alludes to the scene being filmed as Mandell wrote that "For
an early sequence in *Gorgo* where divers are attacked by an octopus, a deep
tank was used on the main stage." Though we can't find any evidence of the
scene being shot, it was at least included in the film's comic book adaptation.

ROOTS OF REPTILICUS
TO FLY OR NOT TO FLY?

ORIGINALLY PUBLISHED IN *THE LOST FILMS FANZINE PRESENTS MOVIE MILESTONES* #4

Still from the infamous flying scene of *Reptilicus.*

RELEASE DATE February 20, 1961 (Denmark), January 1963 (U.S.)

DIRECTORS Sid Pink [U.S. version] Poul Bang [Danish version] **SPECIAL EFFECTS** Kai Koed & Orla Høyer **SCREENPLAY** Ib Melchior & Sid Pink **MUSIC** Sven Gyldmark **CAST** Carl Ottosen (General Mark Grayson) Ann Smyrner (Lise Martens) Mimi Heinrich (Karen Martens) Bent Mejding (Svend Viltorft) Asbjørn Andersen (Professor Otto Martens) Bodil Miller (Connie Miller) [Danish version] Marla Behrens (Connie Miller) [American version] Povl Wøldike (Dr. Peter Dalby) Dirch Passer (Peterson) Ole Wisborg (Captain Brandt)

Spherical, Pathécolor, 82 Minutes (U.S.) 92 Minutes (Denmark)

LA GLOBE FILMS INTERNATIONAL PRESENTA UNA ESCLUSIVITA' AMERICAN INTERNATIONAL PICTURES

REPTILICUS

CARL OTTOSEN
ANN SMYRNER

SOGGETTO DI SID PINK   SCENEGGIATURA DI IB MELCHIOR E SID PINK
PRODOTTO E DIRETTO DA SIDNEY PINK   UNA PRODUZIONE CINEMAGIC

TECHNICOLOR

PLOT As a mining crew drills into the earth, they bore into the still fresh remains of a prehistoric monster. A severed tail is found and transported to Copenhagen, where it is studied by Professor Otto Martens. There, too, is the man who discovered it, Svend Viltorft,

235

who falls in love with Martens' youngest daughter, Karen. When the sample begins to regenerate into a new lifeform, General Mark Grayson is called in to keep an eye on it. Eventually the specimen, dubbed Reptilicus, grows too large to be contained and escapes. It ravages the countryside and develops strange new abilities (flight in the Danish version and green acid in the U.S. cut). Professor Martens becomes despondent when explosives are used on the monster and has a heart attack. Martens is smart enough to realize that if the monster is blown to bits more monsters will spawn from its remains. As such, it is decided to launch a massive tranquilizer into the monster's mouth as it attacks Copenhagen. Grayson fires the shot, knocking the monster out so that it can be destroyed thoroughly. However, on the ocean floor, a severed foot belonging to the monster is already spawning.

THE LOST PROP? According to Danish publicity materials from the time, a 32-foot-long Reptilicus model was created which had the ability to shoot smoke from its nostrils and had flashing eyes. It would seem this was either an invention of the press or something that went unused entirely though the former is more likely. Most likely, one of the two props seen above were all that existed.

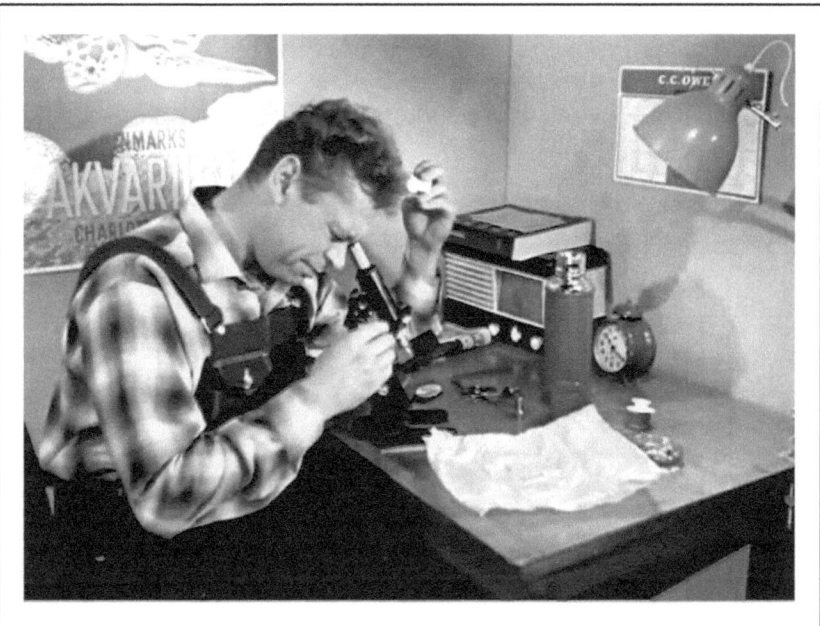

Dirch Passer, above as Peterson, was so popular at the time that Saga Studios flirted with titling their version of the film *Dirch and the Dragon.*

COMMENTARY *Reptilicus* began life with *The Angry Red Planet* (1959), a hit release for American International Pictures, which was written and directed by Ib Melchior and produced by Sid Pink. AIP wanted more pictures from the duo and signed them up for two more. And, because Melchior and Pink both had connections to Denmark, it was decided to shoot the two new pictures there in conjunction with AIP and Danish studio, Saga Productions. One of the films would be similar to *The Angry Red Planet*, and was titled *Journey to the Seventh Planet*, and the other was an as yet unnamed monster movie. Like the King Bros with *Gorgo*, AIP was encouraged by the giant monster genre from Japan in suggesting a giant monster flick (they may have been aware of *Gorgo's* production, too).

When AIP suggested this, Melchior essentially created a new storyline out of two lost projects. For the basic story structure and characters, he resuscitated an old script called *The Volcano Monsters*. The other was a non-monster movie Melchior had dreamed up that had to do with scientists creating a serum that could regenerate severed limbs and body parts (the idea being to

237

create an "indestructible society"). That idea had come to him from the regenerative properties of starfish and lizards, the latter of which has the ability to regenerate its severed tail. In this case, Melchior decided to do the opposite, the severed tail would regenerate into a new monster!

His opening scene, where the tail is discovered by a mining crew, was also lifted from another unproduced script from 1958 called *The Micro-Men*. (The unmade story told of an ancient meteor, buried underground, that is found to contain microscopic spores of intelligence that virally infect the discoverers to take over their minds). According to Melchior, AIP's rather unimaginative story pitch simply had the monster showing up from out of nowhere, and Melchior felt the regeneration idea would set the story apart, and it did.

The initial story meeting had occurred in early March, and by March 14th, AIP had officially greenlit the film. As far as we know, Ib Melchior's story for *Reptilicus* didn't change much in terms of the basic outline, but the monster's design/abilities definitely evolved along the way. Originally, Melchior envisioned Reptilicus as a "serpent with a bat's head," and later he described it as a combination between a sauropod-type dinosaur and a Pteranodon. As for the monster's wings, it's unknown who for sure added them (they may have been purely ornamental as far as Melchior was concerned), but it was Sid Pink's idea to make the monster fly. In Melchior's mind, it made sense for the monster to escape the lab and continue to grow in the canals of Copenhagen, where it would be confined to the city. Melchior told Brett Homenick:

I did not describe him as flying. Sid put that in. I like logic. I like things to be explained, and I want it to make sense. Now Reptilicus is confined to Copenhagen. He can't go anywhere else than Copenhagen. If he's there, he has to do what he does in Copenhagen because he's really trapped there. But if he could fly, he could fly anywhere he wanted! If they started shooting at him in Copenhagen, then he could fly down to Africa or whatever he wanted to do. So it didn't make sense to have him fly.[1]

Another thing that wasn't originally in the picture was the silly Peterson character, written specifically for Danish superstar Dirch Passer. Along with Passer came a few Danish musical numbers too. Of course, we could go on and on about the minute differences from script to screen concerning the dialogue and the "people parts," but you want to know about the discarded monster scenes, so here they are:

During the first confrontation with the military, there was to be a scene of Reptilicus chasing a soldier. The man, a machine gunner, abandons his post, and the monster slithers after him. Minus the shot direction, the script reads:

> He is following the running soldier with his hideous head – Then he opens his mouth wide – and begins to lower his head towards the ground..... Far below the soldier is running – terror stricken; he stumbles, and falls; across him. Reptilicus is bending down; with his gigantic jaws he picks up the screaming man – and crushes him..... Like an enraged Terrier with a rat the monster shakes the lifeless body of the soldier – and flings it into the trees.....[2]

Another exciting deleted scene occurs towards the end of the depth charge sequence. The scripts states:

> Out of the swirling, bubbling water the hideous head of Reptilicus is rising... In front of the patrol boat the head and long neck of the monster rises out of the deep – looming over the boat..... Still nakedly hairless – still staring with blinded, scorched eyes – it crashes down on top of the boat with a deep roar, smashing it – and carrying the shattered pieces and the crew with it beneath the turbulent, seething water....![3]

Notably it is at this point that the doctor has a heart attack at the sight of the accident.

As scripted, the flying scenes were also much more ambitious. When the monster flies over Hamburg, Germany, it was intended to land: "The big, ornate, German Renaissance City Hall building looms large in the F.G.......... Reptilicus comes flying towards it – and lands thunderously on its roof; one of the beast's huge wings strike the tower – shearing it off............ The tower topples – and crashes down on top of several other buildings...."[4]

The script describes several other buildings tumbling down like dominoes and then returns to the monster who, on top of the building, flaps his wings and roars. Reptilicus takes off again as his tail and rear legs "hit and demolish some tall buildings nearby..." Reptilicus continues his flight through the city as various German soldiers fire upon him:

> Reptilicus is flying low over the dock area; below can be seen the skeletal structures of the huge cranes and lifts........... A searchlight beam hits him square in the face – blinding him............ He throws his head back and bellows angrily; he makes a sharp turn in the air........... Reptilicus momentarily blinded by the searchlight, crashes into one of the tall cranes..... He makes a heavy, destructive landing on the docks, tearing and ripping buildings and equipment alike.[5]

Some more destruction ensues, and the script states that with "a lumbering run" the monster takes off and flies away from the heart of the city.

Just as *Gorgo* had a deleted scene involving a circus elephant, here too Reptilicus was to scuffle with animals. The monster was to fly over a zoo where elephants would trumpet in horror which would in turn get all of the other animals to "roaring, shrieking, howling and trumpeting their fear... In a cacophony of bloodcurdling noise..."[6]

Reptilicus answers the cries of the animals with a roar of his own then, "suddenly Reptilicus makes a swooping pass at the lion compound; with his huge, powerful rear legs he levels the moat that isolates the compound; his tail lashes out – felling trees and leveling small structures...." As such, the lions escape to terrorize the people at the zoo as the monster flies away, leaving the city in ruins.[7]

Later in the script, the monster's wings, which had been damaged in the previous scene, are described as simply skeletal remains which the monster flaps in a vain effort to fly. Among the more amusing deleted bits from the climactic city destruction was a sequence of a man who runs into a house of mirrors to seek shelter. As he tries to find a way out he only sees "grotesquely distorted images of himself..." Eventually the monster crushes the mirror house in what sounded to be a frightening scene. There was also to be a scene of a mother and young daughter taking refuge from the monster inside of an abandoned building which it passes by and demolishes.

The monster was also supposed to single out and destroy a couple of machine gunners on a rooftop. Specifically, he was going to use his tiny arm to somehow knock them off the roof.

The comically tiny arms come in to play again in the script, clearly written before the monster prop was created. The shot envisioned the monster seeing a big electric sign on one of the corners of the buildings. For some reason he becomes angry at it and "with his grotesque little forelimbs he rips the structure from the building hurtling it to the ground, as sparks and puffs of smoke crackle and explode from the shorted live wires."

After this, the screenplay plays out as in the finished film.

THE LOST CUT Today, the original English language audio has never surfaced, making it a lost cut in a way (though, who really wants to see it?). Apparently this lost version was similar to the Danish version aside from excising the musical numbers (the flying scenes were still present at this point.) Sid Pink said, "AIP converted my version. My version doesn't exist anymore."[8]

Melchior, being fluid in Danish and English, was supposed to get to direct the English version of the film. But, for some strange reason, Pink directed it instead. (In retrospect, perhaps Melchior should be glad that he did.) The reason for the switch may have been due to the Danish production partner, Saga Studios, which Pink had connections to.

THE GERMAN REPTILICUS??? In addition to the Danish and English versions of *Reptilicus*, there was almost a third German version according to several sources. According to an article on actress Hanne Smyrner, entitled "Hanne's Big Ambitions" and appearing in the August 6, 1960 issue of *Billedbladet*, the actress had to relearn her role in three languages! She also mentions that the Germans were unable to "partake in the great work." Likewise, the actor who played Svend (Bent Mejding) said that, "We did two versions: one in Danish and one in English. We also should have done a German version. But the Germans slipped out of it before the shooting started." Despite those two comments, producer Sid Pink ascertains that the film was only ever a Danish and U.S. co-production.

Reptilicus is also unique because two distinct versions of the film were planned from the beginning. (Unlike *Godzilla, King of the Monsters!*, where new actors were inserted later.) Two versions of the film would be shot simultaneously with Pink directing the English language version, and Poul Bang directing the Danish version (though Pink reportedly hovered in the background to backseat direct). Basically, the same actors filmed their scenes twice. Once for the Danish version and again for the English speaking version. As such, you can watch the same scenes not just in a different language, but from different angles and with different dialogue.

242

The film was shot in the summer of 1960 over 86 days. Denmark welcomed the production with open arms, allowing the producers the needed publicity to generate extras for the "panicked crowd" shots necessary for any giant monster flick. (Around a thousand extras participated in the famous drawbridge scene, including the Bicycle Club which happily agreed to plummet into the waters below – so apparently those weren't trained stuntmen!) Also thanks to Saga Studios owner, Fleming John Olsen, who had a great deal of influence in the Social Democratic Party, the Danish Army and Navy were used extensively for the battle scenes. In other words, all the military footage is new, unlike *Gorgo's* stock shots. As such, *Reptilicus* has a grand polished look unbefitting of its Z-Grade monster puppet.

As it was, the Danish effects technicians from Saga were not up to the task of creating a convincing monster. Reptilicus certainly had a cool design, it just wasn't brought to life adequately. (It wouldn't even pass muster in a peplum movie where it wasn't the focus of the story.) Going off of rare behind the scenes photos, the two Reptilicus puppets looked to be between four to seven feet long. (Truthfully, had they really cared about the film, they should have scrapped the existing footage and hired Ray Harryhausen to create the monster in post-production.)

When the film premiered in Denmark in February of 1961, it was not surprisingly met with laughter and heckling. Reviews were naturally also poor. When AIP executive/founder Samuel Z. Arkoff saw the film he was mortified, not only by the monster but by the performances as well. Since the actors were Danish, they therefore had thick Danish accents in all of their scenes. As such, the English footage would still have to be dubbed over to mask the thick accents of most of the cast. (In a way, they shot it twice for nothing, the only benefit in this method was that the mouths would at least match the words coming out of them unlike the Godzilla movies.) For a time, AIP decided not to distribute the movie at all, hence the fact that Pink sued them. However, when Pink's own lawyer looked at the awful footage he advised Pink to drop the case!

However, Arkoff eventually talked to Melchior about the troubled film, asking him if he thought it was possible to save it through a recut. Melchior told Brett Homenick on Vantage Point Interviews:

So I doctored up *Reptilicus*. There were no close-ups, so we had to do some close-ups of objects, so we could have something to cut away from it. And I did some re-editing, and I put in a couple of extra scenes that we could do without the actors, and the end result was that AIP accepted the film and distributed it.[9]

AIP ultimately decided to cut out the now infamous scenes of the monster flying, nor did the new dubbing script ever reference the creature's ability to fly. Instead, the U.S. version gave the monster its own unique power, the ability to spew a green slime from its mouth. (As such, this necessitated new dialogue to be looped in that was never in the shooting script.) The green slime also served as a way for the monster to greater menace the extras, as there seemed to be a disconnect between the monster and the fleeing humans, which never shared the same shot together.

In addition to cutting the shoddier footage, they also shortened shots of the monster that they did retain. To try and improve the scenes of the monster that they kept, it was double-frame printed and slowed down. This added a sense of scale to the monster and the double-printing helped to hide some of the pesky wires. (This is why the U.S. version of *Reptilicus* has "grainy" footage of the monster that seems mismatched.) Smoke and fire burning in the background were also optically inserted into shots as well. Because they had little faith in the film and were on the cheap, AIP hired the Ray Mercer Company to do the optical printing. As the cheapest optical printers in the business, AIP got what they paid for.

Reptilicus was dubbed at Titra, which often handled Toho's Godzilla and special effects films. Furthermore, writer Ib Melchior also dubbed half a dozen characters according to his testimony. The film was finally released in the U.S. in 1963, two years after its Danish premiere. Though poorly reviewed, the film still grossed around $800,000 in U.S., which was respectable for the time.

Amazingly, *Reptilicus* has managed to endure all these years, perhaps thanks to rather than in spite of the terrible puppet similar to *The Giant Claw*. It's actually possible that the movie would be less well-remembered if it had a good monster on screen!

REPTILICUS - THE DANISH CUT

Cast photo featuring the Danish version of Connie (third from left) played by Bodil Miller.

For many years, before the internet made things easier for lovers of rare films, western fans long bemoaned that the Danish cut of *Reptilicus* had extra monster footage. Specifically, most all sources acted as though the only extra monster footage comprised of the famous flying scene, but this is not the case. Not only does the Danish cut of *Reptilicus* contain more unique monster footage than just that, as it turns out, so does the AIP cut. Considering that both cuts had very little precise footage in common (as both shot their own versions of each scene), an exhaustive study of the differences between the two versions will not be attempted in this section. Instead, we'll just hit the highlights.

The two cuts differ from the start, as the Danish version has credits that play over a serene landscape to like music. AIP's version has only a few moments of this, just long enough to show the AIP logo for a few dramatic bars of music. This landscape footage is also narrated, telling us where we are, while the Danish version is not. Furthermore, when the flesh is discovered on the drill, the title, in blood dripping red letters, displays over Svend's

245

bloody gloves. This is much better than Danish version which superimposed the title in rather bland font over the landscape footage. (The title placed over the bloody gloves is also how Melchior scripted it, so the Danish version deviated from his vision in that case.) The gore in the discovery is different too. The U.S. version utilizes closeups of the flesh caught on the drill, but the Danish version uses a longshot. The Danish cut also shows a brief shot of what looks to be a tiny Reptilicus foot in the wheel barrel, though it's hard to tell (whatever it is, it's not in the U.S. version).

Jumping ahead a bit, the U.S. version has some wide exterior shots of Copenhagen identifying it as such, while the Danish version does not. Most of the extra ten minutes worth of footage in the Danish version is dedicated to the relationship between the Martens sisters and Svend. There's a scene of the two sisters together in their room that isn't in AIP's version, which reveals to us that Lise is coming off of a bad breakup. There is also an extra scene of Svend and Karen on the beach together, where Svend seems frustrated.

There's also a significant casting change we need to discuss before we go any further. The Connie Miller character is played by a different actress in both versions. The U.S. version of the character is blonde (Marlies Behrens) while the other is dark-haired (Bodil Miller). Regarding Connie, after the reporters observe the creature in the tank for the first time, there's a short, heated exchange between General Grayson and Connie in the Danish version only. On the note of the tank, the U.S. version shows fluid circulating within it, while the Danish cut does not (this was likely new footage filmed by AIP in the States for the recut). The U.S. version follows the tank scene with a barrage of headlines, while the Danish version follows it with Professor Martens listening to a recording he made. It describes Reptilicus growing in a fetal position, and its bodily characteristics including the bat-like wings that the U.S. cut ignored. (This scene is in the U.S. version, but placed elsewhere and minus mention of the wings.) Martens' scene in the Danish cut is followed by another, happier beach scene between Svend and Karen, where they profess their love.

For the most part, the Danish version of *Reptilicus* is just fine up until the thirty minute mark. Up until this point, it's like watching the U.S. version from different angles and in a different language. But then comes the song and dance number... As Peterson sits outside reading the paper, he is suddenly surrounded by a group of children and they all break into song together about Reptilicus (shortened to 'Tilicus for the song)! It's truly bizarre tonally speaking. But, such scenes were common in Danish films back then, so for them it wouldn't have been odd apparently. On the note of Peterson, two of his comical scenes are compressed together for the U.S. cut, which features the scene of him eating a sandwich and playing with a microscope back to back with the electric eel scene. (The Danish cut splits those two scenes up.) In the infamous eel scene, Peterson cries for his mother in Danish, too.

In the U.S. version, following Peterson's scare, we get the scene of Professor Martens listening to his tape recorder that occurred earlier in the Danish cut. As the tape plays, here we get shots of the infantile Reptilicus, but they are so close up its difficult to know what we are looking at. Notably, Martens' narration includes mention of the corrosive slime added into AIP's version, and no mention of the wings.

After this, both versions feature a little travelogue sequence featuring the Tivoli Nights musical number. In both, Grayson takes Connie out on the town, though a different actress figures into each cut. The Danish version has some extra footage in this section of the film. After Peterson's microscope scene in the Danish version, we cut to Martens' country home, where the family and Svend are vacationing—nothing of any real consequence happens. (We do get a scene of Lise trying on dresses in a hope that she can steal Grayson away from Connie.) The sequence ends with Grayson and Connie driving up to the house for some social time, and we cut back to the lab. There, the Danish version lacks shots of the slimy Reptilicus stirring in its tank present in the AIP cut (again, that was likely new footage that Saga never had access to). The scene tries to play it for horror and laughs both, as we get suspenseful shots of Dr. Dalby getting a gun to check on the monster, and Peterson trying and failing to ride a bike in the rain. As for one last difference, both cuts have a shot of the monster rising up out of the lab, but both are different. The Danish version shows the silhouette of the wings, while the AIP version shows the neck. (Also, AIP inserted a shot of a downed telephone pole to further emphasize that the power was out during the scene.)

Reptilicus's big reveal in the country is different between the two cuts. In both versions we begin with the farmer standing by his dead cow and AIP's version follows this with the military fighting the monster right away. The Danish version goes to the scene where Reptilicus terrorizes a poor farming family in their country home first, a scene that takes place later in AIP's version. Furthermore, AIP re-edits the scene to make it look as though Reptilicus eats the father, something he doesn't do in the Danish cut, which likewise includes a shot of what looks to be a full-scale foot prop crashing through the roof. At the end of the confrontation, as the charred monster slithers into the sea, Connie remarks about Reptilicus regenerating in both. But, in the Danish version, she says that maybe next time he'll use his wings.

For the underwater bombing scenes, the Danish version uses overhead longshots of the monster, while AIP uses extreme close-ups.

And now onto the infamous flying scenes. Even if the effects are poorly done, the music and direction for the flying scenes are great and have a wonderful sense of urgency and momentum. (Considering the effects were pretty shoddy overall anyway, it's too bad AIP cut them.) There are about four brief flying shots, three at night, one in the day, and all mostly in a darkened profile. Instead of charting the monster's flight path, the U.S. version reports a trail of capsized ships at sea. When the monster emerges at the beach later, it slimes all the beachgoers, presumably killing them.

The ending, where Grayson fires the chemical rocket into the monster's mouth, uses different angles and shots. In the Danish version, we can see the rocket launcher in the same frame as the monster, but not so in the AIP cut. The music also seems to be different in both. Furthermore, Grayson ends up with different girls in each version. In the Danish version he ends the picture romantically involved with the doctor's daughter, Lise, while the U.S. version ends with he and Connie together. Lastly, the Danish version ends with an instrumental version of Tivoli Nights over a black end card with no text. The AIP cut ends with the same music, but with the credits against a blue background.

Which version is better? That's tough to say as both have their pros and cons. The AIP version wins in terms of Reptilicus's roar, which is better. The green slime is also pretty unique... but we don't get the flying scenes. If anything, I'd love to see a fan do a hybrid edit that excises the silly song and dance number from Peterson, but reinstates the flying scenes. Currently, the U.S. *Reptilicus* Blu-Ray is out of print, but here's hoping that a new release down the road will include both versions.

NOTES

[1] Homenick, "The Imagination of Ib Melchior," Vantage Point Interviews. vantagepointinterviews.com/2017/05/18/the-imagination-of-ib-melchior-a-conversation-with-the-danish-monster-movie-maker/

[2] p. 47 of the script as reprinted in *Reptilicus – The Screenplay*

[3] Ibid, p.58

[4] Ibid, p.63

[5] Ibid, p.64

[6] Ibid

[7] Ibid, p.63-66

[8] *Reptilicus – The Screenplay*, p.15

[9] Homenick, "The Imagination of Ib Melchior," Vantage Point Interviews. vantagepointinterviews.com/2017/05/18/the-imagination-of-ib-melchior-a-conversation-with-the-danish-monster-movie-maker/

FILM THAT TIME FORGOT VALLEY OF THE DRAGONS BY MATTHEW B. LAMONT

RELEASE DATE November 1961

DIRECTOR Edward Bernds **SCREENPLAY** Edward Bernds, and Donald Zimbalist (story) based upon the novel by Jules Verne **MUSIC** Ruby Raksin **CAST** Cesare Danova (Hector Servadac) Sean McClory (Denning) Joan Staley (Deena) Danielle De Metz (Nateeta)

1.85 : 1, B&W, 82 Minutes

PLOT Two enemies must learn to survive together in a land of prehistoric monsters.

251

COMMENTARY The story takes place in Algeria on May 16th, 1881, during a duel between Michael Denning (Sean McClory), a soldier of fortune from County Clare, Ireland, and Captain Hector Servadac (Cesare Danova) of the French Army. Both have a purpose: to kill one another over the woman they love. However, the duel is interrupted by a comet that transports the two men into a strange prehistoric world. There they fight off a Neanderthal tribe (but the trailer refers to them as "gorilla people") and an ottoman-sized spider. They also run afoul of footage from Hal Roach's *One Million B.C.* (1940) where the alligator with a dorsal fin (representing a Dimetrodon or Spinosaurus) fights a tegu lizard (trying to portray a Lystrosaurus or T-Rex).[1] For good measure, the title character from *Rodan* (1956) appears as a pterodactyl via stock footage as well.

One night, the stranded men look to the stars and see the Earth. They realize that the comet's power and wind swooped close to Earth, swiped the men, and took them to another time zone. The comet has used that power since Earth was millions of years younger, hence prehistoric plant life, dinosaurs, and cave people there. After looking around, the two men find a cave with food and clothing. After putting on the animal skins (so as better to match Tumak from *One Million B.C.*), Hector is chased away by a wooly mammoth (an elephant with a fur coat). He climbs up a tree where the primeval pachyderm pushes it off a cliff and he splashed into a river (again via *One Million B.C.* footage). After the long trip through the river with footage from that film, he gets picked up by Deena (Joan Staley), a cave girl, and settles down with her tribe, enjoying their interaction. Meanwhile, Michael is involved with the enemy tribe and is attracted by a cave girl named Nateeta (Danielle De Metz), but he has to fight with her boyfriend Anoka (Mike Lane).[2]

Back at the other clan, Hector has invented gunpowder. "Sulphur, charcoal, potassium nitrate, boom!" Hector and Deena go into a cave to look for the chemicals needed to make the explosives only to be attacked by the dreaded humanoid beasts from the trailers. She escapes the cave leaving Hector to fight the creatures (which the film's trailer announcer called "hideous underground demons"). She goes through the forest dominated

CESARE DANOVA · SEAN McCLORY · JOAN STALEY

in MONTASCOPE

Though Toho's Rodan indeed appears in *Valley of the Dragon*, for some reason his co-stars from 1973's *Godzilla vs. Megalon* popped up on this particular re-release poster!

by dragons (i.e. dinosaurs from that 40s movie) and gets kidnapped by cavemen who turn out to be from Michael's tribe. Michael sees the girl and finds out that she belongs to Hector because of the words she was saying "chére" and "friend". He comforts her with water and this makes Nateeta jealous, so he explains to Nateeta that Deena is just a friend. Back at Hector's tribe, he heard the news that Deena was kidnapped, so they went to find her. Michael prepares his tribe to take Deena back to Hector's. Just as they are about to meet, a volcano ruins the moment and we see the film's dragons get killed by nature's wrath, and Rodan files away. (In other words more footage from that Hal Roach monster movie.)

After that is over, Michael brings Deena to Hector, and they are happy to see her safe. The other caveman finds the three and tells them that a giant beast is blocking them. Hector returns to his tribe to tell them that they need to find the ingredients to make the explosive. After testing it, they go off to save Michael's clan from the giant beast played by a tuatara lizard standing in for what I presume to be either a Brontosaurus, Stegosaurus, or... you know what? I don't care anymore. It's just another clip from that "lizards for dinosaurs" movie is all that really matters. From the top of the mountain, they see down below many big reptiles (more stock footage), so they decide to activate the explosives to make a rocky avalanche, crushing the monsters. The two tribes meet and make peace, and everything is hunky-dory. Hector tells Michael that he has been studying the sky and has arrived at the conclusion that the comet will come close to the Earth again in seven years. "Seven years," says Michael. "That's not too long."

"No, not long at all," replies Hector.

What a life! One day they were in a sophisticated world having a duel over the love of one woman, and the next, they both have their cavegirl.

In the 1950s and 1960s, Jules Verne's work was a popular subject to adapt into film. Disney made *20,000 Leagues Under the Sea* (1954), United Artists cooked up *Around the World in 80 Days* (1956), and Twentieth Century Fox did *Journey to the Center of the Earth* (1959) since RKO failed to make a film adaptation with Eugene Lourié and Ray Harryhausen six years earlier (i.e. 1953). However, 1961 was a big year for Jules Verne's stories to hit the big screen. There were three films: American International Pictures conceived *Master of the World*, and Columbia Pictures made *Mysterious Island* and *Valley of the Dragons*. The latter is mostly forgotten and is based on the 1877 story *Career of the Comet* (a.k.a. *Off on a Comet*). This movie is *loosely* based on the novel.

This movie was directed by Edward Bernds, who was known for directing Three Stooges shorts that incorporated stock footage in them.

Joe Dante, the director of *Piranha* (1978), *Gremlins* (1984), *Matinee* (1993), and *Looney Tunes Back in Action* (2003), did a commentary on *Valley of the Dragons* on the web series, *Trailers from Hell*. Dante said that Charlie Largent, the art director to this web series, pointed out that this was a Three Stooges movie without them.[3] It sure was, except it was serious, and there was violence, but not the slapstick variety. The film feels as if someone like Ed Wood or Roger Corman made it because this movie is a Frankenstein's Monster made up of clips from *Rodan* (1956) and *One Million B.C.* (1940). Even the "new" monsters are leftovers: the spider was a prop from *World Without End* (1956), also directed by Bernds, making its black and white debut, and rejected Morlock suits from George Pal's *The Time Machine* (1960) played the underground "demons". Even some of the sets were from the war film *The Devil at Four O'clock* (1961). The only good thing about this movie is the actors and the brilliant score by Ruby Raksin.

Ultimately, *Valley of the Dragons* is a fun film that was often shown on kiddie matinees and late-night television shows with horror hosts like Svengoolie. That said, in the words of Joe Dante, "*Valley of the Dragons* makes you want to track down a good print of *One Million B.C.*"

NOTES

---

[1] According to Hector, he said it was a Plateosaur. A plant-eater from the Triassic era.
[2] He was a pro wrestler and played Frank N. Stein in the children's show, *The Monster Squad* (1976).

DINOSAURS ON
MYSTERIOUS ISLAND

COLUMBIA PICTURES presents JULES VERNE'S **MYSTERIOUS ISLAND**, A. CHARLES H. SCHNEER Production in SUPERDYNAMATION starring MICHAEL CRAIG, JOAN GREENWOOD, MICHAEL CALLAN, GARY MERRILL, BETH ROGAN and HERBERT LOM as CAPTAIN NEMO. EASTMAN COLOR.

As it turns out, the phororhacos was the lone prehistoric holdover from a version of *Mysterious Island* to star dinosaurs.

RELEASE DATE December 20, 1961

DIRECTOR Cy Endfield **SPECIAL EFFECTS** Ray Harryhausen **SCREENPLAY** John Prebble, Daniel B. Ullman & Crane Wilbur **MUSIC** Bernard Herrmann **CAST** Michael Craig (Captain Cyrus Harding) Joan Greenwood (Lady Mary Fairchild) Michael Callan (Herbert Brown) Gary Merrill (Gideon Spilitt) Herbert Lom (Captain Nemo) Beth Rogan (Elena Fairchild) Percy Herbert (Sergeant Pencroft) Dan Jackson (Corporal Neb Nugent)

1.66 : 1, Technicolor, 101 Minutes

PLOT Castaways on a mysterious island find themselves at the mercy of Captain Nemo and his creations.

COMMENTARY Believe it or not, some early versions of *Mysterious Island* pictured it as being populated with prehistoric lifeforms including dinosaurs. It was also envisioned as something of an in-continuity sequel with Disney's *20,000 Leagues Under the Sea*, even though Columbia was the producer. In that line of thinking, James Mason was courted to come back as Nemo. In the end, what we got was Herbert Lom on an island populated by giant animals, though Ray Harryhausen did sneak in one prehistoric animal in the form of the phororhacos.

Along with the dinosaurs, this giant plant, beautifully illustrated in Harryhausen's concept art, got the ax.

As you might guess, Harryhausen was the biggest proponent for the dinosaurs. Harryhausen has never specified what dinosaurs exactly would appear, though.[1] In *Ray Harryhausen: An Animated Life*, he makes mention of a prehistoric mole creature erupting from the walls of the volcano to battle a giant snake-like creature. The battle ends with both tumbling into the lava. It's possible that the prehistoric beasties would have been saved for the very end, as Harryhausen also said that during the climactic eruption, prehistoric creatures would emerge from the cracks in the ground.[2] Along with the dinosaurs was also dropped a prehistoric forest of mushrooms[3] and a mechanical spider used by Nemo as a digging device.

When James Mason proved too costly, Herbert Lom was signed to play Captain Nemo instead and did a fine job of it.

259

Initially, novelist James Whitfield Ellison was signed to write the script but it's unclear if he did. However, it was writer Crane Wilbur's script that was first given to Schneer and Harryhausen. This version of the script had no dinosaurs or monstrous creatures of any kind in keeping with the novel.[4] (Apparently the big draw for the ending would be the discovery of Nemo and the *Nautilus*.) But we all know that's no good, so Harryhausen and Schneer began creating monsters. Among them was the phororhacos that made the final cut (as though it were a giant chicken), a man-eating plant with poison-tipped tentacles, and a huge cephalopod which also survived. Ken Kolb took the next jab at the script and suggested removing Nemo and the monsters alike! In the end, they only removed a dog character from the book, named Tops, as animals could prove difficult during filming of a picture such as this.

Nigel Green was cast as the character of Thomas Ayerton, who lived on the titular island for years in the novel version. Due to eating certain mushrooms, his skin became green. As such, he was called The Green Man. In the script, he was to be eaten by the giant plant towards the end of the movie. Instead the character was reduced to a skeleton in the final film, though Columbia kept both the Ayerton character and the carnivorous plant in the press book:

> Later when Herbert is trying to free a rabbit from an animal trap plant, he himself is grasped by the leg and lifted into the air by a long, sticky vine. He screams and the plant emits pink-colored fumes, rendering him unconscious. His screams attract the others who are thwarted from rescuing Herbert by the fumes. The victim is about to be swallowed when a strange looking creature, wearing skins, heavily bearded and his skin a bright green in color, comes to the rescue. Impervious to the fumes, he cuts Herbert loose and pulls the others out of danger.
>
> The group tries to thank him, but he just smiles and nods. He can't speak, but he understands English. His name is Tom Ayrton (Nigel Green) and he was marooned on the island by pirates, who first cut out his tongue. He introduces them to the giant mushroom as an antidote for the plant's poisonous fumes, but warns them that eating too much will cause one to turn green, which is exactly what happens to Pencroft, who becomes drunk on the delicious food.[5]

Ultimately, it was probably for the best that the dinosaurs were scrapped from *Mysterious Island* since Harryhausen did so many stop-motion dinosaurs throughout his career. Instead, they were swapped for giant animals being grown for food, an idea of which came from an aborted production Harryhausen was involved in for H.G. Wells' *Food of the Gods*. All that said, it's still too bad that the giant plant and the Green Man got the boot, though.

NOTES

[1] That said, he did include a storyboard frame where a Mesosaurus confronts the divers underwater.

[2] Harryhausen seemed to like this idea, as he envisioned it for his planned remake of *The Deluge* as well.

[3] As for the mushrooms and their similarity to the ones in Twentieth Century Fox's *Journey to the Center of the Earth*, it should be noted that *Mysterious Island* was developing before *Journey's* release. Perhaps it was unknown at that time that *Journey* used the mushroom forest, and perhaps after that became known that's why it was dropped from this version.

[4] Though not a monstrous creature, there was a notable animal in the form of an intelligent, trained ape in his script.

[5] Reprinted in *Master of the Majicks Vol.3*, p.47.

FILM THAT TIME FORGOT
EEGAH
BY MIKE BOGUE

ORIGINALLY PUBLISHED IN *THE LOST FILMS FANZINE PRESENTS MOVIE MILESTONES* #1

RELEASE DATE June 8, 1962

DIRECTOR Arch Hall Sr. **SCREENPLAY** Bob Wehling **MUSIC** André Brummer **CAST/CHARACTERS** Arch Hall Jr. (Tom Nelson) Marilyn Manning (Roxy Miller) Richard Kiel (Eegah) Arch Hall Sr. (Robert Miller)

1.66 : 1, Eastman Color, 92 Minutes

COMMENTARY In 1973, the ad tagline for George Lucas's *American Graffiti* was, "Where were you in '62?" No doubt some denizens of that bygone year were at the drive-in, and some of them were probably watching 1962's *Eegah*, a low-budget production from Fairway International. The film chronicles the tale of a somehow still-alive caveman who cavorts with the California cast until his inevitable demise.

Some might be tempted to call the production "prehistoric" in terms of not just its title character, but also its film technique. Indeed, many consider it one of the worst films ever made. For example, *Rotten Tomatoes* gives it a "fresh" rating of 0% out of eight reviews. Certainly the movie is no winner, and yet . . .

Richard Kiel, years before fame as "Jaws" in 1977's *The Spy Who Loved Me* and 1979's *Moonraker*, portrays Eegah. The movie never adequately explains what this caveman is doing alive in the 20th century; the heroine's father opines that the sulfur in Eegah's cave has kept him young all these years. Naturally. So why hasn't anyone seen him before the heroine literally runs into him with her sports car? Again, the film's explanation lacks credibility, and reminds one of the similarly insufficient rationale for the giant arachnid's sudden appearance in 1958's *Earth vs. the Spider*.

Much of the film takes place in Eegah's cave, where Eegah holds Roxy (Marilyn Manning) and her father Mr. Miller (Arch Hall Sr.) captive. Here the movie often strives for comedy, such as Roxy sickened by sulfur water, pretending she is talking to Eegah's mummified relatives, and giving Eegah a shave (no, I'm not

263

kidding), in which he licks shaving cream and squirts it on his face (maybe he's a relative of Larry, Moe, and Curly?). But it's also clear Eegah has other plans for the heroine, and here the movie becomes uncomfortable.

Richard Kiel, as the title character, menaces the damsel in distress.

Tom (Arch Hall Jr.), the hero, helps rescue Roxy (his girlfriend of course) and her father from the smitten caveman. Strangely, they choose not to tell anyone about Eegah, the heroine's father claiming that authorities would take him away to turn him into a lab exhibit. But of course, we haven't seen the last of this caveman whose name is "written in blood."

Eegah is portrayed as a semi-tragic character—not unlike Universal's Gill Man, Eegah is a stranger in a strange land. The 7 foot, 2 inch Kiel gives a lively performance, and his overdubbed caveman grunts and groans prove effective, somewhat recalling Paul Frees' vocals for 1957's *The Cyclops*. Naturally, in the finale the caveman goes in search of the heroine, and is killed by law officers. Roxy and her father express the usual ritual sadness over his inevitable demise.

The movie scores a few points for imagination. For example, Eegah's aforementioned desiccated relatives are a nice idea, and he talks to them as though he thinks they are still alive. The opening credits, though undeniably cheap, resonate with a crude inventiveness. Indeed, the movie evokes the undeniable feel of drive-in movies of the 1960s, and as such has a certain cockeyed charm for hopeless nostalgia addicts such as myself.

Although credits say the movie was produced and directed by Nicholas Merriwether, this was actually a pseudonym for Arch Hall Sr.—the film's hero Tom is Mr. Hall's son, Arch Hall Jr. Hall Sr. participated in various functions on a number of 1960's low-budget films. His son Hall Jr. appeared infrequently; probably his best-known film is 1963's *The Sadist*, in which he stars as a psychotic killer. This one gets 2 ½ stars from Leonard Maltin, who found Hall Jr.'s performance "distressingly believable."

Well, it's pretty safe to say no one will find anything "distressingly believable" about *Eegah*. But therein lies its appeal, what there is of it. No doubt twentysomethings would be stunned to hear old guys like myself actually paid money to see movies like this. But we did. Of course, I can't blame others if they're not eegah to see this one. But if you could withstand that previous pun without throwing this book across the room, *Eegah* might be right up your retro alley.

FILM THAT TIME FORGOT
VOYAGE TO THE PREHISTORIC PLANET
BY BLAKE MATTHEWS

RELEASE DATE April 14, 1962 / August 1, 1965 (U.S. version)

DIRECTOR Pavel Klushantsev \ Curtis Harrington (U.S. version) **SCREENPLAY** Pavel Klushantsev & Aleksandr Kazantsev / Curtis Harrington (U.S. version) **SPECIAL EFFECTS** V. Shelkov & Anatoly Lavrentyev **MUSIC** Iogann Admoni & Aleksandr Chernov / Ronald Stein (U.S. version) **CAST/CHARACTERS** Vladimir Yemelyanov (Cmdr. Brendan Lockhart) Georgiy Zhzhonov (Hans Walters) Gennadi Vernov (Andre Ferneau) **US VERSION** Basil Rathbone (Professor Hartman) Faith Domergue (Dr. Marsha Evans)

1.37 : 1, Color, 78 Minutes / 74 Minutes (U.S. version)

COMMENTARY The 1962 Soviet science fiction *Planet of Storms* is best known today as being the film that B-movie overlord Roger Corman cannibalized not once, but *twice* for American distribution. Interestingly enough, the first of these, *Voyage to a Prehistoric Planet*, is practically the same exact movie, moreso than, say, *Godzilla, King of the Monsters!* (1956) in comparison to *Gojira* (1954). In recent years, the original Russian-language version has become available in the West for sci-fi geeks like me to appreciate, although there's not a whole lot of "new" footage to take in.

Set sometime in the future, three Soviet spacecraft are approaching Venus: the Cappella, the Vega and the Sirius. As they approach the second planet's orbit, a random meteor strikes the Cappella and destroys it. The crews of both the Vega and the Sirius are ordered by mission control—a disembodied voice—to remain in orbit until a fourth ship arrives to serve as a fuel ship.

The crew of the Sirius consists of three cosmonauts: Ilya Vershinin, Bobrov, and Alyosha. The Vega is staffed by four cosmonauts: Scherba; his wife/lover, Masha; Dr. Alan Kern; and Kern's creation: the robot John. Bobrov suggests to Ilya that they land on Venus anyway, to which Vershinin suggests that Kern ask John to make the necessary calculations so that Vega's "glider" and the entirety of the Sirius can make landfall on Venus. The two men and John are to enter the glider, while Masha has to stay behind and maintain contact with mission command.

The glider ends up crash landing on the surface of Venus, but the Sirius makes it okay. The crash of the former damages the radio, so Masha's isn't able to contact her crewmates. The crew of the Sirius thus begins a 30-mile odyssey across Venus to rescue their comrades, encountering killer plants and dinosaurs along the way. Meanwhile, John and the two men from the Vega start off in the direction of the Sirius, encountering danger in the form of aggressive lizard men and volcanic eruptions.

Meanwhile, Masha starts suffering from isolation inside the Vega, which is compounded by the eventual loss of radio contact with both the Sirius *and* mission control. The radio silence starts weighing on Masha's mind to the point that eventually she is ready to disobey orders and land on Venus herself. Will the cosmonauts of the Sirius be able to rescue their compatriots and return to orbit before Masha's mental instability botches everything?

Despite the interplanetary setting, *Planet of Storms* is structured like your typical lost world film. You could replace the

267

spaceships with helicopters or light aircraft and Venus with an uncharted island in the Pacific (or Antarctica) and the result would be the same. Strangely enough, the main difference between this film and its American contemporaries is the way it treats the prehistoric flora and fauna. For the most part, American filmmakers would flaunt their antediluvian behemoths no matter the quality of the special effects: monster suits; immobile puppets; slurpasaurs (i.e. photographically-enlarged lizards); or stop motion; the monsters are always displayed in all their glory.

On the other hand, the beasties in this film are almost portrayed as background details. With the exception of the man-eating plant and the pterodactyl, the other prehistoric reptiles are generally shot from a distance, giving us little opportunity to appreciate the craftmanship that went into the models and suit design. The "big" action scene between the crew of the Vega and the lizard men has no build-up, no suspense, no close-ups of the monsters, no real excitement. They're just there. Near the end of the film, we get a glimpse of some non-slurpasaur Dimetrodon (American viewers hadn't gotten that since 1948's *Unknown Island*), but once more, they are filmed from afar and only for a few seconds.

Moreover, there is little sense of awe that the astronauts/cosmonauts demonstrate when encountering these creatures. "Oh, there's a brontosaurus. That's interesting. Huh." These creatures don't even merit an amusing pseudo-scientific conversation about how they would have evolved on another planet or why they are so similar to dinosaurs on Earth. The lack of filmmaking technique in crafting the monster sequences—and the characters' reactions—just add to the already-leaden pace of the film as a whole. There is some pretty good art design, thanks to V. Shelkov, who also did the effects for *Doroga k zvezdam*.[1] The miniatures of the spaceships are probably on par with what Japan was doing at the time, if not a rung or two lower. But there's just no *life* to these creations.

Planet of Storms is little more than a curio to people who have already watched the Corman cuts. The Russian acting is generally flat and lifeless. Music is used sparingly, but the silence fails to undercut the suspense of any scene in which a character may be in mortal danger. The film is too much walking and driving across Venus and not enough excitement and daring-do. There are no Alpha Male Scientist-Heroes with degrees in "manly" areas like engineering. Just a bunch of regular-looking schmos and a lady who might be going crazy doing "stuff" in space.[2]

As it stands, the Corman version called *Voyage to the Prehistoric Planet* is the more widely seen version. And how exactly did it come to be? By the mid-1960s, American International Pictures (AIP) was doing a lot of distribution of international films, be they Japanese *kaiju eiga*, German *krimi*, or Italian *pepla* and Gothic Horror films. At one point, Roger Corman was able to make it to the other side of the Iron Curtain and pick up the rights to several Soviet space films, like *The Heavens Call; A Dream Come True;* and *Planet of Storms*. Obviously, at the height of the Cold War and only a few years following the Cuban Missile Crisis, it would have been impossible to simply dub the films and release them as they did their other imports. Nope, Corman had to Americanize these, cannibalizing the effects footage to support new stories...except for the first incarnation of *Planet of Storms*.

For all intents and purposes, *Voyage to the Prehistoric Planet* is the exact same movie as *Planet of Storms*. The differences between the two films are noticeable, but have very little effect on the resulting movie. All scenes involving the character Masha have been excised, replaced with scenes of Faith Domergue (*It Came from Beneath the Sea* and *This Island Earth*—starting to look surprisingly haggard at age 41) as an astronaut named Marsha interacting with the Russian actors. Marsha's character arc is the same as that of her Russian counterpart, although Domergue plays her character as being less unstable and more anxious. And the small set that her scenes are filmed on is a bit more colorful than the drab (if realistic) spaceship set of the original film. According to director Curtis Harrington, filming was done in half a day.

In the original film, mission command was little more than a disembodied voice heard over the radio. However, director Harrington and producer Roger Corman filmed new scenes with a slumming Basil Rathbone, who plays the scientist running the space station (played by footage from *A Dream Come True*). Thus, the mission command dialogue is replaced with dialogue from Rathbone, in addition to scenes of him interacting with bit-part actors on the space station.

The bulk of the movie is the original footage dubbed into English. The names are changed into something more palatable to American audiences: Ilya Vershinin is now Professor Lockhart; his crewmates are now Andre and Hans (giving the film an international feel). Scherba is now "Sherman." Only the names Alan Kern and John remain the same. The dubbing has been dismissed as inane by some viewers, but the voice actors give the characters a lot more life than their wooden Russian counterparts. Ronald Stein's score is also more appropriate for the film than the minimalist music of *Planeta Bur*, giving it a more typical B-movie feel. Neither of those save the film from Pavel Klushantsev's glacial approach to the material, but they alleviate the slowness at least a little.

Ultimately, both versions qualify as Movies That Time Forgot as many dino-film fans are unaware of either the Corman re-edit or the original production.

One of the picture's more emphasized dinosaurs: the pterodactyl.

NOTES

---

[1] Footage from that film was cribbed for the Mexican film *Ship of Monsters*.
[2] Apparently, the Soviet censors did not like the portrayal of Masha as an unstable threat to the mission.

APPENDIX I

MORE LOST PROJECTS AND DISCARDED IDEAS

Though they do contain dinosaurs or dinosaur-like monsters, none of the entries from either the Godzilla or King Kong movies will be included in this appendix as those can all be found in either *Kong Unmade* or *Japanese Monsters Unmade*.

THE LOST WORLD Before completion of the 1925 version, there were two other planned *Lost World* adaptations from different studios in 1917 and 1919, one of which had Lon Chaney slated to play the villainous Pedro Gomez.

SHE Early version of *She* (1935) with prehistoric megafauna such as wooly mammoths and saber-toothed tigers. Was also to be shot in color. Though the explorers do find a frozen saber-toothed tiger in *She*, it never comes to life, and Cooper had wanted O'Brien to animate a herd of mammoths for the film. (Said mammoths would attack the explorers.)

MICKEY'S SEA MONSTER (1935) Even Mickey Mouse was the star of a planned dinosaur short in the form of *Mickey's Sea Monster*, which would have seen Disney's mascot encountering a sea monster along with Donald Duck and Goofy.

BEFORE ADAM (c.1930s) One of the influences behind Hal Roache's *One Million B.C.* was Jack London's 1907 novel, *Before Adam*. It featured a modern-day man who dreamt of being a caveman. Notably, it had tribes at varying levels of development, much like *B.C.* In the case of *Before Adam*, it featured the Cave People, the Tree People, and the Fire People. As to why Hal Roach didn't simply adapt the novel, he couldn't. RKO's David O. Selznick had bought the rights years earlier with Lon Chaney Sr. in mind to star.

ATLANTIS (1938) How, or even if, this ties into Harry Hoyt's *The Lost Atlantis* of the late 1930s is unknown, but around the same time, Ray Harryhausen was playing around with his own version of the story. In Harryhausen's case, he had the idea that dinosaurs would attack Atlantis (or, perhaps it was Lemuria, he couldn't remember) as volcanos erupted in the background. In several books, Harryhausen mentioned the project, along with the fact that he had since lost his step outline for it and retained only two concept drawings. Likely it was just a coincidence and was unrelated to Hoyt's *Lost Atlantis*.

ABBOTT AND COSTELLO MEET THE DINOSAURS On his wonderful audio commentary for the Blu-Ray of *Africa Screams*, film historian Ron Palumbo revealed a heretofore unknown Abbott and Costello project. After finishing up *Africa Screams*, producer

272

Edward Nassour wanted to bring the comedy duo back as archeologists who somehow discover and then run afoul of prehistoric monsters. Nassour had an affinity for dinosaurs and was also involved in *The Lost Atlantis* in the mid-1930s. Considering Abbott and Costello met most of the Universal monsters, it's too bad they never met dinosaurs as well. (No, the giant lizard in *Abbott and Costello Meets the Mummy* doesn't count.)

THE GREAT ADVENTURE (1949) This concept, to be produced by Merian C. Cooper from a script by Cyril Hume based on a story by Ruth Rose, was derived from an unfilmed scene from *Mighty Joe Young*. Remember the deleted sequence where Joe and co. were supposed to crash on an island and be attacked by lions? Well, Ruth Rose had been so disappointed that the scene wasn't used that she concocted a whole story around it for a new film! (And no, it wasn't a *Joe* sequel, though it's possible that it had a heroic gorilla in it.) All we know is that Cyril Hume wrote the full script. Ray Harryhausen was set to work on the picture with Willis O'Brien and recalled in *An Animated Life* on page 39 that,

> I never saw a script and in truth I remember little about it, apart from the fact that it was based on the rejected sequence from *Mighty Joe Young* in which the adventurers were stranded on an island where Joe saves them from lions. This was seen to be such a visual idea that Cyril attempted to 'flesh it out' so that it became a story of a bring-'em-back-alive showman marooned on a Pacific island inhabited by prehistoric monsters. I suspect it was dropped because the story had been too near the *Mighty Joe Young* storyline to be considered as viable.

ROCKETSHIP XM (1950) This 1950 Kurt Neumann thriller about a moon expedition gone awry landing on Mars was meant to have dinosaur scenes... somehow. According to Robert Skotak in an issue of *Filmfax*, there were plans of including dinosaurs via the oft-used *One Million B.C.* stock footage. In the end, the sequence was scrapped and the picture was released sans any prehistoric beasties.

MONSTER STORY (1951) The simply titled "Monster Story" from Ray Harryhausen brings to mind the machinations of Willis

O'Brien, particularly some of his old drafts of *Umbah*. Harryhausen envisioned his story in the Rockies, where a scientist experimenting with a new weapon called A-2 has mutated the valley wildlife, making some of it gigantic and somehow bringing back dinosaurs. Specifically, we would begin with brothers David and Al Winder, who have a small cabin in the Rockies. David is a newspaper writer, and his publisher, Eleanor Landing, is coming for visit. The story is really set into motion when David's dog goes missing, and the trio traces it to the hidden valley where they find Professor Paul Hendrix and his experiments. A giant ant and spider would come into play, as would a battling brontosaurus and pterodactyl. A neanderthal caveman would also be discovered to have been a former scientist who regressed to a prehistoric state from the experiment. At the story's conclusion, Al is killed by the caveman and David and Eleanor are the only two to get away in time before the valley is destroyed when another experimental weapon derived from A-1 detonates.

UGALA (1953) This idea from Ray Harryhausen was another that resembled his mentor Willis O'Brien's ideas, as Ray envisioned a lost world of dinosaurs found in Mexico. To differentiate it from *The Lost World*, Ray added in giant men and giant spiders. Rather than a plateau as in *The Lost World*, this would be a prehistoric valley accessible only by helicopter.

"SOUTH AMERICAN ADVENTURE" Perhaps the same as *Ugala*, this entry is included in *Ray Harryhausen: An Animated Life*. The setting is South America, where a couple named Joe and Toni are sent to Guatemala to explore for oil. They tumble across a native tribe worshipping a statue that looks just like a dinosaur. When they learn there is a forbidden valley nearby, they decide to explore it. There they find a cave that they blast to test for oil. After the blast, they hear strange noises and that night their camp is attacked by a huge, unseen animal. The next day they explore the cave and within it find a huge lake of oil. An allosaurus emerges from it. To defend themselves, they toss their torches into the lake and set it afire killing the beast.

TARANTULA! (1955) Supposedly the initial version featured multiple spiders. *Variety* columnist Louella O. Parsons claimed in her February 25, 1953, column that tarantulas plural would appear "on the screen the size of elephants." She also stated that when "slashed with a knife" that the parts would "live on independently." Lastly, she reported that the plan was to shoot the picture in Honduras.

JOURNEY TO THE CENTER OF THE EARTH (mid-1950s) Before the 1959 version starring James Mason and Pat Boone, there were plans for another version. After the success of Disney's 1954 release of *20,000 Leagues Beneath the Sea*, other studios sought to adapt Jules Verne's other great work, *Journey to the Center of the Earth*. Specifically, in 1956, both Columbia Pictures and RKO began working on competing versions of the project. For RKO's version, Stanley Rubin would produce. Columbia's plans were more ambitious, as they planned to make not only *Journey to the Center of the Earth* but also *Mysterious Island*. Both pictures were to be produced by Bryan Foy. Somewhere in the mix was also Eugène Lourié, who was the proposed director for one of the competing *Journeys*, though we know not which. All that is known is that in *Keep Watching the Skies,* it's said that Lourié's version was to be shot in Italy as an independent production. Because Lourié had worked on *Beast from 20,000 Fathoms* with Ray Harryhausen, it is thought that perhaps Harryhausen would helm *Journey's* effects. However, since *Harryhausen: The Lost Movies* makes no mention of this, it may be internet conjecture.

THE GIANT SLOTH (c. 1950s) Nothing about this one is known apart from the title. Though it may not sound intimidating, in terms of cryptozoology, tales of vicious giant sloths in the jungles of South America were semi-common in the early 20th Century, so perhaps it stemmed from that. Furthermore, a giant sloth appeared in *Unknown Island* (1948) as one of the primary monsters.

UMBAH (mid-1950s) Southwestern monster adventure from Willis O'Brien with similarities to *King Kong*. Has a lost valley with giant Gila monsters.

HUMAN HISTORY OF 500,000 YEARS (mid-1950s) We don't know exactly what it is, or where it is now, but in the 1950s Japan produced some sort of caveman movie. It was titled *Human History of 500,000 Years*, which I suppose could translate to *500,000 B.C.* The director's name is listed as Miyachi. Another source identified it as possibly being a Japanese poster for a French film from Nouvelles Éditions de Films. Thanks to Niels Petter Solberg for finding the poster. See poster on page X.

THE DEADLY MANTIS (1957) Though a volcano frees the titular menace in the finished film, it was U.S. atomic testing in the original story. Because the producers needed the assistance of the U.S. military during production, they changed it to a volcano.

BEHEMOTH, THE SEA MONSTER (1957) This proto version of *The Giant Behemoth* had no dinosaur at all and was more akin to *The Blob* as it would have featured a giant, crawling mass of radioactive sludge as said sea monster, still named Behemoth apparently. Though there's not a good source to back this up, some say that at the picture's end the radioactive mass would take some type of more tangible form. Eugène Lourié agreed to direct the film because it was different from his *Beast from 20,000 Fathoms.* Ironically, upon his signing, the producers got excited and essentially turned the film into a remake of *The Beast.* Essentially, what began as an ecological science fiction thriller turned into another dinosaur on the loose picture, the only vestige of the original idea being the radioactive waste left in the monster's wake. Furthermore, *Fantastic Films* #15 featured Paul Mandell's article on *The Giant Behemoth*, which revealed that Eugene Lourié was scheduled to direct *The Black Scorpion.* When he had a disagreement with the producers, he came onto this project instead. Some say the monster was basically invisible apart from its glow, while Lourié described it in his autobiography as "a blob of expanding radiation." Over only ten days, Lourié rewrote the script "plagiarizing" himself.

THE ADVENTURES OF SINBAD (1957) As we all know, *The 7ᵗʰ Voyage of Sinbad* (originally simply *The Adventures of Sinbad*) features a reptilian menace in the form of the dragon. However, there was originally to also be another serpentine menace in the form of a giant snake meant to fight the Cyclops. The giant snake was meant to pursue Sinbad's men up a tree before the cyclops comes along. However, Charles H. Schneer hated snakes and felt they frightened pregnant women in particular and axed the idea.

BEGINNING OF THE END (1957) Originally, the giant locusts, portrayed by real, enlarged grasshoppers in the film, were meant to be stopmotion locusts.

EVE AND THE DRAGON (1958) This project exists only as a title. It sprang from American International Pictures and was to be directed by Stanley Shpetner, who was predominantly a producer. Considering that AIP found success in distributing Italian Sword and Sandal epics, this sounds to be one of them but perhaps with a Biblical slant going off the title.

THE ELEPHANT RUSTLERS (1960) Another of Willis O'Brien's unique variations on the Western, this one had cowboys going to India to wrangle and ride elephants. The climax would have had them traversing a prehistoric swamp inhabited by giant lizards.

FIVE BILLION B.C. (AKA FIVE MILLION B.C.) (1960) Before Hammer remade *One Million Years B.C.* in 1966, Edward G. Ulmer (director of 1934's *The Black Cat*) planned to make a prehistoric epic called *Five Billion B.C.* This is all according to Mark Berry's *The Dinosaur Filmography*, and the project is listed as being in development around 1960. Very little is known about it other than the fact that it was never finished. Jim Danforth recalled to Berry that he did some storyboards for the project, but that was it. Gene Warren was said to be involved with the visual effects as well. It was to have not only stop-motion dinosaurs, but a cartoon-animated opening sequence done by Danforth.

BREAKOUT OF THE LOCH NESS MONSTER (1963) No details given apart from the title and the fact that a script outline exists within the Ray and Diana Harryhausen Foundation archives. Said script came apparently not from Ray Harryhausen himself, but from brothers Donald and Derek Ford.

BIBLIOGRAPHY

Articles

Branch, Glenn. "Censoring Darrow." NCSE. (August 22, 2014)
https://ncse.ngo/censoring-darrow

Galbraith, Stuart IV. "Long Ago Before Jurassic Park." *Filmfax* #48 (January 1, 1995)

Homenick, "The Imagination of Ib Melchior," Vantage Point Interviews. (2018) vantagepointinterviews.com/2017/05/18/the-imagination-of-ib-melchior-a-conversation-with-the-danish-monster-movie-maker/

Lamont, Matthew B. "Harry Hoyt's Dinosaur Dream." *Lost Films Fanzine* #6 (Summer 2021).

Powers, Lee. "Son of the Volcano." *The Lost Films Fanzine* #4 (Winter 2020).

Shay, Don. "Willis O'Brien - Creator of the Impossible." *CINEFEX...the Journal of Cinematic Illusions* #7 (1981)

Books

Archer, Steve. *Willis O'Brien: Special Effects Genius.* McFarland & Company, Inc., 1993.

Berry, Mark F. *The Dinosaur Filmography.* McFarland & Company, Inc., 2002.

Conover, David and Philip J. Riley. *War Eagles.* BearManor Media, 2011.

Cotta Vaz, Mark. *Living Dangerously: The Adventures of Merian C. Cooper.* Villard Books, 2005.

Danforth, Jim. *Dinosaurs, Dragons & Drama: The Odyssey of a Trick-Film-Maker.* CD-Book distributed by Archive-Editions, 2015.

Debus, Allen. *Prehistoric Monster Mash: Science Fictional Dinosaurs, Fossil Phenoms, Paleo-pioneers, Godzilla & Other Kaiju-saurs.* By the author, 2019.

Derendorf, Kevin. *Kaiju for Hipsters: 101 'Alternative' Monster Movies.* Maser Press, 2018.

Hankin, Mike. *Ray Harryhausen: Master of the Majicks: Volume 1: Beginnings and Endings.* Archive Editions, 2013.

-------------------- *Ray Harryhausen: Master of the Majicks: Volume 3: The British Films.* Archive Editions, 2010.

Harryhausen, Ray and Tony Dalton. *The Art of Ray Harryhausen.* Billboard Books, 2006.

------------------------- *Ray Harryhausen: An Animated Life.* Billboard Books, 2003.

LeMay, John. *The Big Book of Japanese Giant Monster Movies: The Lost Films.* Bicep Books, 2017.

Pink, Sid and Kip Doto (Ed.). *Reptilicus – The Screenplay.* CCP Bayou Publishing.

Rovin, Jeff. *From the Land Beyond Beyond: The films of Willis O'Brien and Ray Harryhausen.* Berkley Pub. Corp, 1977.

Turner, George E. and Orville Goldner with Michael H. Price and Douglas Turner. *Spawn of Skull Island: The Making of King Kong.* Midnight Marquee Press, 2002.

Turner, Douglas. *Willis O'Brien's Gwangi Documents (Skull Island Archives: Raw Data).* By the author, 2014.

Walsh, John. *Harryhausen: The Lost Movies.* Titan Books, 2019.

Webber, Roy P. *The Dinosaur Films of Ray Harryhausen.* McFarland & Company, Inc., 2004.

Workman, Christopher and Troy Howarth. *Tome of Terror: Horror Films of the Silent Era.* Midnight Marquee Press, 2016.

Archival Collections

L. Tom Perry Special Collections. Brigham Young University. Merian C. Cooper Papers.

Blu-Rays

Dinosaurus! (Special Edition) KL Studio Classics. Audio Commentary by Kris Seaworth.

The Land Unknown. KL Studio Classics. Audio Commentary by Tom Weaver and David Schecter.

INDEX

281

ABOUT THE AUTHOR John LeMay was born and raised in Roswell, NM, the "UFO Capital of the World." He is the author of over 40 books on film and southwestern history such as *Kong Unmade: The Lost Films of Skull Island* and *Tall Tales and Half Truths of Billy the Kid* in addition to Western novels like *Once Upon a Time in Fort Sumner.* He is also the editor/publisher of *The Lost Films Fanzine* and *Strange West.* He has also written for magazines such as *True West, Cinema Retro, G-Fan, Xenorama,* and *Mad Scientist* to name only a few. He is a Past President of the Board of Directors for the Historical Society for Southeast New Mexico, the host of the web series *Roswell's Hidden History,* and the co-host of the popular story-telling podcast Plot Pit with William Atkinson.

THE BICEP BOOKS CATALOGUE

The following titles are available for purchase on Amazon.com, and are available to bookstores at a wholesale discount via Ingram Content Group (ISBNs of available editions listed for this purpose)

THE BIG BOOK OF JAPANESE GIANT MONSTER MOVIES SERIES

The third edition of the book that started it all! Reviews over 100 tokusatsu films between 1954 and 1988. All the Godzilla, Gamera, and Daimajin movies made during the Showa era are covered plus lesser known fare like Invisible Man vs. The Human Fly (1957) and Conflagration (1975). Softcover (380 pp/5.83" X 8.27") Suggested Retail: $19.99 SBN:978-1-7341546-4-1

This third edition reviews over 75 tokusatsu films between 1989 and 2019. All the Godzilla, Gamera, and Ultraman movies made during the Heisei era are covered plus independent films like Reigo, King of the Sea Monsters (2005), Demeking, the Sea Monster (2009) and Attack of the Giant Teacher (2019)! Softcover (260 pp/5.83" X 8.27") Suggested Retail: $19.99 ISBN: 978-1- 7347816-4-9

This second edition of the book covers un-produced scripts like Bride of Godzilla (1955), partially shot movies like Giant Horde Beast Nezura (1963), and banned films like Prophecies of Nostradamus (1974), plus hundreds of other lost productions. Softcover/Hard-cover (470pp. /7" X 10") Suggested Retail: $24.99 (sc)/$39.95(hc)ISBN: 978-1-73 41546-0-3 (hc)

This sequel to The Lost Films covers the non-giant monster unmade movie scripts from Japan such as Frankenstein vs. the Human Vapor (1963), After Japan Sinks (1974-76), plus lost movies like Fearful Attack of the Flying Saucers (1956) and Venus Flytrap (1968). Hardcover (200 pp/5.83" X 8.27")/Softcover (216 pp/ 5.5" X 8.5") Suggested Retail: $9.99 (sc)/$24.99(hc)   ISBN:978-1-7341546 -3-4 (hc)

This companion book to The Lost Films charts the development of all the prominent Japanese monster movies including discarded screenplays, story ideas, and deleted scenes. Also includes bios for writers like Shinichi Sekizawa, Niisan Takahashi and many others. Comprehensive script listing and appendices as well. Hardcover/Softcover (370 pp./ 6"X9")   Suggested   Retail: $16.95(sc)/$34.99(hc)ISBN: 978-1-7341546-5-8 (hc)

Examines the differences between the U.S. and Japanese versions of over 50 different tokusatsu films like Gojira (1954)/Godzilla, King of the Monsters! (1956), Gamera (1965)/ Gammera, the Invincible (1966), Submersion of Japan (1973)/Tidal Wave (1975), and many, many more! Softcover (540 pp./ 6"X9")   Suggested   Retail: $22.99 ISBN: 978-1-953221-77 -3

Examines the differences between the European and Japanese versions of tokusatsu films including the infamous "Cozzilla" colorized version of Godzilla, from 1977, plus rarities like Terremoto 10 Grado, the Italian cut of Legend of Dinosaurs. The book also examines the condensed Champion Matsuri edits of Toho's   effects   films. Softcover (372 pp./ 6"X9") Suggested Retail: $19.99 ISBN: 978-1- 953221-77-3

Throughout the 1960s and 1970s the Italian film industry cranked out over 600 "Spaghetti Westerns" and for every Fistful of Dollars were a dozen pale imitations, some of them hilarious. Many of these lesser known Spaghettis are available in bargain bin DVD packs and stream for free online. If ever you've wondered which are worth your time and which aren't, this is the book for you. Softcover (160pp./5.06" X 7.8") Suggested Retail: $9.99

THE BICEP BOOKS CATALOGUE

CLASSIC MONSTERS SERIES

Kong Unmade explores unproduced scripts like *King Kong vs. Frankenstein* (1958), unfinished films like *The Lost Island* (1934), and lost movies like *King Kong Appears in Edo* (1938). As a bonus, all the Kong rip-offs like *Konga* (1961) and *Queen Kong* (1976) are reviewed. Hardcover (350 pp/5.83" X 8.27")/Softcover (376 pp/ 5.5" X 8.5") Suggested Retail: $24.99 (hc)/$19.99(sc) ISBN: 978-1-7341546-2-7(hc)

Jaws Unmade explores unproduced scripts like *Jaws 3, People 0* (1979), abandoned ideas like a Quint prequel, and even aborted sequels to *Jaws* inspired movies like *Orca Part II*. As a bonus, all the *Jaws* rip-offs like *Grizzly* (1976) and *Tentacles* (1977) are reviewed. Hardcover (316 pp/5.83" X 8.27")/Softcover (340 pp/5.5" X 8.5") Suggested Retail: $29.99 (hc)/$17.95(sc) ISBN: 978-1-7344730-1-8

Classic Monsters Unmade covers lost and unmade films starring Dracula, Frankenstein, the Mummy and more monsters. Reviews unmade scripts like *The Return of Frankenstein* (1934) and *Wolf Man vs. Dracula* (1944). It also examines lost films of the silent era such as *The Werewolf* (1913) and *Drakula's Death* (1923). Softcover/ Hardcover(428pp/5.83"X8.27") Suggested Retail: $22.99(sc)/ $27.99(hc)ISBN:978-1- 953221-85-8(hc)

Volume 2 explores the Hammer era and beyond, from unmade versions of *Brides of Dracula* (called *Disciple of Dracula*) to remakes of *Creature from the Black Lagoon*. Completely unmade films like *Dracula* (1975) and *Godzilla vs. Frankenstein* (1964) are covered along with lost completed films like *Batman Fights Dracula* (1967) and *Black the Ripper* (1974). Coming Fall 2021.

NOSTALGIA

Written in the same spirit as *The Big Book of Japanese Giant Monster Movies*, this tome reviews all the classic Universal and Hammer horrors to star Dracula, Frankenstein, the Gillman and the rest along with obscure flicks like *The New Invisible Man* (1958), *Billy the Kid versus Dracula* (1966), *Blackenstein* (1973) and *Legend of the Werewolf* (1974). Softcover (394 pp/5.5" X 8.5") Suggested Retail: $17.95

Written at an intermediate reading level for the kid in all of us, these picture books will take you back to your youth. In the spirit of the old Ian Thorne books are covered *Nabonga* (1944), *White Pongo* (1945) and more! Hardcover/Softcover (44 pp/7.5" X 9.25") Suggested Retail: $17.95(hc)/$9.99(sc) ISBN: 978- 1-7341546-9-6 (hc) 978- 1-7344730-5-6 (sc)

Written at an intermediate reading level for the kid in all of us, these picture books will take you back to your youth. In the spirit of the old Ian Thorne books are covered *The Lost World* (1925), *The Land That Time Forgot* (1975) and more! Hardcover/Softcover (44 pp/7.5" X 9.25") Suggested Retail: $17.95 (hc)/$9.99(sc) ISBN: 978-1-7344730 -6-3 (hc) 978- 1-7344730-7-0 (sc)

Written at an intermediate reading level for the kid in all of us, these picture books will take you back to your youth. In the spirit of the old Ian Thorne books are covered *Them!* (1954), *Empire of the Ants* (1977) and more! Hardcover/ Softcover (44 pp/7.5" X 9.25") Suggested Retail: $17.95(hc)/ $9.99(sc) ISBN: 978-1-7347816 -3-2 (hc) 978 -1-7347816-2-5 (sc)

THE BICEP BOOKS CATALOGUE

CRYPTOZOOLOGY/COWBOYS & SAURIANS

Cowboys & Saurians: Prehistoric Beasts as Seen by the Pioneers explores dinosaur sightings from the pioneer period via real newspaper reports from the time. Well-known cases like the Tombstone Thunderbird are covered along with more obscure cases like the Crosswicks Monster and more. Softcover (357 pp/5.06" X 7.8") Suggested Retail: $19.95 ISBN: 978-1-7341546-1-0

Cowboys & Saurians: Ice Age zeroes in on snowbound saurians like the Cceratosaurus of the Arctic Circle and a Tyrannosaurus of the Tundra, as well as sightings of Ice Age megafauna like mammoths, glyptodonts, Sarkastodons and Saber-toothed tigers. Tales of a land that time forgot in the Arctic are also covered. Softcover (264 pp/5.06" X 7.8") Suggested Retail: $14.99 ISBN: 978-1-7341546-7-2

Southerners & Saurians takes the series formula of exploring newspaper accounts of monsters in the pioneer period with an eye to the Old South. In addition to dinosaurs are covered Lizardmen, Frogmen, giant leeches and mosquitoes, and the Dingocroc, which might be an alien rather than a prehistoric survivor. Softcover (202 pp/5.06" X 7.8") Suggested Retail: $13.99 ISBN: 978-1-7344730-4-9

Cowboys & Saurians South of the Border explores the saurians of Central and South America, like the Patagonian Plesiosaurus that was really an Iemisch, plus tales of the Neo-Mylodon, a menacing monster from underground called the Minhocao, Glyptodonts, and even Bolivia's three-headed dinosaur! Softcover (412 pp/ 5.06"X7.8") Suggested Retail: $17.95 ISBN: 978-1-953221-73-5

UFOLOGY/THE REAL COWBOYS & ALIENS IN CONJUNCTION WITH ROSWELL BOOKS

The Real Cowboys and Aliens: Early American UFOs explores UFO sightings in the USA between the years 1800-1864. Stories of encounters sometimes involved famous figures in U.S. history such as Lewis and Clark, and Thomas Jefferson.Hardcover (242pp/6" X 9") Softcover (262 pp/5.06" X 7.8") Suggested Retail: $24.99 (hc)/$15.95(sc) ISBN: 978-1-7341546-8-9\(hc)/978-1-7344 730-8-7(sc)

The second entry in the series, *Old West UFOs*, covers reports spanning the years 1865-1895. Includes tales of Men in Black, Reptilians, Spring-Heeled Jack, Sasquatch from space, and other alien beings, in addition to the UFOs and airships. Hardcover (276 pp/6" X 9") Softcover (308 pp/5.06" X 7.8") Suggested Retail: $29.95 (hc)/$17.95(sc) ISBN: 978-1-7344730-0-1 (hc)/ 978-1-73447 30-2-5 (sc)

The third entry in the series, *The Coming of the Airships*, encompasses a short time frame with an incredibly high concentration of airship sightings between 1896-1899. The famous Aurora, Texas, UFO crash of 1897 is covered in depth along with many others. Hardcover (196 pp/6" X 9") Softcover (222 pp/5.06" X 7.8") Suggested Retail: $24.99 (hc)/$15.95(sc) ISBN: 978-1-7347816 -1-8 (hc)/978-1-7347816-0-1(sc)

Early 20th Century UFOs kicks off a new series that investigates UFO sightings of the early 1900s. Includes tales of UFOs sighted over the *Titanic* as it sunk, Nikola Tesla receiving messages from the stars, an alien being found encased in ice, and a possible virus from outer space!Hardcover (196 pp/6" X 9") Softcover (222 pp/5.06" X 7.8") Suggested Retail: $27.99 (hc)/$16.95(sc) ISBN: 978-1-7347816-1-8 (hc)/978-1-73478 16-0-1(sc)

LOST FILMS FANZINE BACK ISSUES

THE LOST FILMS FANZINE VOL.1

ISSUE #1 SPRING 2020 The lost Italian cut of *Legend of Dinosaurs and Monster Birds* called *Terremoto 10 Grado*, plus *Bride of Dr. Phibes* script, *Good Luck! Godzilla*, the King Kong remake that became a car comm ercial, Bollywood's lost *Jaws* rip-off, Top Ten Best Fan Made Godzilla trailers plus an interview with Scott David Lister. 60 pages. Three variant covers/editions (premium color/basic color/ b&w)

ISSUE #2 SUMMER 2020 How 1935's *The Capture of Tarzan* became 1936's *Tarzan Escapes*, the Orca sequels that weren't, Baragon in Bollywood's *One Million B.C.*, unmade *Kolchak: The Night Stalker* movies, *The Norliss Tapes*, *Superman V: The New Movie*, why there were no *Curse of the Pink Panther* sequels, *Moonlight Mask: The Movie*. 64 pages. Two covers/ editions (basic color/b&w)

ISSUE #3 FALL 2020 Blob sequels both forgotten and unproduced, *Horror of Dracula* uncut, *Franken-stein Meets the Wolfman* and talks, myths of the lost *King Kong* Spider-Pit sequence debunked, the *Carnosaur* novel vs. the movies, *Terror in the Streets* 50th anniversary, *Bride of Godzilla* 55th Unniversary, Lee Powers sketchbook. 100 pages. Two covers/editions (basic color/b&w)

ISSUE #4 WINTER 2020/21 *Diamonds Are Forever's* first draft with Goldfinger, *Disciple of Dracula* into *Brides of Dracula*, *War of the Worlds* That Weren't Part II, *Day the Earth Stood Still II* by Ray Bradbury, *Deathwish 6*, *Atomic War Bride*, *What Am I Doing in the Middle of a Revolution?*, *Spring Dream in the Old Capital* and more. 70 pages. Two covers/editions (basic color/b&w)

THE LOST FILMS FANZINE VOL.2

ISSUE #5 SPRING 2021 The lost films and projects of ape suit performer Charles Gemora, plus *Superman Reborn*, *Teenage Mutant Ninja Turtles IV: The Next Mutation*, *Mikado Zombie*, NBC's *Big Stuffed Dog*, King Ghidorah flies solo, *Grizzly II* reviewed, and War of the Worlds That Weren't concludes with a musical. Plus Blu-Ray reviews, news, and letters. 66 pages. Two covers/editions (basic co-lor/ b&w)

ISSUE #6 SUMMER 2021 Peter Sellers *Romance of the Pink Panther*, Akira Kurosawa's *Song of the Horse*, *Kali - Devil Bride of Dracula*, Jack Black as Green Lantern, *Ladybug, Ladybug*, *The Lost Atlantis*, Japan's lost superhero Hiyo Man, and *Lord of Light*, the CIA's covert movie that inspired 2012's *Argo*. Plus news, Blu-Ray reviews, and letters. 72 pages. Two covers/editions (basic color/b&w)

ISSUE #7 FALL 2021 *Hiero's Journey*, Don Bragg in *Tarzan and the Jewels of Opar*, DC's *Lobo* movie, Lee Powers Scrapbook returns, Blake Matthews uncovers *The Big Boss Part II* (1976), Matthew B. Lamont searches for lost Three Stooges, and an ape called Kong in 1927's *Isle of Sunken Gold*. Plus news, and letters. 72 pages. Two covers/editions (basic color /b&w)

ISSUE #8 WINTER 2021/22 The connection between Steve Reeves' unmade third Hercules movie and *Goliath and the Dragon*, *The Iron Man* starring Tom Cruise, Phil Yordan's *King Kong* remake, *The Unearthly Stranger*, *Saturday Super-cade* forgotten cartoon, the 45th anniversary of Luigi Cozzi's "Cozzilla" and *Day the Earth Froze*. Plus news and letters. 72 pages. Two covers/editions (basic color /b&w)

MOVIE MILESTONES BACK ISSUES

MOVIE MILESTONES VOL. 1   VOL. 2

ISSUE #1 AUGUST 2020 Debut issue celebrating 80 years of *One Million B.C.* (1940), and an early 55th Anniversary for *One Million Years B.C.* (1966). Abandoned ideas, casting changes, and deleted scenes are covered, plus, a mini-B.C. stock-footage filmography and much more! 54 pages. Three collectible covers/ editions (premium color/ basic color/b&w)

ISSUE #2 OCTOBER 2020 Celebrates the joint 50th Anniversaries of *When Dinosaurs Ruled the Earth* (1970) and *Creatures the World Forgot* (1971). Also includes looks at *Prehistoric Women* (1967), *When Women Had Tails* (1970), and *Caveman* (1981), plus unmade films like *When the World Cracked Open*. 72 pages. Three collectible covers/editions (premium color/basic color/b&w)

ISSUE #3 WINTER 2021 Japanese 'Panic Movies' like *The Last War* (1961), *Submersion of Japan* (1973), and *Bullet Train* (1975) are covered on celebrated author Sakyo Komatsu's 90th birthday. The famous banned Toho film *Prophecies of Nostradamus* (1974) are also covered. 124 pages. Three collectible covers/ editions (premium color/ basic color/ b&w)

ISSUE #4 SPRING 2021 This issue celebrates the joint 60th Anniversaries of *Gorgo, Reptilicus* and *Konga* examining unmade sequels like *Reptilicus 2*, and other related lost projects like *Kuru Island* and *The Volcano Monsters*. Also explores the Gorgo, Konga and Reptilicus comic books from Charlton. 72 pages. Three collectible covers/editions (premium color/basic color/b&w)

MOVIE MILESTONES VOL. 2   VOL. 3

ISSUE #5 SUMMER 2021 *Godzilla vs. the Sea Monster* gets the spotlight, with an emphasis on its original version *King Kong vs. Ebirah,* plus information on *The King Kong Show* which inspired it, and Jun Fukuda's tangentially related spy series *100 Shot/100 Killed.* 72 pages. Three collectible covers/editions (premium color /basic color/b&w)

ISSUE #6 FALL 2021 Monster Westerns of the 1950s and 1960s are spotlighted in the form of *Teenage Monster, The Curse of the Undead, Billy the Kid Versus Dracula, Jesse James Meets Frankenstein's Daughter,* and Bela Lugosi's unmade *The Ghoul Goes West.* 50 pages. Special Black and White exclusive!

ISSUE #7 WINTER 2022 This issue is all about Amicus's Edgar Rice Burroughs trilogy including *Land That Time Forgot, At the Earth's Core, People That Time Forgot* plus unmade sequels like *Out of Time's Abyss* or Doug McClure as John Carter of Mars. All this plus *Warlords of Atlantis* and *Arabian Adventure!* 100 pages. Three collectible covers/editions (premium color /basic color/b&w)

ISSUE #8 SUMMER 2022 *Godzilla vs. Gigan* turns 50 and this issue is here to celebrate with its many unmade versions, like *Godzilla vs. the Space Monsters* and *Return of King Ghidorah,* plus *The Mysterians* 65th anniversary and *Daigoro vs. Goliath's* 50th.

NEW RELEASES

COWBOYS & SAURIANS/THE REAL COWBOYS & ALIENS/HISTORY

Cowboys & Monsters features potentially true stories of real vampires, werewolves, and even mummies unique to America's Wild West period. Examples include the cursed mummy of John Wilkes Booth, New Orleans immortal vampire Jacques St. Germain, precursors to the Beast of Bray Road, and the origins of Skinwalker Ranch. Softcover (316 pp/5.06" X 7.8") Suggested Retail: $19.99 ISBN: 978-1-953221-46-9

Featuring cases the authors missed, *The Lost Cases* covers things such as the skyquakes recorded by Lewis and Clark, airships and the Spanish American War, Pancho Villa and crystal skulls, lost alien tribe of the Tundra, invisible alien monsters, the Great Moon Hoax of 1835, hellhounds and airships, the Sonora Airship Club and more. Softcover (252 pp/5.06" X 7.8") Suggested Retail: $18.99 ISBN: 978-1-953221-55-1

UFOs in the Roaring Twenties takes a look at UFO sightings in the 1920s just as the title suggests, along with accounts of Mothman in Nebraska, Lincoln LaPaz's first UFO case, Men in Black investigating an airship crash in Braxton County, West Virginia, Camden's Cosmic Sniper, and much more! Softcover (248 pp/5.06" X 7.8") Suggested Retail: $19.99 ISBN: 978-1-953221-51-3

This biography, for the first time ever, tells the history of western journalist Ash Upson, who ghostwrote Pat Garrett's *The Authentic Life of Billy the Kid* and also reproduces many of Upson's letters that detailed the harsh realities of frontier life in New Mexico during the turbulent Lincoln County War. Softcover (318 pp/5.5" X 8.5") Suggested Retail: $16.99 ISBN: 978-1953221919

FICTION/FILM HISTORY

The first novel from historian John LeMay weaves a fantastic web of fiction via real life mysteries and legends of New Mexico, namely the puzzling theft and return of Billy the Kid's tombstone in 1976, the legend of the Lost Adams Diggings, the villainous Santa Fe Ring, and the enigmatic Acoma Mesa. Softcover (300 pp/4.25" X 7") Suggested Retail: $13.99 ISBN: 978-1-953221-89-6

The first book ever devoted solely to the Pink Panther franchise, *Trailing the Pink Panther Films* features production history and commentary on all eleven films including outliers *Inspector Clouseau* (1968), *Curse of the Pink Panther* (1983) and *Son of the Pink Panther* (1993) along with the two Steve Martin films. Softcover (205 pp/5.83 X 8.27") Suggested Retail: $14.99 ISBN: 978-1-953221-47-6

The 2nd Edition of *Kong Unmade* revises and expands the original chapters and also adds new entries on lost films like *Island of Sunken Gold* (1928), *Ingagi* (1930), plus more unmade scripts like *War Eagles*, *Umbah* and lastly charts the complicated development of *Godzilla vs. Kong*. Softcover (372 pp/8.25" X 11") Suggested Retail: $34.99 ISBN: 978-1-953221-69-8

This combined edition features Volume 1 & 2 of Classic Monsters Unmade in full color. The tome runs the gamut of Universal and Hammer's heydays and the films that never were such as *Cagliostro, King of the Dead*, *Wolf Man vs. Dracula*, *The Mummy's Return*, *Frankenstein and the Monster*, and many more! Softcover (454 pp/8.25" X 11") Suggested Retail: $37.99 ISBN: 978-1953221674